Clive Wilkinson

Sept. 2019

To Donna,
with admiration!

Clive

The Theatre of Work

FRAM3

"I can't help but dream about a kind of criticism that would not try to judge, but bring an oeuvre, a book, a sentence, an idea to life; it would light fires, watch the grass grow, listen to the wind, and catch the sea-foam in the breeze and scatter it. It would multiply, not judgments, but signs of existence; it would summon them, drag them from their sleep. Perhaps it would invent them sometimes – all the better. All the better. Criticism that hands down sentences sends me to sleep; I'd like a criticism of scintillating leaps of the imagination. It would not be a sovereign or dressed in red. It would bear the lightning of possible storms."

MICHEL FOUCAULT 'THE MASKED PHILOSOPHER' 1997

"A book, any book, is a form of criticism."

CLIVE WILKINSON 2019

Contents

3

Preface

4

Back in the 1970's, riding a wave of Freudian thinking, people would say that everything one does is driven by the need for sex. And further, that the need for sex was a subterfuge, concealing a deeper need to return to the womb. The exciting side of this self-serving fantasy was the idea of the journey: the journey back into the womb. Writing a book then seemed like a way of exploring this path, with all its manifold diversions and digressions, into the chasms of mystery. Exotic, subterranean, darkly exciting – but beyond that, it could be an experience of simultaneity where the exploration, the documenting and recording, and the unravelling of mystery could all be captured in the pages of a book. The book thus becomes a platform for the poetics of experience. And a book on interior design may become a voyage into the poetics of spatial experience.

Most writers, I imagine, write books in order to tell stories. I undertook this book mostly as an exercise of discovery: as a way to dive into the complexity with which we work and try to better understand what it is and where it is leading. This might account for certain open threads and unanswered questions that follow, since the subject matter is rich, and I simply have not uncovered the answers to many of the questions. Questions in any event are more valuable than answers, since they are the initiating drivers for creative projects. It is said that for learning to consistently occur in the world of work, every project must be regarded as a unique project. And therefore, every project is a journey of discovery. I think this also explains why some of our clients want to be regarded as pirates.

Since the establishment of our firm, Clive Wilkinson Architects, in 1991, we have undertaken the formulation and design of workplaces for a variety of businesses, chiefly creative companies. Our first clients were ad agencies and film production companies in Los Angeles. The conversations we engaged in were specific to creative space, the needs of creative workers and what could be done with tight budgets. There is considerable mythology around the actions and behaviors of corporations at large, much of which ignores the basic survival missions that underpin them. They do in fact work like ecological organisms and are susceptible to failure like any other ecological organism. This vulnerability makes them subject to life cycles – even ephemeral at times – and fascinating subjects for design investigation.

After completing several workplace design projects, we discovered that our process and product bore two distinct layers: that of a research and investigative process leading to a specific set of ideas and strategies, and that of a designed creative product as an environment that is inserted into the physical world. The responses we got from clients, users and media commentators concentrated on the surface of what was produced. Locating, defining, categorizing and evaluating the success of work on its visual qualities alone was somewhat frustrating.

Beyond such cursory readings of our work, there is a deeper encircling position, a kind of 'weltanschauung', that underwrites the work and needs to be understood. No physical man-made thing exists in a world exclusively of its making – it engages, willingly or not, in the vast complex world we live in. Consciously or otherwise, we promote certain values, political beliefs and socio-economic ideas through our work, and we must therefore try to be cognitive of these, in order to communicate responsibly. All human objects communicate, and we have a responsibility be in control of what is communicated. A need to clarify and explain the ideas developed in our studio has led to this book, more than 10 years in the making.

For my part, I grew up in South Africa in the 1960's and 70's. The country was ruled by white conservatives, who had institutionalized an elitist policy of racial segregation, and called it 'apartheid', or 'separate development'. As someone approaching adulthood, like many of my peers, I gradually became aware that the entire system was fundamentally wrong. We could not pretend to understand the plight of our black fellow South Africans, as we had been so effectively separated from them, but we could sense that one law for the privileged and one for the poor was fundamentally unfair. The system made mixed race, or Asian, colored people second class citizens, and black people third class citizens, with job restrictions, and restrictions on where they could live. It stripped people of their basic human rights, and was essentially inhumane. From the time of this realization, I had serious problems with authority and top down control. It had showed its potential to be both fallible and morally bereft.

Coming out of these conditions in Africa, it became impossible to work in the highly privileged developed world without constantly thinking about what the rest of the world experiences. So while much of what follows in this book is written in the context of the developed world in which I work, the source of this book is the lesson of Africa. We have a responsibility to the earth to use its riches frugally, and with respect, in order to aspire to an ecological balance, and of course simply to survive.

This book has truly been undertaken as a process of discovery. After 25 years of working with many exceptional creative companies focused on rethinking their organizations and their mission, we needed to reassess the products of that work. While our projects have received considerable media coverage, too much of it revolved around the hero image – the unfortunate 'starchitect' phenomenon – and not enough focused on our practice's worldview: our strategic, sociological and behavioral approach. Indeed, it is our ambition in the corporate world to help enable nothing less than organizational transformation: a transformation necessitated by a massively changed world. This book hopefully serves as a vehicle to communicate that broader and more valuable viewpoint.

Towards the end of his life, the artist, Paul Gauguin, stated that his work was not in itself worthy of greatness or critical acclaim. Rather, it was his influence across the field of art that made his work great. Its value was not intrinsic, but lay instead in the extent to which it facilitated an opening up of the territory, of creating new freedoms for artists that came after him. This act of projecting new models of thought into the world, of the disruptive proposition, is what truly contributes to the discourse of culture. This is how we would like our work to be understood, as a contribution to the discourse that favors the useful and practical role of design in the service of humanity, notwithstanding its undoubted philosophical, political and aesthetic dimensions.

With so much resistance to change in contemporary society, (witness the belligerent refusal to accept climate change), our world has become an over-engineered vehicle with too many options for putting on the brakes and too little fuel to move forward. And yet we can only survive by constantly changing and adapting to a fast changing world. Projecting back to the middle of the 19th century, we might honor the words of that scion of declining Italian aristocracy, Prince Fabrizio di Salina, in Guiseppe di Lampadusa's grand novel The Leopard, observing how the modern industrial world was disrupting their lives: 'Things must change, in order for them to stay the same'.

Introduction

Interior of the Palais Garnier in Paris – The Auditorium as Theatre.

6

Architecture frames the theatre of human experience. Winston Churchill said that we shape our buildings, and thereafter they shape us: a relationship that is deeply synergistic. We are affected profoundly by much of the architecture around us, by the interiors of buildings, and not necessarily in good ways. When the toils of all those who make buildings pay off in wonderful edifices and spaces, we are grateful for what are really the stage sets to support life. This book endeavors to examine the various and fluctuating forces that weigh upon the making of buildings that accommodate workplaces, or, in particular, of buildings for creative communities.

Work is simply a function of human survival – something almost everyone engages in to a greater or lesser degree. Up until the late 20th century, the forms of work were largely based on combinations of muscle and mental power and changed little over time, though the subjects of work evolved. With the emergence of digital communications and the internet, everything changed. During the life of our office, we have witnessed the correction of the former scarcity of information with a constant abundance of information, and the introduction of a new interpersonal connectivity and processing power that has radically changed our ways of working and

7

"An objective study of the ways in which meanings are transmitted has shown that much more is relayed from one man to another through and in silence than in words. Words and sentences are composed of silences more meaningful than the sounds. The pregnant pauses between sounds and utterances become luminous points in an incredible void: as electrons in the atom, as planets in the solar system. Language is a cord of silence, with sounds the knots – as nodes in the Peruvian 'quipu', in which the empty spaces speak."

IVAN ILLICH – CELEBRATION OF AWARENESS

communicating with one another, and indeed the entire culture of society.

Driven by a fundamental shift in the forms of labor, a new work culture has emerged with three distinctly different facets: the physical culture of the workplace, the virtual culture brought on by digital communications, and the behavioral culture that is evolving under pressure from this new digital world. While change is happening beyond our control, the importance of re-assessing the role of the workplace is more urgent than

ever. If organizations are to survive, they need retooled and transformed corporate culture. In assisting this transformation, architects and designers need better information and better understanding of the complex organism of the workplace.

This book explores historical precedents around the culture of work and its related spatial environments. In this way, the book seeks to inform and contribute to a developing body of research and practice, delving into historical narratives and their causal chains, which in turn provide background to the current world of work. However, we have less of a concern with historical evolution than with developing 'an analytics of change' using history as a comparative source. The massive change in which we are submerged in today has numerous precedents, though the forces which propelled those earlier convulsions could be markedly different.

What really connects the workplace to theatre? We tend to think in narrow terms about both of these subjects. Many people think of work as a droll activity that absorbs one's day, and they think of theatre as a play performance, or a similar form of entertainment. The reality is that work in its most engaging form has the potential to become theatre – which is a total experience, immersive and engrossing at its best. In theatre itself, beyond the processional space of vestibules and halls, the audience space is part of the experience, as the audience is in truth part of the play. In this image of The Palais Garnier in Paris, with the rustling sounds of the audience, the theatre experience begins well before the curtain is up.

It is said that the true theatre of humanity plays out in city streets. As such the city creates the stage for human drama. In no lesser sense, we can propose that the workplace itself can and should function as theatre, where workers are alternatively the players and the audience. And through this drama, and the unveiling of a corporate culture of permissiveness to engage fully, the work community may constantly invigorate itself.

There are multiple levels upon which we can examine a history of work in the community. All of them may be valid. We can examine the subject from the poetics of space. We can examine it from sociological, phenomenological, economic and political perspectives. We can examine it from the perspectives of business and management theory. We can examine it from the specialist perspectives of architecture, urban design, industrial design and even landscape design.

This book proposes that it is important to encircle all possible perspectives within itself, even if such a layered approach invites contradictions. All vital organisms in nature are profoundly complex, even as they attenuate their systems. The willingness to attempt too much is how evolutionary progress is made – to push the organism to the limit of stress, in order for new muscle growth to emerge.

We can also examine the history of work as simply as possible: as affirmation of community, affirmation of engagement, affirmation of mindfulness and of presence. In its idealized form, the place of work can become that moment of being entirely equipped and prepared, which is the moment preceding perfect execution. While this can sound almost spiritual, it is really nothing more, nor less, than a compression of preparedness. It is also a celebration of awareness. Ivan Illich's book *Celebration of Awareness* was profoundly influential for many in the post-hippie 1970's. Amidst the indescribable rightness of his socio-political purpose, the most resonant concept was also the humblest: the celebration of silence. For Illich, silence communicates at multiple levels, which may be dissected and analyzed, and indeed more is communicated through silence than through words. The same may apply to the space of work.

Two people facing each other offer a vast potential in rich communication. Visual gestures, expressions and body language supplement the spoken word, which is further modulated by handling of silence, tone, tempo and pitch. It is possible to extract great nuance, and learn an enormous amount about a person's concerns in this manner, and it will always be the richest and most valued method of interacting in business and social affairs. This simple fact underpins the immense value of bringing people together physically in a new social workplace.

So, lastly, we can examine the workplace from the perspective of functionality. The office, or workplace, is the support environment for human productivity. It is a place where most people spend the most vital hours of their day. From a time perspective alone, the workplace is one of the two most important human environments in existence (the other is, of course, the home). This makes it worthy of serious study. In the early 21st century, the office is undergoing a radical re-evaluation driven by massive technological change. The routine service function of white collar work has changed, particularly within developed nations, into an innovation-oriented function of the self-managed, collarless worker.

It is well understood that rapidly evolving technology is responsible for the massive change in which we are immersed. Since information has become independent of time or place, the traditional office has in many ways lost its reason for being. The resulting massive dislocation has forced a reappraisal of the role of the workplace – and driven many to promote mobile working as the mode of the future. The phrase 'work whenever, work wherever' has become a cliché of the new generation. What has emerged, however, is a consensus for accepting and embracing a new exciting communal work environment. Humans are fundamentally social and need their tribal environments to function. Telecommuting and remote work have lost much of their initial attraction and people are returning to offices. For this reason, the office is in the process of not only being revived, but in being redefined and elaborated as the inspiring, vibrant heart for new business communities: the new palaces of work.

Of course, the modern workplace is now a central component of modern commerce, and therefore, of the modern city. Its precedence is owed to the rise of the new knowledge (or creative) economy that has largely superseded the hegemony of the service economy of the 20th century. Where the old workplace was conceived and ordered around the idea of rigidly stratified management hierarchies and routine clerical production, the new workplace is ordered around the collective exchange of ideas and knowledge, enabled by digital tools, in service of the rapid development of new products and services. Since its role is fundamentally different, it

9

"**Theatre is the amplification of human life, the re-energizing of memory and experience, the re-awakening of passion.**"

ANTONIN ARTAUD – THE THEATRE AND ITS DOUBLE

has become a sensitive and sensuous space, and it now functions on multiple levels. Its effectiveness is measured on the extent to which it supports and enhances creativity, problem solving, team working and innovative productivity.

For many large innovative organizations today, the workplace has become a kind of theatre. The action of work becomes a play. It is no accident that for many societies, the theatrical drama is called a 'play'. Where human activity is freed from excessive management and control, work can become serious play and the associated activity become a state of flow, as described by Mihaly Csikszentmihali in his book: *Flow, The Psychology Of Optimal Experience*. Indeed, this state of consciousness called flow is an optimum desirable condition to be strived for in creative communities. Flow works like the movement of water, inspiring and connecting people and processes in an efficiency of movement and productivity.

The function of theatre extends further: while there is an assumption of both audience and performance, a heightened value comes from energizing both the observer and the observed, which feed off each other. In the workplace, this means that the drama of work performance feeds on both the energies of the participants and their role as visible theatre on the open stage of the office. While design and architecture cannot create this drama, it can intentionally set the stage for the play, shaping an environmental culture and driving the play into existence.

We have seen that cultural change today occurs slower than technological change. The notion of style being victim to fashion shifts has become secondary to an exponentially increasing redundancy trail of technology. The technological devices that support modern life are constantly changing and evolving. Once 'ancient technology' was 500-year old technology. It is now five-year old technology. The notion of basing strategic commercial decisions on functional requirements, of developing a 'fashion proof' design proposal, has become futile in the face of the changing parameters of functionality. Only one constant remains unchanging – the basic human interface – and even this is measurably altering. Our interaction with the modern world has forced us to become 'information processors' on a scale that would have been shocking to our ancestors. We live immersed in an electronic world.

In the developed countries today, one fifth of the world's work and workforce, society and polity are all qualitatively and quantitatively different from both the first

"In 2006 for the first time, more transistors were produced than grains of rice."

SEMICONDUCTOR INDUSTRY ASSOCIATION

years of the previous century, and indeed from anything ever before experienced in human history. They are different in their configuration, in their processes, in their problems and in their structures. Fifty years before we awakened to it, Marshall McLuhan talked at length about the pain associated with technological change. Each new technological offering that penetrates our world does so because it executes certain human tasks more efficiently – it replaces human capabilities with faster, often better, technical devices. In doing so, it renders both those skills and the related human physical capabilities redundant. Each new technology amputates us. Metaphorically and literally, we replace our limbs with more effective mechanical and electrical armatures. Whatever parts of our bodies we do not use, as with any biological organism, will die. However, it is equally true that our biological systems will develop entirely new 'armatures', or perhaps cognitive capacities, to address the new needs of an immersive digital age.

So, in this book, we will focus on the driving entrepreneurial force of today's knowledge-based organization: on the necessary tools, and the habitation structure and organizational forms which support change. We need to understand these businesses as highly evolved, integrated organisms, and to search for new ways of organizing a company's workplace or physical structure to make the 'organism' a balanced and ecologically refined commercial entity focused on the future as a journey. Beyond 'classical design', which prioritized elegance, craft and perfection in execution, we must now include 'design thinking', which requires empathy and addresses the customer or user experience, and 'computational design' which influences everything

10

about our peripatetic digital experience and work flow.

In the face of massive change and an unpredictable future, the old notion of a perfectly ordered architectural system has lost its persuasive power: the organization of the future is by necessity relatively formless. It needs to be a shape shifting organism, stripped of unnecessary baggage, and equipped more with a toolkit of strategies, than dumb technological power alone. The new world is light, swift and ephemeral. Anything which anchors you down, will be an encumbrance. To quote a saying of the nomadic Tuareg Arabs of the African Sahara desert: "that which you do not require, will kill you".

On the subject of change, it's worth noting the observation of Amazon's Jeff Bezos in response to the question: "What's going to change in the next 10 years?" He said, "What's not going to change in the next 10 years?"And he submitted that that second question is actually the more important of the two "because you can build a business strategy around the things that are stable in time. When you have something that you know is true, even over the long term, you can afford to put a lot of energy into it."

Part One of this book looks at the evolution of society and the workplace from various historical perspectives, leading to what we understand to be the workplace of today. Since computers have begun the job that artificial intelligence will soon complete, of appropriating most routine work activities, the dominant form of work today is knowledge based. Old hierarchies are being challenged and organizations are in a process of transformation. The new workplace has become a major focus of attention due to its role in the new knowledge economy.

Quite simply, a great workplace which fosters productive work effectively, is a major attraction for talent, and a powerful business tool. In research that we undertook with one of our banking clients, we learned that a 2.5% increase in productivity would pay for the entire capital program for a new corporate workplace. Measurement of productivity is difficult as so many factors come into play, but in the one instance where a client completing a large workplace project commissioned independent research, an 11% increase was attributed to the new workplace within the first year. It should become immediately apparent that a comprehensive workplace transformation can more than pay for itself in a short time.

Before completing this review of the workplace in time, we look at the factors that contribute to the success or failure of workplaces, and what can assist in bringing resilience into play. We consider that ignoring any of these issues will jeopardize success. The organisms of work communities have fragilities and vulnerabilities which must be addressed: they range from structural and organizational challenges to behavioral and social sensitivities.

The open office is itself under fire from numerous sources as a dysfunctional nightmare. It is our belief that the open office is not a panacea. Rather, what is really under fire is poorly conceived design solutions which fail to take into account the range of human needs, and drop the ball with issues such as densities, personal space, concentrated working, lighting and acoustics. Good workplace environments should be conceived and developed in close collaboration with client stakeholders to ensure that gaps do not emerge, and that solutions are evolved that can be embraced by the employees to the extent that they are truly empowered by the new office environment and can fully utilize all of its tools and amenities.

The second and major part of this book, Where Are We Going?, addresses seven concepts about the workplace that we believe contribute to great new workplaces. They build upon the lessons of the intermediate section called What Did We Learn? These ideas address the paradigm of knowledge work and the goal of building creative communities.

Like so many chefs writing about their work, we have been 'cooking' with these ingredients in all of our projects since the founding of the firm in 1991. We have had the opportunity to study their effectiveness and to adjust the 'recipes' as we go along. Consequently, we have used our projects as case studies to illustrate the ideas. Fourteen projects have been included and used as examples, though of course there is considerable cross-over for most of them. The other important consideration in the case study model is to impart an understanding of process, of how the various ideas emerged – so the project illustrations in many instances include early models and sketches which foreshadow the final designs.

11

Part One

How Did We Get Here?

"Each epoch dreams the one to follow."

JULES MICHELET

"Each epoch, in fact, not only dreams the one to follow, but in dreaming, precipitates its awakening."

WALTER BENJAMIN

"Nothing changes, except in a condition of stress."

CLIVE WILKINSON

The Rise of Humanism

> **"Structuring and identifying the environment is a vital ability amongst all mobile animals. Many kinds of cues are used: the visual sensations of color, shape, motion, or polarization of light, as well as other senses such as smell, sound, touch, kinesthesia, sense of gravity, and perhaps of electric and magnetic fields."**
>
> **KEVIN LYNCH**

14

How we arrived at that peculiar place for devoting our energies – the office of the 21st century – is part of the story of human evolution and of urbanization. Everything we do is founded on behavior systems that evolved through millions of years of adapting to the natural world. Our immediate physical system, the human body, is attuned to sustaining life through the apprehension of both prey and predator. When threatened by a superior force, we flee. When tracking prey, we alternate rapid movement with stealth movement. We function in bursts of power. What we have now come to understand as best practice in fitness training in a gym, is fundamentally rooted in our animal behavior past.

Civilization, as we know it, is an idea that first came to prominence during the Enlightenment period, and was again popularized at the beginning of the 20th century. As the story goes, civilization emerged from the Dark Ages 1,000 years ago. Of course, this is a singularly Eurocentric point of view, since several other civilizations, most notably the Arabic and Chinese, were much more developed at that time. Chinese cities were the largest and most advanced in the world – they had invented paper and gunpowder amongst other things, and standardized bureaucracies that streamlined commerce, and even facilitated transportation networks through regulating the width of the carriage chassis to ensure that the grooves in dirt roads would not impede wheel movement.

Around the 12th century, surprisingly, the world enjoyed its greatest global connectivity prior to the 21st century. Genghis Khan organized the Mongol hordes so effectively that they overran all of Asia and the Middle East, securing and opening the flow on all major trading routes, largely freed thereby from the threats of lawless and corrupt local officials and bandits along the way. The Mongol Empire became the first great global empire and the rapid and wide-spread exchange of cultures and commodities transformed the world beyond recognition. New trade allegiances were formed and the exchange of knowledge escalated technological progress in Western Europe. It is not insignificant that Italy thus obtained its obsession with pasta from China, whose affair with noodles had a much earlier origin. All of which is to say that any history of humanity must accept that history is often a matter of perspective and interpretation – non-linear, layered and often contradictory.

The Late Medieval period, which evolved in parallel with the great Mongol Empire to the East, was also the moment of a dramatic rise in scholasticism in the West, emerging as it was from centuries of theological domination. Much of its revitalization was owed to the transmission of knowledge from Byzantium and the Arabic states, which were more advanced civilizations at that time, and whose scholars were the primary custodians of historical knowledge in the various Mediterranean languages, including classical Greek and Roman literature. The intellectual freedoms that flourished in the unfolding scholastic milieu influenced all the arts. Architecture reached a new pinnacle of achievement with the series of enormously influential and richly expressive Gothic cathedral edifices. While the Renaissance caused a dramatic break from religious oppression and mysticism of the feudal past, Scholasticism in this era paved the way for the innovations that followed.

A central tenet of the subsequent Renaissance period, was that man was at the centre of the world, and in the centre of all images of the world. This act created a decisive schism with the deeply religious medieval world that preceded it, where man was reduced to an undifferentiated unit of the human species, subjugated under the structures of the church, and blended into the species of all earth's creatures, the totality of whom withered in the light of an almighty Christian God. Accomplishments under this religious regime were not individual but communal accomplishments, like the erection of the cathedral masterworks, which had no identifiable authors, though the content of their communication was encyclopedic in scope and variety. The cathedral was a book before books could be widely published and circulated, a compendium of biblical stories inscribed in stone.

Architecture itself served a deeper purpose of memorializing the story of humanity and it's sacred beliefs. At a time when few could read, the visual representation of narratives carried immense weight. Indeed the Christian church at that time was also the place, for each town, where people heard all the news of their (limited) world. Preachers were also the town criers! As Victor Hugo described in *Notre Dame de Paris*: "Architecture has been until the 15ᵗʰ century the principal register of humanity: in the interval there appeared no complicated thought that was not worked into a building; that every popular idea has, like all religion's laws, its monuments; that, in short, human beings thought of

Saint Jerome in his Study.
Antonello da Messina, c. 1475.

15

nothing of importance that they did not write in stone." Hugo's character Claude Frollo, archdeacon of Notre Dame, touching a book and observing a cathedral, declares "This will kill that". He concludes that architecture is dead because it no longer represents the most efficient means of preserving ideas, now owned by the book.

While we lack a developed history of the office, we can retrieve early pictures of man engaged in working at a desk. The early Renaissance portrait by Antonello da Messina of Saint Jerome, an 'irresistible model of the scholarly life' with his lion, in a spacious study, pouring over his books, is itself rich in information and symbolism to the extent of providing considerable narrative depth to that moment in time.

Certainly, some dichotomies of time are at play here: da Messina dresses his Saint in contemporary clothing, in a building of

Chiat/Day office, Los Angeles in 1995 –
the first highly publicized virtual office.

contemporary stylistic design, while the
actual milieu was 1,000 years earlier in the
4th century AD. He achieves hereby a com-
paction of time in order to render the story
more immediate to his contemporaries. Saint
Jerome is sitting on a raised dais, at his desk
with objects and library shelves adjacent, and
his head, arms and book describe a circle that
forms the visual centre of the painting. While
all seems frozen in a state of calm repose,
there are a number of allegorical signs. In
as much as they function historically, some
of these signs may no longer be accessible or
worthy of accessing (the peacock, the hunting
bird, the towel, the lion) but they speak of the
picture functioning as narrative.

In his book *Species of Spaces and
other Pieces*, Georges Perec observed of this
scene: "The whole space is organized around
the piece of furniture (and the whole of the
piece of furniture is organized around the

book). The glacial architecture of the church
(the bareness of the tiling, the hostility of the
piers) has been cancelled out. Its perspectives
and its vertical lines have ceased to delimit the
site simply of an ineffable faith; they are there
solely to lend scale to the piece of furniture, to
enable it to be inscribed. Surrounded by the
uninhabitable, the study defines a domesticated space inhabited with serenity by cats,
books and men."

Saint Jerome was known for trans-
lating the scriptures from Hebrew and Greek
into Latin, and for supposedly extracting a
thorn from the paw of a lion. More significant
for our time is the relationship between the
strange positioning of secular furniture, and
the bleakness of the gothic church. It could
only be a renaissance folly that the windows
of this church at once shattered of the veil
of stained glass, are further rusticated or
barbarized in rectangular forms indicating

a later 'change of heart' or 'change of faith' in the church's builders. The alarmingly open view to fields and sky permits an almost limitless reading of Saint Jerome's world, one populated with innocent nature even as it is overshadowed with Christian iconography, and further mediated by the strange insertion of the authoritative secular study structure, which alone speaks of literacy, worldliness and the then new conception of man's supremacy over the natural world.

From this locus in time, the civilized and politicized vision of man became the measure of cultural progress for the next several centuries. With lesser grandeur but scarcely less density of meaning, we can compare the contemporary image (to the left) of a mobile worker at the offices of the advertising agency Chiat/Day in Los Angeles in 1995. The photograph was intended for publication to illustrate the new working environment for this cutting-edge advertising agency. It is the interior of the Frank Gehry Binocular Building of 1991, substantially redesigned by Lubowicki Lanier in 1995 to facilitate the company's change to the new 'virtual office' model.

The complex messages here function at the levels of informative, obvious and obtuse meanings. The obvious meaning is the radical liberation of the worker. The domesticated armchair setting speaks of a new insertion of domesticity into the office – however, the office architecture beyond is clearly ordered with different intentions. Most of the pre-existing shelving is empty, and frankly redundant for a mobile working scenario. The visual connection to other workers modulated by a system of acoustic glazing indicates that concentrated work was taken seriously, as was inter-personal connectivity. However, the ergonomic condition of the worker is challenged through the overly soft armchair and the awkward cubic work surface (obtuse meaning). Clearly, the appropriation of old tools from dislocated environments (the home) were not going to function perfectly for office activities. The worker is simultaneously radically liberated and significantly compromised. As with Saint Jerome, work is transfixed between two modes of habitation.

What further dramatizes the conflicting messages of these two images is the role of the individual in society and the world. Da Messina's vision in a sense is a resurrection and celebration of the individual divorced from both the theological and the social world. In 1460, this was emblematic of the Renaissance celebration of man as distinct from the prior homogenized and humiliated vision that negated or subjugated individuality in the Medieval period. Placed within an idealized environment, Saint Jerome could freely indulge in thought and construct a humanistic and spiritual view of the world without help, interference or censure.

The Chiat/Day employee, by contrast, is part of a larger work community from which she obtains her identity as a knowledge worker. She is visually connected to it and in a state of transition between attending to her personal mobile worker needs as well as her work productivity, in so doing she is separated from a clear role within the larger community. Here, the architectural environment is unresolved: while it facilitates her work, it simultaneously obstructs it.

Both images aspire to promote interior environments within which the individual can be empowered to produce 'enlightened' creative work – beyond whatever their milieu offered. These are worksettings rich with meaning, not consistently supportive of their inhabitants' goals, and yet perhaps an entirely naturalistic situation. The ambiguity and complexity that accrues with the individual's place in larger communities and the environmental or architectural support structure, drives the workplace design investigation that follows.

"Being Human is an art form. Human – the form(,) being (–) the art."

NERI OXMAN VIA TWITTER 4-29-18

An Age of Transformation

History books tell the stories of how societies have evolved over time. Somehow, the measure of time in chronological years has become the measure of history, although the reality is that almost everything that surrounds us in our modern world was invented and produced within an absurdly short period of time. Humanity has effectively reeled under the onslaught of a technological revolution unlike any the world has ever seen. Our ancestors of only four or five generations ago would not recognize anything in the modern world other than the rural landscape beyond the towns and cities, and the relics of certain streets within those cities. What this may press upon us is that we have invented our world today in a complete and enveloping sense, whether we realize it or not. Since we have participated in the creation of the monster of modernity, it follows that we should assume deliberate and intentional control of where the beast leads us. Progress rarely reverses, except when supreme monarchical power intervenes, and little of that remains today.

The city and the architectural interior are both shaped by human use. In order to understand the workplace of today, we need to understand where it comes from, which is not a simple story. The city itself contains all the threads of utility and meaning that we grapple with in workplace design and is thus a great place from which to trace the story of the modern workplace. United by a common interest, urban design and interior design are both uniquely concerned with how people use places. Both promote logical ordering of needs and propinquities within a spatial and circulation logic which relies on the connective characteristics of flow.

As such, there is an enormous responsibility placed upon us to shape our streets to support our dreams and ambitions. And to resist the dumbing down of this commonplace 'place' which has too often been shaped by landowners, engineers and property developers who have narrowed their responsibilities to the public realm. For engineers, a street is merely a device to move from point A to point B. For a landowner or property developer, the property on either side is financial asset to be leveraged for maximum profit. It is left to design and designers to be held accountable for infusing the city and its streets with meaning, albeit tempered by commercial constraints.

Working and learning, which has historically been the process whereby knowledge and skills are acquired, came to need the comforts of shelter. Shelter was 'found' where agreeable conditions existed. The cave, the tree umbrella, the tree clusters gave some shelter from wind, rain and predators. The tree became an archetype of shelter. And humans used its strong limbs and trunks to create the first huts. The primitive hut became the archetype for 'house' and so the process of building began to inform the image of architecture. Order, clarity and economy were conveyed by accepting and growing appreciation for the 'look' of how things were made. The fluted columns of the Greek Doric order express the mark of the wood chisel from when these columns were cut and shaped from the trunks of trees.

All human environments emerged as adaptations of the first primitive shelter: the cave which became the room. Rooms became houses, houses became sacred and civic institutions, and later offices. For most of the world's population, the simple house people shared was a single room, which served multiple purposes. Apart from housing the family and in some cases servants, it might house livestock, feed and farming tools. All lived together in often smoke-filled space, since chimneys were a late invention, and fire was needed for cooking and warming the interior. Activities like work occurred in this space, including transactions with the outside world.

The Medieval house that was a single room, in a time of relative prosperity became subdivided into multiple rooms, and its footprint extended. A large hall would have rooms carved out, and a second level added for bedrooms. If the main house was too small, room extensions were added. The space which is a room was also the building block that evolved and moderated domestic culture from the 16th century to our own. Within the house, a kind of individual ownership occurred too. Bedrooms became owned and decorated accordingly. The embellishment of the interior evolved from the pragmatic housing of farm tools and kitchenware with simple furniture to a display of luxuries that represented measures of worldly success. The house became capable of supporting a mythic world, and in so doing became its own archetype.

The act of entering a person's house or home became the act of entering their deliberately shaped, and embellished world. The house and the property it sat on fortified and extended an owner's identity and self-image. The value of ownership thus became mythical beyond its pecuniary value – and indeed valuable to how we consider work communities today. The first offices that followed were the rooms for governance, such as the Uffizi complex (meaning 'offices') designed by Giorgio Vasari in 1560 in Florence, and where scribes and clerks recorded on scrolls of papyrus, parchment or paper.

Five hundred years ago, as populations grew and local economies flourished in Europe, circumstances converged to see the feudal system rapidly replaced by the new private (non-communal) enclosure of land, which brought the wholly new concept of private and individual land ownership into being. As it happened, the land grab that occurred via the opportunism of feudal lords and monarchs violently dispossessed vast peasant communities who had enjoyed communal use of land that was regarded as God's sole possession. In England, from the time of King Henry VIII, a series of acts of parliament ensured protection for the new owners, who themselves constituted the parliamentary body. Landowners would thenceforth frustrate urban improvements first in English cities and later across the globe, wielding as they did more legislative power than the monarchy. Indeed, since the signing of the Magna Carta, the system of law in England was primarily designed to protect property, not people, since property represented real value.

The societal disruptions caused by the royally sanctioned campaign of land appropriation were considerable. Those in favor, and generally those who profited thereby, would offer the argument that it was human nature to possess and exploit property, which would ultimately lead to the greater benefit of the community. The British 'founding' of America was a case in point. The Mayflower settlers of 1620 arrived in Virginia on a charter that was positively communist: they were committed as a community to exploit all economic opportunities in the new world for a period of seven years, and thereafter to pay dividends to the European shareholders who funded their voyage. Instead, their communal efforts quickly fell apart and were superseded by land subdivisions that allowed individual ownership and exploitation.

GLOBAL TRADE AND CROWD SOURCED SCIENCE

In the European Renaissance, a new merchant class emerged as the dominant social class, replacing the aristocracy and trade guilds in power and influence. The merchants organized themselves as trading powers, and the trading company was brought

"Nothing is experienced by itself, but always in relation to its surroundings, the sequences of events leading up to it, the memory of past experiences."

KEVIN LYNCH – THE IMAGE OF THE CITY

The Primitive Hut, illustrated by Charles-Dominique-Joseph Eisen, as envisioned by Marc-Antoine Laugier in *Essai sur l'architecture*, 1755.

into existence. Trade with the Far East was a huge attraction, and voyages of discovery by the British, Dutch, Spanish and Portuguese lead to new sea routes to the Spice Islands and a corresponding 'contraction of trade distance'. Spice had become highly sought after in Europe, both a vanity of the wealthy and essential for preserving meats. By virtue of minimal weight by value and durability, it became a lucrative cargo to offset the financial burden of long and expensive ship voyages around the heel of Africa.

Early companies like the Dutch East India Company and the English East India Company had military arms, and with their sovereigns' blessings, subjugated native people in the Americas, Africa, India, the Spice

Islands and the Far East (from 1150 AD, the word Company described a 'body of soldiers' and so the term was, from the start, confused with a military meaning). The company became a body organized to overcome competition and dominate a market. In the early days this extended to utilizing any violent means necessary.

The foundation for the age's exponential growth was provided by massive advancement in scientific discovery. A landmark event in 1665 saw the creation of The Royal Society in London, formed to foster the growth and sharing of scientific knowledge. At this time, several knowledge 'societies', such as the Royal Geographic Society and the Royal Botanic Society, were expressly established to help commercialize knowledge of far-off resources, and exploit far-off colonial ventures. They were driven by the love of minerals, spices, crops and homewares, not simply the love of shared knowledge.

Henry Oldenburg, the first secretary of the Royal Society, 'pioneered the idea that secrecy was inimical to scientific progress, and convinced scientists that they should give up their sole ownership of their ideas in exchange for recognition they would receive as creator or discoverer of those ideas' (J. Surowiecki, *The Wisdom of Crowds*). The modern age would grow rapidly on the first flowering of 'open science' shared freely with the public – essentially the renewable resource of knowledge sharing – acting for the public good.

This newly unified international scientific community could now build on knowledge from numerous sources, and benefit from multiple intelligences applied to any problem, like an early form of multiple platform processing. While large groups, or 'crowds', may be poor idea generators, they excel at broadening the scope of subjects and editing propositions through analytical debate, which greatly speeds both the development of inventions and delivery to market. In many ways, this foreshadows the essential values of cohesive teamwork that is vital to the workplace today.

THE EMERGENCE OF THE CONSUMER SOCIETY

From the early 17th century, the French Ancien Regime had been obsessed with the culture of refinement. From the pinnacles of robust Baroque invention, they had increasingly detached themselves from the real world, inspired by their monarch Louis XIV's claims to divinity, and endeavored to create a heaven on earth, where nature was trained, guided and controlled by man. The vegetable garden of the palace of Versailles, Le Potager du Roi, created between 1678 and

1683, moved beyond the simple provision of fresh fruit and vegetable produce for the kings' table to become a laboratory for the subjugation, instruction and reinvention of nature. Fruit bearing vines were trained for optimum production, plants were cross-bred and new fruits were harvested out of season using a novel system of suntrap walled enclosures to form micro-climates 50 years before greenhouses were invented in Holland.

Science was on the ascendant, and controlling nature was its validation. A hundred years later, in a whimsical attempt to represent man's harmonious relationship to nature, Marie Antoinette had a faux rustic village built at the foot of her garden at Versailles so that she could observe rural life, and watch cows being milked. The wigs she wore were either white or grey, in keeping with the time, intentionally lending her a sense of age and experience beyond her years.

In society, wisdom, rhetoric and refinement were revered, passion and the rustic were not. Faces were powdered white, as nothing was more gauche than a suntan. Signs of physical exertion were the signs of a commoner. Beyond powder, perfumes were used liberally to mask unhygienic scents. Personal bathing was still rare and people quite literally smelled like animals. It was not till the late Victorian era that indoor bathrooms became accepted and even then they were rare. In 1912, the Savoy Hotel in London boasted the most modern facilities of any hotel in the world: one bathroom was provided for every 12 rooms.

As much as it was presided over by a declining, and aging, aristocratic class, the 18th century culture of maturity and refinement in tradition is diametrically opposed to that of today. The evolution of modern advertising through the middle of the 20th century led to a realization that mature adults had made their consumer choices in early adulthood, and would not easily shift brand loyalties. Youth however, were not only open to choice, but actively curious about new product ideas. Marketing to youth proved highly effective, often achieving lifelong brand loyalties. Promoting youth as the 'taste makers' also helped convince their elders to shift loyalties. Our world's obsession with youth, with never growing old, is ultimately consumer driven.

In 1789, the French Revolution and the associated Paris upheavals brought in cultural changes that were to accelerate the social advancement of the masses. In 1793, with the capture, eviction from their home, the Louvre palace, and subsequent execution of the royal family, parts of the Louvre palace were opened up to the public. This single act was in itself a major paradigm shift in creating the first public exhibition of art. For the first time, the riches of the secular art world were on display to the people. Not only had all prior art been commissioned by and for the rich, but it had been effectively hoarded and sequestered by the rich. To be an artist was to be the vassal of merchants and aristocrats. Before this moment, art was an exclusive luxury commodity and culture completely beyond the reach of the common man.

The Salon Carre in the Louvre was used to host the first public exhibition of painting and sculpture by contemporary artists of the time. Although the art works were neither political nor socially engaging – they were traditional paintings of landscapes, nudes, and religious or mythological themes – the experience completed a transformation of both art and the common man. The audience for this show was the first real 'public' – comprised of citizen subjects who had just violently gained political power and instituted the democracy of France's First Republic. As art found a new audience in the masses, the masses were invited into the spectacle of consumption. Art would henceforth re-enter the world, from its long confinement in the cloisters of the wealthy, and the masses would embark on a new journey of aesthetic consumerism.

The marketplace of the time would also undergo a massive transformation in response to the enfranchisement of the masses. The typology of the marketplace, in so many ways the ancestor of the modern office, had remained unaltered for centuries. As the city grew into a system of social communication, urban dwellers adopted the streets as their dwellings. The facades of houses became the four walls of the social life of the crowd. The street had become a (newly sanitized) dwelling. With the discovery of an iron architecture, married to industrial glass, the first arcades emerged in 1790, offering covered streets of shopping in Paris and other European cities. With gaslighting, the marketplace was effectively extended into the night and shopping in Paris of the time could extend till 10 o'clock at night. The arcades flourished with this new illuminated spectacle and led to the first department stores in 1870's. The marketplace had become a controlled indoor experience focused on seduction.

The great Industrial Age brought with it innumerable changes to the lives of ordinary people. It ushered in the age of mass production, which necessitated mass marketing and mass distribution, engendering the proliferation of new markets for the vast quantities of new goods. Almost overnight, the

21

people, now referred to as 'the masses' themselves, were exposed to something entirely new – a dream-like proliferation of (now affordable) luxury commodities. The scale and clustering of retail stores would similarly change overnight, and the glazed arcade became the grand new interior/exterior for the spectacle of capitalism.

The arcade interior was all the more provocative in that it offered a bridge between the private domestic interior and the public space of the city. It would serve as a metaphor for the extension of a personal world into the collective world, into the crowd. The domestic domain had already been dismantled as the workplace became permanently separated. What would also follow was the great escalation of urban waste and garbage as the inexpensive products of mass production were easily disposed of, upending the old practice of literally leaving all your possessions to your family. Prior to this, domestic possessions were preciously treated: for instance, a man's suit would be carefully repaired and maintained, and passed down for several generations.

Writing in his book *Paris, Capital of the 19th century*, Walter Benjamin observed: "Most of the Paris arcades came into being during the decade and a half which followed 1822. The first condition of their emergence was the boom in the textile trade. The magasins de nouveauté, the first establishments that kept large stocks of goods on the premises, began to appear. They were the forerunners of the department stores. It was the time of which Balzac wrote: 'The great poem of display chants its stanzas of color from the Madeleine to the gate of Saint-Denis'. The arcades were the centre of the luxury goods trade. The manner in which they were fitted out displayed Art in the service of the salesman. Contemporaries never tired of admiring them. An illustrated Paris guide pronounced: 'These arcades, a new contrivance of industrial luxury, are glass covered, marble floored passages through entire blocks of houses, whose proprietors have joined forces in the venture. On both sides of these passages, which obtain their light from above, there are arrayed the most elegant shops, so that such an arcade is a city, indeed a world, in miniature'."

Conventional history announces the achievements of an age as technological wonders, but more significant are the social wonders as a measure of the impact of technological change. The mass influx of people into the cities to serve the new industries created the condition of the crowd, whose first incarnation had spelled disaster for the privileged classes: in destroying the monarchy the French revolution effectively cut a line across history. From the revolutionary crowd emerged the new class of consumers, the true urban masses. And the intelligentsia struggled to uncover a means of coping with the startlingly new world: mass production had been followed by a fetishistic culture of consumption. The city began a metamorphosis to supply this new demand.

In the *Society of the Spectacle*, Guy Debord would observe: "The first stage of the economy's domination of social life brought about an evident degradation of being into having – human fulfillment was no longer equated with what one was, but with what one possessed. The present stage, in which social life has become completely dominated by the accumulated productions of the economy, is bringing about a general shift from having to appearing – all 'having' must now derive its immediate prestige and its ultimate purpose from appearances."

THE PRIMITIVE HUT: A RETURN TO ELEMENTAL ARCHITECTURE

Prior to the beginning of the industrial revolution, the building typologies ranged from peasant hut to palace to temple, with few examples between. If a building had a civic function, it was not much more than a large house with multiple rooms, acquiring corridors where rooms became numerous. Architecture was concerned with the application of style, utility was a factor to be solved simply to make time for the love of embellishment. The service of Architecture was an exclusive luxury of the rich within a highly structured, hierarchical society.

At the tail-end of the Baroque Period, in his essay on architecture of 1753, the Jesuit priest Marc-Antoine Laugier, condemned the frivolous late Baroque architectural practices of the day and advocated powerfully for a return to fundamental, authentic principles. As has been done so many times before in history, he admonished architecture for forgetting its origins in the principles of basic construction. The concept of the primitive hut exemplified these original principles, and Laugier argued for a new authenticity that would adopt this type of approach:

"The savage, in his leafy shelter, does not know how to protect himself from the uncomfortable damp that penetrates everywhere; he creeps into a nearby cave and, finding it dry, he praises himself for his discovery. But soon the darkness and foul air surrounding him make his stay unbearable again. He leaves and is resolved to make good by his ingenuity the careless neglect of nature.

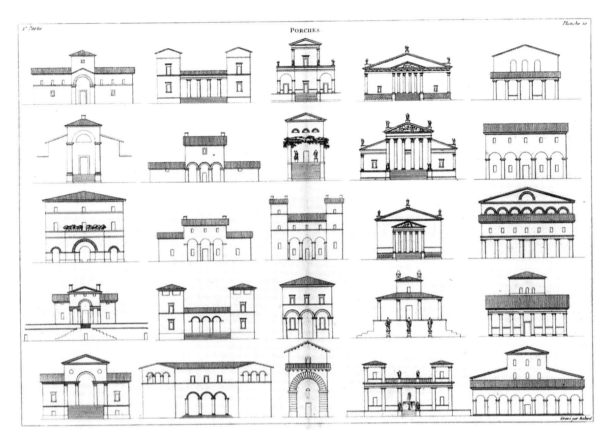

Building elevation typologies identified in
Precis des leçons d'architecture données à l'École royale polytechnique, J.N.L. Durand, 1809.

He wants to make himself a dwelling that protects but does not bury him. Some fallen branches in the forest are the right material for his purpose; he chooses four of the strongest, raises them upright and arranges them in a square; across their top he lays four other branches; on these he hoists from two sides yet another row of branches which, inclining towards each other, meet at their highest point. He then covers this kind of roof with leaves so closely packed that neither sun nor rain can penetrate. Thus, man is housed. The pieces of wood set upright have given us the idea of the column, the pieces placed horizontally on top of them the idea of the entablature, the inclining pieces forming the roof the idea of the pediment."

This elemental approach to elegance in architecture produced a profound new direction in architectural theory. Enlightenment architects would present a new milieu of classical purity in conception, and even as historicist styles ebbed and flowed through the 19th century, new directions would use the same yardstick to justify a new evolution. In 1920, Le Corbusier and his peers would appeal to a rationalist purity cloaking a socialistic program of housing and urban development. His much lauded statement that "a house as a machine for living in" was little more than industrial fetishism applied to the primitive hut.

THE RATIONALIZATION OF BUILDING TYPES

From the 1780's, the pressures on towns and cities in adapting to expanding populations and new civic needs produced entirely new building types, ranging from hospitals to schools to prisons to factories to warehouses. The milieu of the Age of Enlightenment assisted in the rationalization of these new types, with powerfully influential examples like the lexicon of architectural typologies produced by J.N.L. Durand. Through scores of typological plans, his rationalization lead to a persuasive modular unitization, foreshadowing the wide scale industrial production to come.

As a former army engineer, Durand had just two governing criteria for his model types: convenience (or efficiency) and economy. Napoleon had proposed that architects who caused overruns in building budgets should be thrown into debtors' prison, and hence economy was paramount! Durand understood nature through a process of scientific quantification, which substituted mathematical logic for metaphor as a model of thought. The Enlightenment principle of rationalism assumed that God/ the creator had made the universe beautiful, harmonious and mathematical, and that through scientific experimentation the principles of creation could be recreated. The objective was to deduce the laws of nature, the general from which all of the particulars may then be derived. His book *Précis Des Leçons D'architecure Donnés À l'Ecole Polytechnique* (Précis of the Lectures on Architecture Given at the Ecole Polytechnique), (1802-1805), formed the major reference source for most architects working on public projects in France in the first half of the 19th century.

For Durand, the grid was the generator of the plan. Architectural method approached scientific method in applying technical rules and abstract formulas to building design and town planning. This cataloging process was a parallel

24

Passage des Panoramas, Paris, 19th century.

development to the extensive illustrated engineering manuals of machines of the time, curiously called 'Theatres of Machines'. The striving for rationalism and scientific validity was carried through architectural education to the modern movement from 1920 onwards, the difference was that Durand was cataloging classical orders applied to pure geometric form, while the modern movement in architecture was to strip away the orders and reduce architectural form to its primitive geometric essence. The world moved thus from a classically elaborated and constrained tradition to a completely new beginning without precedent, and with all the unreflective emptiness that can be associated with newness.

The Parisian city dweller of the 19th century, with his new political superiority, attempted to bring the countryside into town, and initiated a conception of the city as a continuous landscape. Experiments in utopian urban and suburban schemes were rising throughout Europe, and the first garden suburb was built in 1875 by Richard Norman Shaw outside of London, a forerunner of the Garden City Movement. Formalized by Ebeneezer Howard in 1898, the movement promoted self-contained garden cities ringed by greenbelts, like lungs of nature, and many modern cities were planned with these principles in mind. Ultimately, the constraints of a centrifugal planning that created internal ghettoes would cause the idea to capsize itself.

For private individuals, the new Industrial Age of commerce brought with it a fundamental dislocation. The place of work was removed from the home, so each setting was no longer tempered by the other. As the home became a personalized and private landscape, the office became a machine for service and production. The gravitational centre of communal living shifted to the office as the domestic space internalized and shut out the world. The industrial revolution had overturned old ways of living and working, and shattered their interrelationships.

First an adjunct to palaces, later to sacred and civic structures, the office became, in the 19th century, an important appendage to the factory to undertake its administrative functions. Without any idea about what the growing typology of the office meant, people applied their expertise in known sciences. The formal organization of the office was therefore arranged on two paradigms: the classical hierarchical organization of the military, and the spatial divisions of agriculture. Hierarchical organization ensured the smooth operation of labor, the spatial divisions of agriculture guided efficient factory planning.

Thus, the apparently benign modern workplace was a child born of conflicted parents (the farm and the factory) in an age of convulsive and traumatized change. Its grandparent, the early industrial enterprise, was itself a child of an embattled age. The great labor classes of the 18th century – the agricultural workers and the domestic workers – were thrust from embryo to withered octogenarian in so many years, but the transition was less painful for their offspring, who donned the uniforms of the first blue collar factory workers and overnight became the new predominant class in Europe and America: the working class, or the new proletariat of Marx and Engels.

The society of the time, across all classes, struggled with adapting to a new world. Marx accurately diagnosed the newly imposed form of political economy based on capital and the associated disruptions on people's lives. In Northern England, workers that became known as the Luddites destroyed factory machinery in protest, while in Paris, the bourgeois intellectual flaneur walked tortoises in the arcades and streets in protest at the pace of modern life and its overwhelming utilitarian character. Baudelaire himself was to run screaming from the sight of Paris' new technological imposter, the Eiffel Tower.

The invention of photography and machines of reproduction undermined the value system of art, and in so doing, dramatically undermined the production of traditional culture. However, photography itself had been prefigured in the panorama paintings of Jacques-Louis David and his students in the early part of the century who, in parallel to a scientific drive to master nature, wanted to produce scenes of a perfect imitation or reproduction of nature. Their efforts at artificial perfection prepared the way not only for photography and mechanical reproduction, but for silent film and sound film, and, most recently the video game (which as an $8 billion industry in 2007 surpassed the global movie industry).

The industrial era invariably created the molds for so many modern institutions. From boarding houses came hotels, from the arcades came the department stores, from the department stores came the first image of the modern marketplace and total mass consumption. This marketplace, in tandem with the factory office, became the model for new institutions, from hospitality, to government, to healthcare and education, to the workplace. The progressive open office of today functions as a highly refined trading environment or marketplace. The transactions merely involve less audible noise.

FROM THE GLASS ARCADES TO THE GLASS SKYSCRAPER

Though its origin may have been the age-old village marketplace, the 19th century consumer experience of the arcade blurred inside and outside. Following the introduction of iron as a new building material, and the creation of a private sector of speculative building, it began as a functional means of glazing over streets in order to avoid inclement weather obstructing use of the street and disrupting the business of shopping. Whatever prolongs the buyer's exposure to the seller, favors the exchange of capital. The new arcade would appropriate the street as a movement channel and transform the pedestrian experience into a social experience by providing a maze of competing destinations with an endless variety of seductive storefronts. Taking their places first in the arcades, the gas lamps arrived and created a new interior of the night – the crowd now felt safe to wander the city at night without the dangers of darkness.

As the promenade of the newly emancipated urban society of the post-revolutionary era, the arcade soon became a construction typology itself, where buildings were constructed or adapted to create the arcade thoroughfare lined with merchant stores and accept the glass roof in an integrated fashion. The hybridization inherent in the arcade typology – neither street nor building, neither inside nor outside – allowed the advantages of its ambiguities. Even its etymological origin was hybridized: the term 'arcade' referred to an arched and vaulted space typically defined by open columns down one side. It would be simultaneously public and private, and its encircling panorama the constantly changing market display of commodities.

As the new systems of commerce and political reorganization molded the modern world, the people sought enfranchisement in work and society. The new model of the city would proscribe their social relations but not without a profoundly democratic interaction. To the awareness of interior/exterior space and its parallels with the inner and outer lives of people, was added a fascination with the physiognomies of the new urban dwellers in the 1840's, and the struggle for a cultural framework to ground the new world. A hero class was needed to mediate between tradition and modernity in uncovering the identity of modernity, and with his empathetic relationship to literature, this first hero would be the empathetic 'flaneur' of the Parisian cityscape: a new kind of urban man who saunters around observing the new society.

Born into the new age of industry, the middle class flaneur laid claim to the city

25

"It was a thousand years after the Romans left Britain that the country's fledgling and burgeoning press and publishing industry began to invest in hard roads – why? Simply to ensure that newspapers, books and letters were dispatched with the maximum speed. The speed and distribution of information drives economies."

ALAN MOORE – NO STRAIGHT LINES

as his home. His existence attracted considerable attention as the icon of modernity, in its unique blending of privilege, education and liberation from the myopia of industrial life, like the division of labor. The flaneur was to live two equally important lives: one as a real person, whose identity was challenged by the changes in his time, and another, no less significant, as a symbol: a mythical hero figure whose very existence acted as both a critique and a promotional emblem of the new capitalist world.

The flaneur was a construct of three sources: the middle class intellectual, the journalist writer and the newspaper reading public, a wholly new urban class that had grown rapidly as newspapers transformed themselves adding affordability through advertising revenue and entertainment to their news function. They became mass purveyors of the stories of accidents and crime. Their intrusions into the private lives of people accompanied a wide fascination with social types. The

most popular fiction of the 1840s in France was the physiognomies – books that analyzed the behaviors of different urban characters and vocations.

In due course, the flaneur led to the detective of fiction, the private detective, who grows in sophistication, as the hero of the urban condition. The shadow side of the detective was a person with the set of skills to solve the modern mystery of identity, or better, to solve the crime of modern life, and prosecute the offenders. This was the hero whose conquests of rational process against all odds became a model for surviving the decline of routine human labor and led to the model of the knowledge worker. This worker is essentially the mirror of the private detective: isolated by choice, burrowing into the depths of specialism and responsible for his or her results without supervision or accountability as those above him or her would know less and less about the fragmented knowledge structure itself. Where in the industrial economy, wealth was based on ownership of capital, i.e. factories, in the knowledge economy, wealth is based in part upon the access to knowledge and information and the ability to use both to create or improve goods and services.

Whatever it's capitalist and metropolitan drivers, the arcade experience introduced a radically new architectural typology that would begin a commercial restructuring of the city. A great and permanent public 'room' had been created for the spectacle of commerce as a new facility for mass consumption. The ambiguities of inside and outside would serve to extend its attraction. The notion of an embellished public interior would begin to speak to the private interior, and as such facilitate, what Guy Debord saw as the transplanting of culture with fetishism and alienation, in the 'spectacle of the commodity'.

This utterly new urban condition would inevitably change forever the identity of the common man – a crisis already dreamt by Rousseau 50 years earlier, and now taking hold. The hero icon of the 'noble savage' imagined into being by Rousseau was to appear as an increasingly remote mythology, though one that could be carried into the future in different clothing. The noble savage straddled the worlds of pre-history and modernity, of both cowboy and Indian, later emerging as conflicted Hollywood characters like Rambo or Dirty Harry. The spectacle of the commodity would suffuse modern life and make the masses prisoners to consumption. In the 1930's, Walter Benjamin would describe the arcade as the hollow mold from which the image of the 'modern' was cast.

Since the arcade space itself had become both the spectacle and marketplace for the new consumer phantasmagoria, the spectacle demanded to be emulated on a grand scale. In 1851, when one of the first great world's fairs, the Crystal Palace Exhibition, opened in London to popular and almost ecstatic acclaim for its novelty, all that had occurred was the appropriation of the arcade experience onto a greenfield site. Where urban walls were absent, the glass of the roof descended to the ground creating a miraculous crystal box. Glass had made its appearance no longer as embellishment to a solid masonry temple of permanence, but as the total enclosure of shelter, and one that symbolized light, delicacy, modernity, fragility, and the (uncritical) mirror reflection of its surroundings. It successfully emulated the lightness of the commodity.

The arcade type grew in popularity but also convulsively gave birth to a different model of the parade of consumption: the multi-level department store with single ownership and wholly controlled interior atmosphere. Le Bon Marche store in Paris evolved into the first version of this type in 1852 and was an immediate success. The interieur offered by the arcades had become a street again: where the arcades offered the labyrinth of the city for roaming, the department store offered the labyrinth of merchandise – an infinitely more shifting, immersive and fantastic landscape.

The city of the crafts guilds and the aristocrats had given way to the city of the merchants and industrialists and in so doing become a gigantic expression of the marketplace. With massive urban redevelopment, a confusing texture of complexity overlaid the city. It became increasingly difficult to read the transformations that had taken place. The charm of the arcade was in its crystallization of this idea in producing a microcosm of the city, and, at the same time, the cathedral for worshipping the new religion of consumption.

Once built, the Crystal Palace, in composition both grand and elegant, provided an entirely new provocation. Buildings could become light-weight, transparent and sheathed in glass on a massive scale. The first skyscrapers of the 19th century borrowed the heavier language of low-rise traditional masonry buildings, extruded to great heights. But as early as 1920, Mies van der Rohe proposed entirely modern glass skyscrapers for Berlin. Not only did glass solve problems of weathering and weight, but it was inexpensive and easily fabricated and installed. It would take little time for it to become the 20th century standard for speculative and conventional corporate architecture.

With the decline of the centralized city form, as detailed in the following chapter, the department store was gradually superseded by the localized American Shopping Centre typology of the 1950s, serving suburban sprawl, which was closer to the arcade in ownership divisions and experience, but a product of extreme control over the consumer experience. Shopping behavior was studied as in a Petri dish, and the planning led to a fixed design formula, which guaranteed a controlled, formulaic experience. Since organization and control were the shores of reason against the inhuman lunacies experienced within the world wars, as well as the methods of the military machine that had saved the world, this packaged 'comfort food' became entirely acceptable. From its earlier parallel career with the department store, the office gradually converged on the marketplace. The need to accommodate large numbers of staffers to confer, negotiate and respond to mass market conditions drove the office to become an open, dynamic and occasionally very loud environment by the end of the 20th century.

We have seen the monk's cell which becomes an office, the merchant seafarers that create new territories of trade, open source science that becomes first a rapid platform for knowledge sharing, and later, the open source web, the new consumer society that becomes the market for innovative products, the glass greenhouse which becomes the glazed shopping arcade, which becomes the Crystal Palace, and then, ultimately, the basic standard for sheathing commercial office buildings. Out of this new society, new heroes would come.

The world of the worker is itself a progressively changing invention. The flaneur character for a short time captivated the French post-revolutionary imagination, which lead to modern heroes of the masses, in particular the private detective. These fabrications served to provide an ideal human model to which modern workers could aspire, to forget the drudgery of their work lives and reimagine their futures.

The new worker of the 21st century, the knowledge worker, is profoundly different, though it is questionable that the older service industry milieu has fully transformed. Traces of its presence persist and obscure the landscape of the new workplace. We know this new worker has reformed the work process itself, which must invariably disrupt the place of work too.

27

The City as an Organizational Model

There is no better model of organization than the city, when it comes to planning a workspace. The form of workspace in many ways mirrors that of the city: as a system designed to moderate and guide productive human processes. The workplace is an organism in a constant state of change, as is the city, but the city has resolved, over centuries, most of its complexities and contradictions, whereas the workplace is a relatively new invention. We therefore look to the city for guidance in moving workplace design forward.

As our richest platform to create community, the city holds profound meaning for all people. While there may be a million different views on good cityscapes, the attachment to this phenomenal, incremental product of human effort is universal. For this reason, the city as archetype belongs actively within our daily lives.

For centuries, men have proposed dramatic changes to the face and form of the city. It is in the nature of humanity's philosophizing to reduce processes to 'essential descriptions' which capture the essence in as few words, or thought categories, as possible. There have been many propositions about 'correcting the city', and many visions of the utopian city. All of these have been forced to reduce their ideas to essential concepts to be communicable. And yet, the thread of connection between these ideas and the reality of the city is fractured when one compares narrowly framed viewpoints and the almost unfathomably vast, complex, living organism that is the city, which is why it perpetually resists every earnest effort to rationalize or codify its occupation.

As one of humanity's most amazing and enduring inventions, the city is a laboratory for endless experiments in how we can utilize space, interact with others, focus our entrepreneurial efforts and optimize our conditions of production so that we may at the least, survive, and at best, prosper and grow long overlaid over with newer experiments, which themselves were replaced and then lost. How do we explain the distribution of space and the network of streets that facilitate the modern city's working? It is the consequence of numerous trials and errors. What worked well survived, what did not, was scrapped. As cities evolve, their economic base evolves too. There is a correlation between suitable development and intrinsic economic value. This way many good structures find themselves obsolete, so the core of the city is continuously renewed under conditions that maintain the relative density and value of space utilization.

The newness of development is a fundamental factor in urban character. In new cities, land which begins as raw land is cheap. Cheap land begets cheap building, but after each generation values increase. As land lifts in value, so more money is spent on development. The new cities in the Western United States are good examples of this. Any visitor to Los Angeles might be appalled at the shoddy condition of almost all urban development, without realizing that for the most part, the buildings are the first ones to sit on this land. In each case, when one of these 'derelicts' gets knocked down, a better building replaces it. When considering the cities of Europe, it should become evident that every building, however old, is sitting upon many generations of building before it.

The city as artifact is the product of millennia of human effort. Even new cities benefit from this legacy as they adopt

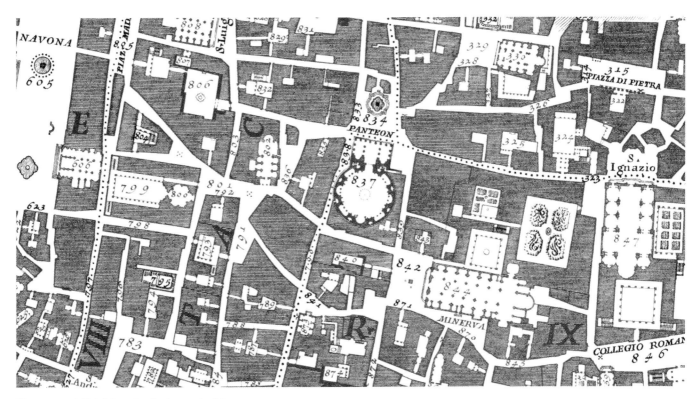

Figure-ground: Detail from *La pianta grande di Roma*
(The Large Plan of Rome), Giovanni Battista Nolli, 1748.

planning strategies that have been proved over time. Its basis of order is the network. One form of that network is a street pattern or grid. All physical activity is dependent on the street network or grid, and all life flows through it. The city has also been described as a place which exists for no other reason than to maximize the opportunities for human interaction. At its most prosaic level, this exists to support the economic system of trade. Trade flourishes under conditions of relatively fast and loosely controlled human agreement. Trust itself may be the corner stone of efficient business since the law, or legal framework, is perhaps too ponderous to maintain a vital and robust exchange system.

The concentration of co-located business has produced the city we experience today. The interweaving of human habitation is a function of movement systems. In early cities, these were unsophisticated, causing people to live in close proximity. In the 20th century, a revolution in mass transportation, combined with a historic distrust of the city's moral fabric and analogous environmental impurity, allowed people to flee the disorder and inconvenience of the city for suburban sprawl, and yet still operate in close business proximity. The city today is therefore more defined by business development than residential, though recent developments following a renewed interest in urban living, have caused an inverse effect.

Although urban environments are perceived as a tableau of solid and negative space, the experiential reality is that it is most profoundly about space and not about objects. We exist in space. We do not exist in objects. The closest we may get to existing in objects is in owning a trophy home, or some fashion designer statement dress. This kind of existence is more than anything else symbolic. The attraction for objects is little more than an existential fascination with 'the other': the outside world, the perfectly circumscribed and complete, the symbolic or the unattainable. This attraction to the fixed symbol in part describes orthodox city planning's focus on bricks and mortar development: the urban block, rather than the negative space of streets.

In 1748, Giambattista Nolli published his figure-ground map of Rome. Although the cartographic style was not entirely new, his representation of built space with blocks and buildings shaded in a dark poché, leaving open space in white, brought a new lucidity to the experience of the city. One could immediately imagine oneself traveling through the articulated scenic canyons of streets and alleys and enjoying the generosity of public moments in squares, temples, markets and libraries.

In her ground-breaking treatise published in 1961, *The Death and Life of Great American Cities,* Jane Jacobs advocated for a city that can be actively ordered, shaped and controlled by its inhabitants. She quoted James Boswell who wrote of the city of London in 1791: "...the intellectual man is struck with it, as comprehending the whole of human life in all its variety, the contemplation of which is inexhaustible". Echoing this view, Boswell's friend Samuel Johnson coined that famous phrase: "When a man is tired of London, he is tired of life".

FROM FRANKENSTEIN UTOPIAS TO DOUGHNUT CITIES

Boswell's hint at the complexity of cities is crucial: it is the multiplicity of uses, inextricably woven into each other, that make the city both vital and open ended. To attempt to define the city by identifying and separating use categories – a major failure of modern planning doctrine – is futile and misleading. The reassembled picture fails to bear resemblance to its subject. It is the combinations and mixtures of uses that need appraisal. To quote Jacobs: "A mixture of uses, if it is to be sufficiently complex to sustain city safety, public contact and cross-use, needs an enormous diversity of ingredients." Monofunctions and monotony are fatal. In essence, she observes that a mixture of uses attracts a mixture of users. A mixture of users will guarantee a diversified time use of streets and these attributes make for successful, safe and lively urban areas.

Thus, the ideal city relies on a great diversity of uses, encouraging the growth and proliferation of diversity itself. It is the natural home to small industries and all forms of specialized business. These endeavors would not survive without the synergistic support of other small manufacturers, suppliers and distributors. For the most part, small businesses could not survive outside of the city which provides clients or customers from its large population diversity. In this sense, the city is a true incubator. Generally, all business ventures must start small, and the city offers a sustainable base from which to grow. Towns, suburbs and villages do not have the breadth of consumer base to support these endeavors – they must be satisfied with monopolistic uses: the supermarket, the multiplex cinema

complex and the big box retailers for one-stop shopping. And these smaller venues can be a natural home for large businesses, which frequently have the resources to handle all aspects of the production chain in house and sell to broader markets; and are thus internally self-sufficient.

As a biological organism, the city is essentially an open-ended system. It relies on unimpeded mobility and fluidity in its boundaries. In order to sustain itself, it must accommodate endless modification and change. Politicians and planners have constantly attempted to institute complete and perfected visions on the city in an effort to create one-time solutions to blighted city areas, or to shape incipient settlements. Many of these visions have been especially seductive: Britain's 19th century Garden City movement,

"It is said that a fish knows nothing about water. It is completely immersed in it, and consequently lacks any experience of what it is not. Water's ubiquity makes it invisible to the fish. The same might be said of our experience of the City. We experience it, move through it constantly, conduct our business in it, connect with friends and colleagues inside and outside its boundaries: as water is to the fish, the city is to us – transparent."

CLIVE WILKINSON

Camille Sitte's industrial city, Le Corbusier's Ville Radiuse are amongst them.

Each of these utopian visions has surgically appropriated special aspects of the city and structured a vision of persuasive clarity. Each of these visions fails for the same reasons. They fail to learn anything coherent about what makes the urban areas work, and achieve clarity at the expense of amputating the city's essential complexity. It is as if doctors were to construct a 'whole new man' from a body on an operating table by amputating only those limbs and organs that are supposedly 'charming and healthy' and reconstituting them in a new body, and at times replicating them to sculpt a new monstrous species. The creation of Frankenstein comes to mind – not coincidentally dreamt up in 1820 by Mary Shelley, whose attachment to the contemporary English Romantic movement in literature no doubt fueled many stories of the appalling human cost of early industrialization.

Another distinct failure in planning theory has been a fascination with closed-system solutions. Simply proposing a static image of the city is tantamount to suggesting that something as frozen in time as the tourist picture post card image could solve urban problems. In the face of a continuously dynamic system like the city, any static image becomes immediately obsolete, a thing of the past, like a picture postcard. Most city plans fail to rise above frozen snapshots of ordered solutions, ignoring the fact that completeness or perfect design is antithetical to the city. A city plan needs to confront and resolve unfolding, evolving and continuously re-adapting physical formations, which are informed by complementary and interrelated use structures.

Curiously, the city's ability to rapidly respond to change also requires a stable base. There is a dynamic balance between fixity and flux. The myriad of enterprises which constitute the city rely on both creating new networks and utilizing established networks. This requires time to grow stability and mesh together, and requires both population stability and cross-use stability. Truly rapid and pervasive change can destabilize areas and frequently leads to urban blight. This kind of dramatic change often emanates from top down 'well intentioned' political initiatives.

The American city landscape was disrupted after World War II when a popular distaste with congestion and attendant social problems, the explosion of car ownership and the dream of safe suburban living, prompted a general flight of big business and people from the city. In relocating to suburban and even rural sites, these large corporations found that they needed to replicate attributes of the city in order to satisfy their employees and attract new talent. It was not enough to provide coffee stations and coat closets, they needed to offer subsidized cafeterias, recreational facilities, travel agents, ATMs, etc. – all to take the place of the mixture of uses that was at everyone's disposal in the city. The economic advantages of relocation were eroded by the new higher space requirement per employee. This reshaping of the corporate environment added a new dimension to how a large company should work, and how it should be composed. The new model of a self-sufficient mega-corporation became a complex organism imitating aspects of the city, although in highly controlled conditions. It relied on a replication of the city for its attraction and this revolved around two issues.

The city functions as a duality; both an image, and a complex concentration of uses. The image feeds our ability to navigate and internalize the body of the city so that we may easily traverse it and utilize all it has to offer. The use concentration feeds our productive needs so that we can use it fully to sustain ourselves. In large offices, corporate leadership was asking what do people need to cause them to spend more time in the office? What supposedly tangential uses are in fact central to a healthy growing workforce? Inevitably, many of these uses replicated uses on a city street, and they replicated the image diversity of the street.

The most common type of public shared space within an office is inevitably meeting space. It helps greatly that most companies recognize the need for many different types of meetings, so that this monolithic use can be broken down or diversified into different types of spaces: formal meetings, AV presentations, video conferences, lounge meetings, etc. The space differentiation enables an architecture of variety even when basic uses are similar.

A dynamic pattern in urban evolution is the cyclical nature of success and failure of neighborhoods, or the self-destructive tendencies of success. When a street or neighborhood becomes successful, based on expanding magnetic diversity, competition for space in the location develops. This competition tends to favor uses that have the resources to buy in, and push out those that do not. A monolithic spread of single use frequently follows the escalated land costs, and diversity and liveliness wither and stagnate. Cities of any age exhibit examples of this: the decline of large precincts like the City of London, and Downtown in Manhattan, the sterilization of Kings Road in London, the commercialization of Soho, New York. These tendencies, often called 'gentrification', can be seen to be destructive, but they are more correctly evolutionary, and proof of dynamic and inevitable change. Similarly, new technology is gradually transforming how cities work. Dependent on technology, the nature of work is changing, and so the requirements for work space change.

SYSTEM UPDATES FOR A POST-DESK WORLD

Over the last 100 years, the increasing refinement and specialization of new technology has facilitated an electronic revolution. At an unprecedented scale, new sophisticated, electronic tools are envisioned, designed and produced for consumption. The notion of culture and style being victim to fashion shifts has become secondary to an exponentially increasing redundancy trail of technology, itself now behaving like a fashion victim. The technological devices that support modern life are constantly changing, evolving and exhausting themselves. Once 'ancient technology' was 500-year-old technology. It is now five-year old technology, or even 'last month technology'.

The effects on culture have been disruptive. If one face of the future is constantly changing, what of the production of culture? Where fashions of culture evolved gradually, we now have a fixation with the rapid introduction of 'new looks' across the spectrum of commodities and consumer interfaces which has confused the world. Almost everything is now new, so that anything genuinely new is lost amongst the proliferation of images, the society of the spectacle. Consequently, the notion of basing strategic decisions on functional requirements, of developing a 'fashion proof' or 'future proof' design proposal, has become futile in the face of the changing parameters of functionality. Only one constant remains unchanging – the basic human interface – and even this is measurably altering. Our interaction with the modern world has forced us to become 'information processors' on a scale that would be shocking to our ancestors. We live immersed in an electronic world, as anticipated by the futurist, Marshall McLuhan, in the 60's: pervasive media 'works us over' with a constant barrage of information.

McLuhan also talked at length about the pain associated with technological change. Each new technological offering that penetrated our world did so because it executed certain human tasks more efficiently – it replaced human capabilities with better performing technical devices. In doing so, it rendered both those skills and the related human physical capabilities redundant. Each new technology amputated us. Metaphorically, we replaced our limbs first with mechanical, and then later with electrical, prosthetics or armatures.

In order to retain their almost abandoned physical facilities, people followed this by devoting considerable leisure time to 'working out' at the gym, the health club or gym related classes and activities. Those who failed to grasp this opportunity drew comfort from 'super sizing' themselves at the great American fast food establishments.

Interfaces with technology change human behavior, and change the nature and form of our communications with each other. The paradigm shift began with the arrival of the earliest telephones inside our homes, where the phone was first wired into the entry hall (not quite accepted as a permanent guest) and those using the phone would feel as if they were somehow outdoors, or in a telegraph office, with the whole world listening in, and that they needed to raise their voices accordingly, to celebrate this public expression of making contact with friends over large distances.

Our current flirtation with technology devolves on miniaturization: the 'nano' world. Scaled down product means lighter and smaller and more mobile. The more we can communicate and create content in a moving world, the more effective we become (I am writing this on a Greek island with a laptop in a backpack in a straightforward merging of a work week and a new kind of weekend). What this further implies is that the old office workstation is ceasing to offer satisfactory utility with its bolted down technology. The next office type is likely to be more like a hotel without beds, but with a whole range of private to public space proportioned to the work that happens there, and changeable as that work type itself can and will change. It may begin to look very much like the famous city clubs of a recent era, which existed to promote more cross fertilizing than socializing, but died out as new trends in communicating and structuring time took over. In recent times, this vision has been realized through the global proliferation of coworking spaces with their club-like offerings.

THE OFFICE AS INVERTED CITY

Today, the office is sounding like, and working like, a city turned outside in. Planning and design of the contemporary office needs to observe some principal factors in city design which can be interpreted

32

for the office. We pair Jane Jacobs on the city street with office planning in the following comparison. In her 1961 book, Jane Jacob's wrote that to generate exuberant diversity in a city's streets and districts, four conditions are indispensable:

"The district, and indeed as many of its internal parts as possible, must serve more than one primary function; preferably more than two. These must insure the presence of people who go outdoors on different schedules and are in the place for different purposes, but who are able to use many facilities in common.

Most blocks must be short; that is, streets and opportunities to turn corners must be frequent.

The district must mingle buildings that vary in age and condition, including a good proportion of old ones so that they vary in the economic yield they produce. This mingling must be fairly close-grained.

There must be a sufficiently dense concentration of people, for whatever purposes they may be there. This includes dense concentration in the case of people who are there because of residence".

In all but the third condition, we can closely match her urban goals in the workplace. In the third which speaks of real city fabric, her observation on obsolescence is still appropriate:

"Uses and shared functions require diversity – a genuine mixture of uses.

Movement (the circulation system) needs to be easily navigable, and fluid, and the settings of neighborhoods open ended to facilitate 'slinky space' expansion and contraction.

Uses need to respond to active use, and need to be retired when the use has become redundant or exhausted. This suggests a plan of office structuring that can attribute different life cycles to functions, and accommodate change accordingly.

A reasonably high 'resident' population density is key to achieving liveliness and a dynamic environment. An absence of people is an absence of energy."

The parallels above are more than fortuitous. The conditions of human settlement or community interaction are common. It is important to note that Jacobs is relentlessly rational in her diagnosis and prescriptions for the city. It is fundamentally about content and use and the associated economic behavior over time. The image of the city flows from the healthy workings of the content, and where the content ceases to be healthy, the physical fabric disintegrates. The organism is never static, unless dead.

The large office becomes a small city when the complexity of the corporate community organism is addressed. It becomes a matrix of places, of meaningful destinations, some open, some closed, and all connected by a circulation network of open paths and alleys. It will have a support infrastructure of services: for refreshing the community, for supplying and removing stuff, for digital connectivity, for security. When the right component pieces synchronize with the right support networks, the theatre of work plays out on this platform in a manner consistent with the theatrical function of the streets of energetic cities.

Taylorism and the Emerging Modern Office

Today, the office is the workshop of the knowledge industry: a prosaic but vital tool in the new economy. It has only recently received attention, which is amazing as it is the singular place where most people spend the most productive hours of their day, and an enormous proportion of their lives. For those with the financial resources, you would think that they would insist on having Chanel or Balenciaga design it for them. It is not a second skin, but it is in a sense their second layer of clothing, and it really should both fit well and look great, or why bother coming to work?

The office as a typology of habitation was formulated relatively late in history. Although there had been organized guilds and crafts shops from Roman times where people co-located for communal work, the physical office typology was invented in the 19th century in response to a need to organize human labor efficiently, both following new factory planning principles and to service the newly accelerated markets that industrial production had fostered. At the end of the 18th century, the advent of the Industrial Age had brought with it the migration of the agrarian workforce to the new industrial cities. Human labor on farms was increasingly replaced with mechanical equipment. The uprooted labor force moved to the new factories in newly built towns to produce more of the machines that had replaced them.

Early factory conditions were deplorable. With little compassion for human labor, the factory bosses exploited their workforces in the much same way they had formerly exploited farm horses. This was quite predictable as the only large-scale reference point that management had was agricultural work. As organized attempts to counteract their mistreatment, the 19th century witnessed the painful rise of worker's movements'. The labor union legislation of the early 20th century finally achieved an uneasy balance of power in the industrial workplace.

For white collar workers, the late 19th century office was characterized by strict hierarchical order – further streamlined following publication of *The Principles of Scientific Management* by Frederick Taylor in 1911 – and was laid out like a factory production

The 19th and early 20th centuries saw a progressive deterioration of rural societies.

34

line, for which human labor provided the most adaptable and effective machinery.

Taylor's ideas were revolutionary in their day. He discovered that, in a rapidly growing economy hungry for labor, great efficiencies in industrial production could be achieved by disregarding skilled crafts which had been protected for centuries by guilds, and redesigning work from first principles. Workmen, who were regarded as units of production were instructed to do exactly what they were told by experts in white coats with clipboards and stop watches. The intention was to fragment work. Control and organization were more important than skilled discretion or individual intelligence. Discipline and obedience in following the formula were vital.

To optimize production, labor was specialized into part servicing and each employee performed a specific fraction of the overall workload – known as division of labor. While this logic fed well into a mechanized factory, it offered nothing but extreme drudgery for the workers. The concept of division of labor dates back to the 'geometrical method' of Descartes which involved breaking down any situation or operation into its smallest constituent parts, then attempting to deal with them mathematically. While this method made perfect sense for production, its effects on humans were terrible. Each worker would have a small highly repetitious task to perform day in and day out. The capitalist employers were regarding machines and humans as complementary tools of production.

Inevitably, this thinking was extended into the early office workplaces. Social problems arose that were not specifically created by Taylorised workplaces, but which this office type could only have exacerbated. Dissatisfaction with inhuman blue-collar labor conditions and remuneration had led to the creation of powerful labor unions which progressively renegotiated worker's conditions. While white collar workers were seen to be privileged and enjoying a life of relative comfort, their lives were equally compromised. Work was seen as drudgery, for all but the few privileged members of the 'ruling class'.

One of the most memorable images that encapsulate this era is the interior of Frank Lloyd Wright's Larkin Building in Buffalo, New York, 1905. White collar workers are lined up with primitive machines and rotating chairs bolted to the desks, clearly ordered and in perfect Taylorist control. Without actually being able to see the management watch tower, you know it is there.

In the absence of specific value being placed on the lives and mental health of employees, there could be little rational

The early industrial workplace.

argument against Taylor's model, and since work itself had not evolved much, its blueprint became the paradigm that lasted until the 1960s. A photograph of the interior of Mies van der Rohe's Seagram Building on Park Avenue, New York City, of 1958 shows the same conditions of order and control repeated 50 years later: here the only difference is in the 'progressive' style of décor. Taylorism applied to the office produced a mechanization of office work. This new order suited real estate practice and led to the standardization of internal and external systems, most clearly visible in ceiling grids and external cladding grids. The building expressed its commercial ideal, and ultimately a political ideal.

THE RISE OF THE COMPANY

The incorporated form of the company dates back to Roman times where the word derives from corpus, the Latin word for body or a 'body of people'. Such bodies had the right to own property and make contracts, to take legal action, etc. In Medieval Europe, churches and legislative bodies incorporated in order to create legal entities that could exist in perpetuity. The guild system utilized incorporation as a method of organizing and controlling membership rights, etc. The modern corporation came into being with dramatic effect following the exclusive Royal Charter granted by the Queen of England to the East India Company in 1600 to exploit trade across all territories east of the Cape of Good Hope. Similar rights were granted the Dutch East India Company (Vereenigde Oost-Indische Compagnie) in 1601, and both companies were

35

Atrium of the Larkin Administration Building, Frank
Lloyd Wright, Buffalo, New York, c.1903-1906.

hugely successful in East Asian sea trade over the subsequent 200 years.

The modern age was brought into life by an avalanche of opportunity precipitated by the steam engine, the new iron railways, structural iron and steel, and the emergence of the telegraph. In the absence of business models to guide them, the American entrepreneurs of the 19th century fell back on the only organizational model that dealt with large scale human deployment: the military and their experience of the 1860's Civil War. Hierarchy and status would parallel the army, as 'the new company' was born from the military company. Assembling divisions and ranks of workers and instituting a command structure, as if at war, could only last so long: scientific analysis of the problem of management was needed. Fredrick Winslow Taylor introduced measurement and systems analysis to the industrial workplace and the factory floor, culminating in his influential 1911 book, *The Principles of Scientific Management*. Henry Ford's Detroit automotive assembly line was the most vivid example of Taylorist time-and-motion studies, but these studies did not remain constricted to the factory floor.

Once the back-office support service of industrialization, the clerks assumed increasing importance as paper became the pre-eminent tool of control for the new economy. Increasing growth in service business saw massive growth in the numbers of service workers which required appropriate workspace.

THE ENORMOUS FILING CABINET

From the 1880's in Chicago and New York, to house the growing service economy, a series of office building projects began to dramatically transform the urban landscape. The modern office building was an invention facilitated by the new electric elevator: work process could now be stacked floor upon floor like an enormous filing cabinet. Indeed, when The Equitable Assurance Company's Manhattan Headquarters were completed in 1915, sociologist C. Wright Mills called the building an "enormous file" for the storage of paper. This structure was the world's largest office building at 1.2 million square feet of rental space, and was furnished with the 'The Modern Efficiency Desk'. The equipment of work itself was now evolving from the embellished desk of the 19th century (no doubt conceived for the merchant barons who were inclined to work), to a mechanical support system. The service economy had arrived and in 1919, Upton Sinclair coined the term 'the white-collar worker' to describe the newly emerging stratum of capitalist worker. By 1921, only two years later, the white-collar worker numerically outstripped the blue-collar worker, and the service economy was launched.

In his book of 1979, *Delirious New York*, Rem Koolhaas expanded the concept for the enormous filing cabinet with his speculative 'culture of congestion' project for the Downtown Athletic Club. With its 'definitive instability', the building highlighted the skyscraper dilemma: a monolithic exterior with capacity for multiple discrete internal functions. The high rise structure offers the opportunity for creating highly varied destinations on every floor, like a layer cake, essentially turning the multi-story silo effect to advantage, and of course utilizing the elevator core as a means of creating a massively effective connectivity to the entire melting pot of uses. This speculative proposition, largely thwarted by the modernist ideology of separating uses, promises to re-enter our mainstream as planning authorities of our cities eventually return to acknowledging the virtues of co-existing mixed and diverse uses.

At the onset of the 20th century, technological change was transforming the landscape, both metaphorically and physically, sociological upheavals were destabilizing the world. The age was plagued with petty nationalistic wars, both small and large. Europe and America were embroiled in labor organization unrest: improvements in work conditions were achieved more substantially through the threat of labor action than through ownership or managerial class benevolence. As the burgeoning middle class of 'middle management' grew in affluence and influence, white-collar fully supplanted blue collar as the predominant class, and the workplace extended beyond its narrowly defined economical parameters, becoming a politically and socially significant landscape as 'the place where the people worked'.

With reliable lack of imagination, each age utilizes the baggage of the previous age to embellish its present. Factory floor layouts initially resembled military formations, office floors initially resembled factory floors. The early desks of the Wooton Desk Company in 1880 resembled the large traveling wardrobes of the aristocracy of generations earlier; in 1910, desks became variants of a mechanized idea of work process, and later they became generic, resembling the collision of a metal box with saddlebags, or as others have put it: the early desks were like cottages, while the later ones appeared like tract houses laid out in grid form emulating suburban lots.

The First World War saw three decisive amputations of the faculties of man. By 1918, an entire generation of the male youth of Europe had been wasted in the fields of France and Belgium; secondly, with the mass desertion of the agricultural countryside, the industrial world effectively amputated man's symbiotic connection to the natural world; and, lastly, in the wake of vast and pervasive disillusionment, the old leadership class and its trappings were all but extinguished. An overturning of political and cultural systems

Women processing mail orders in the Order Entry Department of Sears, Roebuck & Co., Chicago, Illinois, c. 1913.

occurred, art devolved into abstraction and expressionism, 'aristocratic' classical music faded as popular music arose, literature assumed a disembodied stream of consciousness and architecture became simultaneously obsessed with primal form, mass production, mechanized modernity and a socialist utopia. As had taken place so many times before, Technology moved in to offer prosthetic support to Amputated Man.

The origins of this new white-collar class were shallow: their parents and grandparents before them had been compelled to adapt to the new industrial world which promised so much and delivered so little. Their communities had been racked with nationalistic military conflicts which reached a crescendo with the two world wars in which an unfathomable number of people died. The consequent desperate search for stability and normalcy produced a traumatized generation, for whom law abidance and mass conformity was the only answer. To quote the mid-century sociologist, C. Wright Mills: "By their rise to numerical importance, the white-collar people have upset the 19th-century

38

An 1876 advertisement of the Wooton Desk in the *Indianapolis City Directory* – "One hundred and ten compartments, all under one lock and key. A place for everything and everything in its place."

expectation that society would be divided between entrepreneurs and wage workers. By their mass way of life, they have transformed the tang and feel of the American experience. They carry, in a most revealing way, many of those psychological themes that characterize our epoch, and, in one way or another, every general theory of the main drift has had to take account of them. For above all else they are a new cast of actors, performing the major routines of 20th century society."

MID-CENTURY MILITARISM AND THE WORKPLACE

By 1950, the new structures erected for work searched for new social and economic relevance. Nothing fit so well as the image of neatness, frugality and military order that followed from almost half a century subsumed in world war. Just as the new star of the corporate world became 'the man in the grey flannel suit', the sleek and anonymous glass curtain wall was a fitting dress for the new modular steel framed building, now equipped with 'unmanned' elevators and air conditioning to eradicate the influence of weather on work. In the 1950's, the residue of World War II was a painful dream. Coping with life meant being in a constant state of preparation for a military existence as the Cold War reigned. Individualism was an enemy of the state, collective endeavor and conformism were upheld as unquestionable popular virtues.

As much as the organizational paradigms of the military shaped corporate organization, so these paradigms shaped the behavior of 'the organization man'. Once a minor character as clerk in the factory back-office, as the early 20th century unfolded, the white-collar worker came to outnumber the blue-collar factory worker. The command structure of the army was transferred to the corporation. Management was configured into multiple layers of control. In an age when all service and administrative functions were processed by white collar workers, human productivity could be measured, and the analogy of the factory line was not unreasonable.

A key player in this new society, 'the man in the grey flannel suit' became the pawn of industry. A military uniform was exchanged for the business suit where shades of colorlessness defined conformity, and extended the radical depersonalization of work. The male suit was itself intentionally tailored into a strict representation of acceptable activities for the gentleman. Standing and sitting were honored, the extremes of physical labor and unseemly relaxation were 'unsuitable'. When subject to inappropriate uses, the

"The office, as we have come to know it, is an adolescent statement starved for appropriate definition and somewhat oblivious to the forces of change."

ROBERT PROPST, THE OFFICE – A FACILITY BASED ON CHANGE

suit expressed this by puckering, bunching, wrinkling and creasing in reproach.

With the advent first of the telegraph, then the telephone, followed by radio, television and later satellites, the world experienced a new contraction of distance. The new communication systems meant that propinquity or physical adjacency was no longer imperative. Corporate offices moved away from factories, large organizations moved out of the city centres, establishing their own communities in suburbs and greenfield locations. Improved labor relations had led to more sensitive, though paternalistic, corporations and some of the new office buildings were consequently equipped with supportive facilities like child-care, sports centres, food services and retail outlets.

From the 1920's the once prominent role of the secretary began to diminish, threatened by the new stenographers' pool. The ever-growing industrial machine demanded greater efficiency in transcribing the managers' spoken word to paper which delivered instructions to the servants of the machines and maintained records of the process. Speed and accuracy were the only skills required of the (typically female) worker – there was no room for independent thought of any kind. This kind of job required less training, simpler specialization, cheaper labor per unit and thus replaceable employees. As observed by the sociologist C. Wright Mills in 1950: "The new office is rationalized: machines are used, employees become machine attendants; the work, as in the

factory, is collective, not individualized; it is standardized for interchangeable, quickly replaceable clerks; it is specialized to the point of automatization. The employee group is transformed into a uniform mass in a soundless place, and the day itself is regulated by an impersonal time schedule. Seeing the big stretch of office space, with rows of identical desks, one is reminded of Herman Melville's description of a 19th century factory 'At rows of blank-looking counters sat rows of blank-looking girls, with blank, white folders in their blank hands, all blankly folding blank paper.'"

In this context, it is small wonder that mass media of the age lionized the individual with stories of new heroes and individual triumphs: from Mickey Mouse to Superman to mythologies of lone cowboys in the wild west, the latter continued through to Leo Burnett's iconic, rugged and ultra-masculine Marlboro Man, possibly one of the most influential campaigns of the 20th century. These mythical stories offered people escapism and a dream of personal heroism through the multiple alternative realities of packaged commercial entertainment.

The evolving new media provided the pre-eminent vehicle for a new cultural landscape. Though the phonograph had been invented as an office dictating machine in 1909, it was appropriated for music recording and distribution. The transistor radio became the low-cost vehicle for mass distributing talk shows and music. Television became the permanent guest in the living room. The omnipresence of sound and connectivity both

39

The 'grey flannel suit' of the white collar worker (left) resembled the uniforms worn by U.S. Air Force soldiers (right) in the early 1950's.

Exterior and interior of the Seagram Building,
Ludwig Mies van der Rohe, New York, 1958.

ameliorated and invaded people's lives, changing privacy boundaries and creating widely distributed communities, which newly improved transportation, particularly air travel, was simultaneously extending. With its newfound affluence, America became the first country to export multitudes of working class tourists while extending its global business network.

The new electronic guests in the living room were engaged in one-directional communication. They spoke to you, who had become their audience. Technology had not yet evolved to offer two-way communication options, and this doubly emphasized a culture of passive conformity. A newly pervasive culture of materialism was simultaneously promoted by both the need to keep up with your neighbor's latest domestic machines (and to sell product), and via the constant marketing messages that TV brought with it.

In keeping with the post-war material reality, Mies van der Rohe's Seagram Building of 1958 was also an exercise in the aesthetics of scarcity. The building was completed scarcely 10 years after the deprivations of World War II. Due to the war effort, steel had been in shortage for years – and

Seagram packaged office utility in a monk-like box with the only modest decoration being the expressed bronze window I-beam mullions. That those mullions were decorative and not structural, due to state fire regulations, was a small irritation to the great architect. He understood that the message was more important than the means and this stylistic device celebrated construction itself as the new aesthetic. The office interior reflected both the aesthetic of scarcity and the absence of tradition. Desks were simple rectangles like floating planes, the flat ceiling plane was gridded, the floor tiled, the windows screened with horizontal venetian blinds and chairs functional metal seats. The only visual interruption would be the business machines littering the desks. Few photographs exist of this interior, largely because it was so uninteresting, though a strange misplaced nostalgia has been reinvigorated through TV shows like Mad Men wherein the 60's office interior became a platform for subtle artistic experiments in color.

At its time, the Seagram Building accomplished two things on the scale of the city: it provided a new model for the office building, and a new gift to street life through its generous ground level plaza. In the words of Phyllis Lambert, scion of Samuel Bronfman, the builder of Seagram and a pivotal advocate for its architecture, 'the plaza opened the prospect of clearings in the forest of the city' and led to the establishment of New York City's 'Open Space Design Criteria'. William H. Whyte, author of *The Social Life of Small Urban Spaces* called the plaza 'a theatre – you can't tell where the social life of the street and the plaza leaves off. They are inextricable. The plaza offers choice, sittability, permissiveness and activity: there is always something going on'. Why is this relevant? Because the concept of the urban plaza has come indoors in the 21st century, often functioning as the heart or hearth of the new organization.

 The new construction systems led to a new appreciation for the depreciating asset. As observed by workplace strategist Frank Duffy, and tech visionary Stewart Brand, buildings are made up of a system of design lives that ideally should allow each other to be independently sourced and refreshed – to live and breathe separately. This concept is relatively new, largely because the systemization of buildings has developed so much within the last 150 years. Buildings are built out of a series of layers of materials with varying degrees of longevity. Some are long lasting, others respond to a client's shorter term needs. Still others are intended for tenant users on a very temporary basis.

 We expect a long life from the ground a structure sits on, as well as the structure: at least 100 years. Cladding systems should last 50 years. Internal mechanical services like air conditioning should last 15 years. The sets or scenery of office space improvements like partitions, etc. should last five to 10 years in response to changeable organizational needs, while loose furnishings, equipment and spatial arrangements may only last five months (not through obsolescence but portability). It requires unlearning notions of all-encompassing durability in a building to leverage the advantages of layered systems. Where modern building thinking tends to only observe two separate systems: 'shell and core' and 'tenant improvements' – our buildings would become much more intelligent and sustainable through a keener attenuation of life cycles, extending to the point in the near future when buildings can learn, like any other learning machine.

 If the most successful buildings of the future are those that can accommodate multiple interventions by users over time in a welcoming and graceful way, then our approach to making these interventions

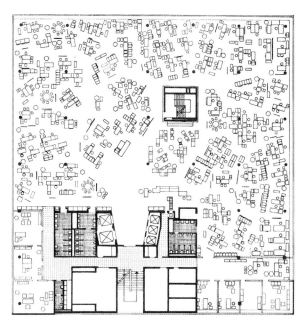

Plan: Osram Headquarters, Walter Henn, Munich, Germany, 1963.

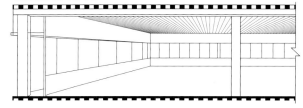

SHELL 50 YEARS

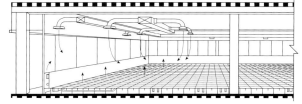

SERVICES 15 YEARS

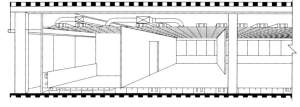

SCENERY 5 YEARS

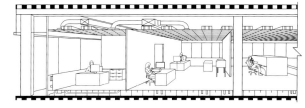

SETS 5 DAYS

Life cycles of building components.

(in workplace projects) might simultaneously respect the limits of the building's integrity, and discover new ways and opportunities of landing lightly on its floors with highly adaptable, reusable and mobile architectures. Far too much of the fabric of tenant improvement build-outs ends up in garbage bins.

'BUROLANDSCHAFT' AND CHICKEN COOPS

In the 1960's, a new conception arose based on an affirmation of worker's rights as well as an astute economy of space. The open office landscape model was conceived as a vision of democracy at work. Originated by the Quickborner Team and called 'burolandschaft' (meaning office landscape) in Germany, the form became rapidly adopted by large businesses who supported the tenets of democracy as well as the density achieved in the open plan office model). The new office format promised workers a new level of comfort and a high degree of control in their surroundings and their work methods. However, the workplace remained subject to an overriding order of top down control: an architecture of preformed modularity (see the Centraal Beheer in Den Haag, The Netherlands, by Herman Hertzberger, 1973) which preconfigured internal relationships with definite limits.

While efforts of political and social activism assisted with improving work conditions, the real savior of the workers was to be technology itself. As more and more sophisticated machines were developed from 1960 to 1990, many of the rote functions undertaken by humans could increasingly be executed (more effectively) by machines. The nature of work began to change. Mass computerization and electronic communications finally proliferated in the late 20th century and consigned most formulaic, repetitive work to the hidden interiors of machines. Two aspects of the new technology provided the life lines to finally liberate work: the internet and micro-computers: the internet for freely supporting communications 'anywhere, anytime' and micro computing for putting individual computers into the hands and homes of people everywhere. It offered the promise for a person in a garage or a coffee shop to market and compete for business on an equal footing with a large corporation. It only required an ability to produce the goods.

Sociological research into the behavior of workers and the productivity of organizations lead to new experiments in the workplace, as well as the emergence of the new disciplines of human relations and facilities management. The regimented office

42

The world's first open-plan office system – Action Office 1, 1964. Developed by Robert Propst and manufactured by Herman Miller, the original version envisioned an agile and free-form supporting role for furniture. Unfortunately, Propst was 40 years too early, and his concept failed in the marketplace.

landscape evolved to the 'burolandschaft' or office landscape concept of the German management consultants, the Quickborner Team.

Their radical 1963 plan for Osram GmbH in Munich demonstrated their principles of placing dynamic interaction, adjacencies and human relationships as the basis of the office plan, rejecting the grid or assembly line as organizing principles. Simultaneously, US furniture manufacturer Herman Miller unveiled their Action Office workstation solution, which proposed a dynamic working environment, which for the first time acknowledged and synthesized a whole range of workstyle issues, and correlated 'body motion' with 'mental fluency'. The proposition was truly revolutionary in both programmatic conception and aesthetic execution, and while it attracted great interest in the media, it was too radical for the market. In an ironic reversal of McLuhan's adage, Action Office failed to use enough old tools, and consequently became a commercial flop.

As the children of the post war generation, the baby boomers rebelled against the conformity and narrow horizons of their parent's world. A youth revolution would invade university campuses across America and Europe, both political and cultural, with civil rights and socialist agendas, culminating in the Paris riots of 1968, Prague spring of 1969, Woodstock, 1970 and an entire 'hippy' alternative lifestyle movement that would eventually dissolve in a pool of self-indulgence and drug induced haze in the early 70's. In the words of Michelet, "each epoch dreams the one to follow", and in spite of the brevity of its ascendance, the influence of hippie culture and its naturalistic, human-centreed ideals would be felt into the next century.

In parallel, by the late 60's, diluted visions of a new workplace landscape and diluted versions of earlier office furniture ideas found their way into mainstream products and the 'open office' entered mainstream corporate life. Herman Miller reined in its radicalism and produced Action Office 2, a furniture system product which 'eased the hard edges' of the early version and became an overwhelmingly persuasive tool for the modern office: the much maligned cubicle. In 1968, Robert Propst, its designer/inventor, published his concise and inclusive treatise *The office – A facility based on change*. The importance of flexibility and the acknowledgment of a permanent condition of change in the modern workplace would shape workspace thinking from this point forward.

Paper management was the currency and the vehicle for control of the new service economy. And paper management essentially

Not a cube farm, but an ancestor of its vision – Monsieur Hulot overlooks a human battery farm in *PlayTime*, the 1967 film from French filmmaker Jacques Tati.

In 1998, around 40 million Americans were working in various versions of Robert Probst's Action Office II, now largely referred to as the cubicle.

ruled the new workstation aesthetic by owning most of the surfaces that comprised it. Almost like a playing field, space to 'spread' had become the defining goal, and what was not a desk layout area, was a paper storage function. Somehow this 'paper ranch' had become the building block of workspace. For effective processing of paper, more machines had arrived, and dictating machines, typewriters, photocopiers, shredders and facsimile machines became the new kitchen tools of modern worklife, later superseded or supplemented by computers, scanners and printers. In decentralizing control to the office workers, the technology simultaneously democratized the office. It was now much harder for management to withhold information, or to assign information to favored staff on a 'need to know' basis. The achievement was a new transparency to the organization, and this

occurred at the same time as newly enlightened management thinking recognized its
benefits. To quote management guru Peter
Drucker, there are four fundamentals of communication: communication is perception,
is expectation, and it makes demands. Communication and information are different and
indeed largely opposite – yet interdependent.

     While much attention had been
placed on the devices for paper management,
much attention had also been directed at
improving the means of communication. After
all, the viral spread of the modern economy
had been predicated on connecting people and
commodities over large distances, and on the
speed of communication to effect the intended
transactions. To the telegraph was added the
telephone, which from its beginning in 1876
formed the network for all business relationships and transactions. When the fax machine
was added 100 years later, it provided the
link with paper to pervasively consolidate
all transactions.

     While acting as the repository of
information and knowledge, paper had exercised a subversive effect on the landscape of
the office and the freedoms of the worker. For
almost every aspect of paper locked down
activity and space usage. Even the convoluted
wired systems of offices were ultimately
serving paper. A new invention popular with
management came to the fore in the 1970's:
the cubical workstation, also known as the
cube. It's initial appearance could be con-
strued as a budgeting committee's attempt to
create an office that saved as much money as
possible by squeezing the footprint, lowering
the walls, removing the door, removing the

ceiling and air conditioning, and connecting them together in grid formations to save
space. To make them acceptable, even desirable, they would cover most surfaces with soft
tackable fabric. Once sitting in your cube, you
could be blissfully unaware of your colleagues.
Although, you could hear everything they said.
You could no longer look out of the window,
but then why would you, when you had so
much work to get through? And you were free
to pin up photos of your kids and your pets.
Management loved it because it reminded
them of factory production – it was efficient.

     After several years, it became
increasingly clear that the cubical was both a
symptom and a symbol of bureaucratic break-
down. Remorselessly regular layouts within
very deep office space, which provide neither
privacy not cohesion could not be interpreted
as a provision of equal benefits. To quote the
workplace theorist Frank Duffy: 'the cube
represents an equal distribution of misery
within which anyone and everyone can be
replaced in any order and at any time – the
essentially heartless utilitarian and eventually militaristic vision, that lies at the heart
of and is the principal strength and weakness
of Taylorism.'

     A rejection of this impersonal, man-
aged work environment occurred in Northern
Europe at the same time. The 'burolandschaft' open workplace was considered too
distracting and dropped in favor of the new
highly cellular 'social democratic' office: every
worker would have their own enclosed office
with good light and outside views. This typology evolved from sociological research with
workers who invariably chose this solution
as making them the happiest. Enlightened
management assumed a happy employee
would be a productive employee, and while
there is truth to this, it entirely neglects the
value of collective knowledge sharing which is
frustrated by the cellular plan. It works best if
you don't need to learn more about your work,
and are undertaking routine tasks.

     As the 21st century approached,
the new electronic communication modes
of the internet, email and mobile telephony
were becoming the primary modes of communication. Paper was on its way out, and the
office that was ruled by militaristic organizational theory, supervisory management and
factory-like production goals was a dinosaur
of the industrial era. By mindless repetition
of a worn-out idea, the office had lost the plot.
What would lead it back to a meaningful
and sustainable plot? The watershed of
information supply: a commodity whose
value did not get expended as it was shared
and passed on.

44

Aerial view of the former SAS (Scandinavian
Airlines) Headquarters, Niels Torp, Frøsundavik,
Stockholm, Sweden, 1987.

The No-Collar Worker

The knowledge workers of the developed world entered the last decade of the 20th century mercifully free of the office uniform, and liberated by an internet that allowed the out-sourcing of routine administrative processes. A revised conception of 'white collar' was needed. The new focus was on innovation to ensure survival in the new economy.

Of course, the mythical ancestor of the knowledge worker was the autonomous Renaissance man. The knowledge worker has evolved to become an 'enterprise unit' and the corporation recognizes the need for a new relationship of trust and support. Cognizant of his or her negotiating abilities, the knowledge worker begins to change work conditions and pushes for acceptance of a new time and place-based fluidity and flexibility. The definition of work changes as the definition of the office changes.

THE INFORMATION REVOLUTION

The last decade of the 20th century saw technology's conquest of information management. The desktop of the office worker literally moved inside the computer, with the functions expressed on the monitor screen in front of him. The new 'desktop' contained electronic folders and documents, word-processing functions, spreadsheets, copy functions, image handling, trash-bins, and the bottomless information network of the Internet. As information was now tamed, routine job functions would no longer be done by humans. For businesses to succeed in the new world, they needed to innovate, or die. This simple fact changed the way business was transacted. Another factor was invading society and culture: new opportunities for connectivity, and new communication devices, were creating new hybrid communities.

In 2004, a US newspaper reported that large numbers of young children in the San Francisco Bay area were maintaining open mobile phone lines to their peers. Phone charging plans allowed unlimited time, and kids were using this new freedom. They would have their phones dialed into a friend's phone for hours on end, and not feel any need to actually converse, but using it to occasionally comment on something they would be doing or experiencing. They would thus be 'in the same room' and connected, although merely in digital space. Connection periods were

> **"In a mass media society, the basic units are the large collective masses. In a networked society, the network becomes a basic unit of organization at all levels (individuals, groups and organizations). Online social networks, media networks, and technology networks act as the catalysts for a networked society."**
>
> JAN VAN DIJK, THE NETWORK SOCIETY

45

typically two to eight hours. The import of this is significant: in the future, with pervasive connectivity, we will lose inhibitions about unusual ways to connect and will begin to explore new modes of connectivity. We will establish peer and family communities in new ways, and support these relationships perhaps more effectively than we do today. And we could be using our brains differently too. The human body is likely to respond to the stress of information overload by developing new capabilities in processing massive data: short attention spans may evolve into rapid processors.

To the benefits of connectivity, it is important to note the vulnerabilities. Social media sites collect our information with supposedly benign intentions, but massive abuses of data have risen to the surface. Data mining opportunities allowed election meddling in the United States in 2014-16. It also undermined the United Kingdom referendum on Europe, contributing to the momentous outcome of Brexit. The shady British consulting firm Cambridge Analytica acquired without permission the personal data of 87 million Facebook users and used this information strategically for campaigns to discredit its employer's opposition candidates. This and other events led to the European General Data Protection Regulation Act (adopted in 2016 and enforced in May 2018) to protect citizens from privacy and data breaches.

In the 1960s, Marshall McLuhan warned that the new technologies were creating a new type of audial space, and that the computer functioned as an extension of the nervous system. "Electric information systems are live environments in the full organic sense. They alter our feelings and sensibilities." He observed that software would undermine the entire industrial establishment so long devoted to hardware, and that it would abolish the division between industrial worker and savant. This last notion will only become true with generational changes in the workforce. Knowledge work requires education, self-management and specialized training.

However, McLuhan exercised remarkable predictive powers in surmising the impacts of the new wave of technology: "All media or technologies, languages as much as weaponry, create new environments or habitats, which become the milieu for new species or technologies." (Marshall McLuhan – *Global Village*). He said this in 1968, and in 2018 we are only now attempting to describe and relate to this new milieu we find ourselves in. We are not certain that it is not still an intervening state, on the road to an entirely new era, and our grappling with new technology are almost futile in the face of its sequentially imminent redundancy.

McLuhan believed further that "electric circuitry confers a mythic dimension on our ordinary individual and group actions. Our technology forces us to live mythically", but we continue to think fragmentarily, and on single separate planes. (Marshall McLuhan – *Medium is the Massage*). Although the physics of human nervous systems and new electronic processes may have much in common, the more fundamental nature of pervasive connectivity and its new forms conceals an invasive new force on the workings of the human brain.

There is certainly a pressure to think mythically and not fragmentarily as any TV viewer will rapidly grasp. Broadcast information has reworked normal human communication by slicing and dicing information into sound bites that connect. Thirty-second advertising, where a large story needs to be shrunk down to high-cost available time, has compounded this trend. In developing new capabilities to comprehend large quantities of information and selectively process it, we have created a fast, wide, but shallow receptive ability, and have transferred this process into our own social and business behavior. If we could compare – we talk faster, think faster and act faster than our grandparent's generation. However, we are not necessarily any smarter, as depth penetration, or vertically accessing multiple layers of meaning, is critically compromised if not virtually absent in this new capability. At its simplest, recent years suggest that the speed, volume and plurality of information in circulation, has degraded our ability, and perhaps our appetite, to differentiate between the true and the false, fact and fiction, science and ideology. Alternative facts are now a thing.

THE NETWORKED SOCIETY

With the disruption caused by new technologies, a profound shift took place. At the closing of the 20th century, mass media society evolved into the networked society. The top-down, heavily managed world of the Industrial Age was finally overwhelmed by its own inventions. The mass media society was the product of mass communications that were intrinsically one-sided. The television, the movie, the radio, the newspaper and even the book, spoke to you as a unilateral communication. Media literally washed over you. In the United States alone, people were averaging more than six hours a day of television consumption. To the extent that community had previously shaped behavior, politics and world views, people were drawn into a critical

The network removes distance restrictions on connectivity – "the death of distance".

and precarious relationship with media that resided in your living room, and would henceforth become your family's most persuasive source of information.

The shift to a networked society profoundly disrupted the old business model. Advertising dollars shifted to the internet, and to platform providers and away from content producers. Television struggled to stay alive and descended into a choice between a mockery of the new social networks with Reality TV, or high quality but paid subscription services, like HBO or Netflix. The positive side was of course a new interactive world wherein anyone could create content and interact with audiences everywhere. This signaled a new and exciting ability to participate in the creation of culture. However, at the time of writing, a dark side is emerging: net neutrality is being eroded in new legislation. The US Federal Communications Commission rules barring internet providers from blocking or slowing content were wiped off the books in December 2017, indicating an uncertain future for internet freedoms.

However, many new players have dived into the field of opportunities that the Networked Society represented. Creative organizations rejected the business models of old business. They positioned themselves as pioneers in a new electronic business world and experimented with new physical ways of working. The West Coast's largest ad agency, TBWA/Chiat/Day became famous for its workplace experiments: first in 1988 with a temporary warehouse conversion by Frank Gehry, then a new Gehry building with a pair of binoculars by Claus Oldenburg outside which they soon transformed into a virtual (mobile) office while the rest of the world was still using paper.

In New York in 1994, Jay Chiat had the Italian artist revolutionary Gaetano Pesce create a version of the virtual office which resembled a Greek nightclub on the 28th and 29th floors of a Wall Street office building. Work was an uphill battle, but it had a big draw with young job candidates. The only desks (numbering about 10 for a population of 160) were equipped with Apple computers and custom designed with a narrow footprint to make it impossible to lay out a piece of paper, which Jay considered dangerous antiquated rubbish. The agency suffered some attrition through these years. Work itself had become a challenge, though the production of creative ideas was, if anything, improved. They learnt that forcing teamwork was a good thing, though people at that time really did need a spot to call home – surprise, a desk!

One obvious discovery from the new interconnectedness was that it was no longer essential to collocate office workers, if they could simply communicate over phones and the internet. This facilitated the networked office – which became a distributed office strategy relying on information technology for connectivity. You could be anywhere and still be working and 'connected'. So to the apparent demise of colocation, synchrony was added: one no longer had to work at the same time as one's fellow workers.

The notion of community itself was changing from merely physical to virtual. And the idea of shrinking the office, as more people became more mobile, was further supported by the 'green' notion of reducing your carbon footprint. Depending on work styles, this approach suited some companies very well. For instance, global management consultants, such as Accenture, PWC and Deloitte, as these professions went virtual, shrunk their office real estate footprint and increased their mobility. They instituted the concept of 'hoteling': named so because staffers would book office space to work much like booking rooms at a hotel.

One of the founders of workplace consultants DEGW, Frank Duffy observed that buildings themselves are fundamentally inert: it is how they are used that matters. He summarized current thinking by saying that "we need cities that are conceived as aggregations and concentrations of multiple overlapping networks." In 2007, we hear this electronic update of Jane Jacob's prescription for the healthy city of 1960 when she wrote of "the need of cities for a most intricate and close-grained diversity of uses that give each other constant mutual support, both economically and socially. The components of this diversity can differ enormously, but they must supplement each other in certain concrete ways".

THE CONTENTIOUS ARRIVAL OF THE OPEN OFFICE

With demise of cubicle-land at the beginning of the 21st century, big business turned to the next big thing: the notorious open office. Furniture manufacturers led the way with their suites of new open office furnishings. Management consultants sang its praises and leadership loved its emphasis on collaboration and space efficiencies which drove down costs. Its primary attributes were in promoting interaction and community – it would also herald a new level of transparency, which aided higher levels of group cohesion and staff engagement. The hierarchical organization was out, the flat organization was in. While wise leadership remained vital, the appearance of flatness empowered workers at lower levels. Indeed, data has emerged that shows that peer pressure (not the boss figure) is the most powerful motivator in work communities. People want to live up to what is expected of them.

Since it was becoming apparent that new business or product innovations could happen at any level of the company, it made sense to promote a sense of universal empowerment. Where things began to get unstuck was in the wide commercial deployment of the idea. Mediocre office design on a large scale managed to barely accommodate the predominant components of the Open Office, and forgot to address the need for quiet individual work. Many large offices were built out too quickly and too thoughtlessly leading to an unnecessarily high level of staff discontent. When too much distraction exists, people cannot get their work done, and stress levels rise.

In most organizations, there is a simple pattern that the work process follows: employees alternate between collaborative work and private work. Collaborative work may involve a team, or one other person. Space could solve for this simple triangle: team collaboration space, private quiet space, and two-person collaborative space. With strategic colocation and appropriate shielding, an effective workspace can be created. Privacy is really about the ability to control information (what others need to know) and stimulation (any kind of disruption).

In its defense, the open office greatly facilitates face to face interactions, which are the single most important activity in the office today. Communication theory has long emphasized that face to face interaction involves an exponential quantity of information exchange. The face and body language, couple with spoken language, communicate masses of information which no electronic interface can fully match. Workplace theorist, Franklin Becker observes in *Offices at Work*: "The reality is that small-scale, team-oriented, open plan clusters designed as part of an activity-based workplace strategy have myriad benefits. More expensive, less flexible closed offices undermine interaction and render tacit learning nearly impossible." Research has shown that the closed office model has limited value for all but a few organizations that have the appropriate workstyles (primarily highly focused individual work).

START-UPS, INCUBATORS AND THE COWORKING PHENOMENON

Around the year 2000, a new form of working came into being, called coworking, because it involves a shared workspace and independent activity within a community setting. Coworking was initiated by small independent ventures like The Hub in Kings Cross, London, and Brad Neuberg's coworking in San Francisco in 2005. Freelancers and start-ups were attracted to the combination of low space rent, internet access and on-site meeting facilities which allowed them the ability to present themselves as legitimate businesses with cool premises. The rise of coworking spaces has occurred in parallel with the rise of IT and mobile working. Mobile computing and communications has empowered a whole new generation of business start-ups, who need somewhere to work. The coworking spaces, and their offerings, have become widespread and attractive. WeWork, founded in 2010, has seen exponential growth and has become perhaps the major player in this field. At the time of writing, it has 449 locations in 86 cities.

The design of WeWork spaces is also influencing the next generation of workplace design, though true innovation in the territory is happening with innovative providers like Second Home. Working with the excellent Spanish design firm, SelgasCano, Second Home truly uses design to promote its values of connectivity, variety, collaboration, frugality and flow. Space is highly transparent, colorful and embellished with cool second-hand modern furniture and a variety of green potted plants, which look strangely like fellow co-workers extracted from nature. The company claims to be a social business with

Second Home Holland Park, a new co-working space in West London designed by Spanish studio SelgasCano.

ECONOMY	LOCATION	WORKFORCE	MOBILITY	PROCESS
AGRICULTURE	RURAL	FAMILY	IMMOBILE	CLIMATE
INDUSTRIAL	URBAN	MANPOWER	STATIONARY	LINEAR
SERVICE	(SUB)URBAN	BRAINPOWER	INCREASED MOBILITY	DEMAND
IDEA	GLOBAL	NETWORKED	UNLIMITED MOBILITY	INNOVATION

Table: Developments in Economic Structures Over Time.

a mission to support creativity and entrepreneurship. They also claim "businesses grow 10 times faster at Second Home".

Surveys of coworkers have demonstrated that given the choice "people will choose workspaces that support their digital style while giving them access to new knowledge, exposing them to different kinds of expertise and accelerating their learning". In addition, proximity is key: "research indicates that interactions and engagement decrease as the physical distance between work groups gets bigger, whereas online engagement increases with the number of users. We must aggressively change the definition of what a workspace is, from where work is done, to how work is done, and then design spaces – physical and digital – around that." (*Harvard Business Review* – Waber, Magnolfi and Lindsay).

Where the model of coworking promises to lead is equally interesting. Software as a Service is now dominant and Space as a Service (SaaS) is the next progressive model. Within the first two quarters of 2017, space consumption of coworking and flex space in the City of London exceeded the tech and financial sectors for the first time.

Larger organizations are increasingly recognizing the need to have flex space within their offices. They see this as a home for more itinerant staffers but also for business partners who might be small outfits with whom it makes sense to collaborate on their premises for limited periods of days, weeks or months. Amazon in Seattle has instituted this kind of shared space. A large workplace can thus become a more diversified and exciting community of specialists who may not all be on payroll.

THE NEW BESPOKE OFFICE

For all the flux and disruption that has occurred in the work space over recent years, and even as technology continues to change many rules, the lesson for office environments is remarkably anodyne: different businesses have different requirements. A standardized office blueprint failed on numerous fronts. Office design needs to accommodate and support change, and there are complex sociological issues that need resolution: like community and corporate/personal identity. The crux of what kind of space was needed finally came down to the type of work undertaken, and it needed participation from greater numbers of employees to adequately determine needs.

Advertising people rely heavily on team-work so they need a range of collaborative spaces and a powerful expression of their creativity. Internet companies crunch highly complex software code and therefore need quiet space for highly focused personal work. Financial institutions are frequently restructuring and need a high density open architecture that is very flexible. Architectural design has finally entered an era that product design has toyed with for years. Since 2000, the new focus is on user interaction and user experience (commonly called UX): the relationship between users and their work tools and workspace. The new promise of the product is a bespoke space – unique to your needs and your brand. You can finally get your Chanel office, or your Mad Max office or your Harry Potter office.

The new workplace is a complex organism deserving research, strategy and creative planning. We call it an organism because it is a vital process: a kind of biological micro environment that is constantly in flux, expanding, contracting and reforming itself. In this sense it resembles the city, and because of this resemblance, we believe there are persuasive lessons in urban thinking and the urban condition that can apply to large office design.

People are unquestionably a company's most valuable resource. In the new economy, they function as both product or service innovators and producers. They need specialized support from the organizations for whom they work. They need intelligent, creative solutions to complex work issues which will make them more effective. And they need obstacles or barriers to work to either be removed or ameliorated.

The issue of 'obstacles to work' is significant. If we were to analyze efficiency in the workplace like a factory process, we would identify a number of conditions that inhibit productivity. These can range from poor collocation of teams, to inefficient circulation, to insufficient equipment support, to siloed departments, to desk bound work machines and phones, to visual barriers to knowing who is where in the office. Early in this process, it took a while for the world to realize that the cables hooking up one's computer were yet another obstacle – in this case to mobility. The theory suggests that if the workplace is 'obstacle free', it is also highly fluid and supportive of all kinds of work processes.

The challenge today is to accommodate new differentiated types of work communities. While these are defined by new approaches to work, and corporate leadership's visions for where they want to take companies, physical design shapes this environment and the human relationships it hosts. In 1926, brushing aside the aesthetically focused design philosophy of the Beaux Art academies, the legendary architect Le Corbusier announced that "the plan is the generator". Architects have trained their sights on the plan ever since, but what this notion failed to address was the question of what goes into the plan? In the absence of examining the required and suitable recipe, it is like starting to cook with all the ingredients that happen to be in your refrigerator and expecting a masterpiece.

The film maker, Jean Luc Goddard, once said that "style is the outside of content, and content the interior of style". This observation stresses the relationship which is truly fundamental to architectural progress. We need to embrace the interrelated complexity of program needs, the user interface, the physical context, the social milieu and the historical trajectory, out of which might come a truly effective, sustainable and rewarding building. There is a decidedly creative aspect to compiling the program or brief for a building, which determines all ingredients and their relative integration in a form of recipe, and does this in a truly inclusive way. By contrast, the editing of real need in the interests of architectural effect is one of the most offensive and intellectually vapid disciplinary failures of formalist architecture. It is really the client program or brief that is the generator of the plan, which is then the generator of the architecture.

In achieving this, thorough research, observation and planning is key to compiling an effective set of requirements and performance standards for each new office type. We need closer observation of how people work today in order to design space and tools that support them in cohesive communities. In the past, people were given a set of tools and asked to use them, whether or not these tools suited the changing conditions of work. In the great human spirit of adaptability, people worked around the inadequacy of their tools to achieve the purpose of the work, as if this was just the way life worked. Marshall McLuhan expressed his frustration with this succinctly when he said "We are a rear-view-mirror society. We continue to use old tools to solve new problems". In so doing we inevitably hamper our productivity.

The second parallel investigation of this book is the idea of urban design entering the workplace. Knowledge of the workings of the city provide an additional set of tools, on the assumption that all circumstances of human occupation have been resolved by the city. It therefore stands as a valuable model for adaptation, and a means to introduce structural ideas about community into the workplace which factor in people's memory. The territory which is most familiar is that most rapidly assimilated. This allows introduction of 'new territory' or culturally provocative material into a familiar landscape and allows the appropriation or extension of that landscape. As with poetry, the focus is on the ordinary, in order to make it extraordinary.

Our last three centuries have seen the most dramatic shifts of all time. The world moved from a predominantly rural agricultural economy, family-based, immobile, and responsive to climate, to an industrial age that caused a flight to cities (automation took over farm jobs) and relied on muscle power and repetitive tasks. It then moved to a service economy of clerks fueling the industrial machine, to a knowledge or idea economy that has shifted global, is networked, mobile and innovation focused. Human work may finally be liberated from drudgery, and become inspiring and invigorating.

51

Intermezzo

What Did We Learn?

"Four-year-olds exposed to television expect, demand and respond to very different pedagogy than four-year-olds did fifty years ago."

PETER DRUCKER 2001

"Today, four-year-olds exposed to smart mobile devices expect, demand and respond to very different pedagogy than four-year-olds did twenty years ago."

CLIVE WILKINSON 2019

Seven Lessons for Building Creative Communities

Since the 1970's, young people had been energized by the idea of the 'global village' and of societies coming together peacefully. Published predominantly from 1968 to 1972, *The Whole Earth Catalogue* was the bible for a new world, bringing people together and living in the now, in harmony with nature and the universe. As an aspirational idea, the global village provided an idealized collective nirvana in which all could participate regardless of their background. Work and personal survival were still on the radar: in the previous century, the world had seen a mass exodus from the countryside with cities becoming the place to live and work. Government and large corporations had become the primary employers. Education didn't happen at home anymore, nor did it happen in small intimate classrooms. People embraced mass learning and working.

Mass culture in the form of pop music, pop art, television and radio and magazines pacified the masses – not unlike Marx's observation that religion was the opium of the masses. In an ascendant economy, the populace could believe that life was great. But economies cycle through down-swings, stretching the capitalist machine in the middle as well as at the edges. Of course, cracks appeared in the perfect edifice.

High culture, which had been the prerogative of the ruling classes was overtaken by the new wide spread pop culture, and the voices of the populace were becoming heard in the marketplace largely due to its newly increased buying power. The workplace itself was late in adapting to the new social and economic realities, and a crisis was emerging at the end of the 20th century. Technology was driving increased mobility and replacing routine service and manufacturing jobs. Around 2000, the so-called dot com economic bust occurred, involving a plethora of digital companies, and forever changed the economic landscape and the workplace. Knowledge work was now ascendant as the office model of the 1980's no longer worked.

My personal experience with workplace design began with TV studios in the early 1980's in England, followed by speculative office buildings, all within the City of London. After relocating to Los Angeles, for the first time, I was confronted with a client who understood much more about the workplace than I did: the West Coast ad agency Chiat/Day. I was working for Frank Gehry & Associates at the time, and designing the interiors of the Binocular Building in Venice, California. At our first meeting, the first thing Jay Chiat asked me was "how big was the house you grew up in?" I was taken aback but replied "moderately big". He then said "I don't want anyone who grew up in a small house designing my offices". While this comment could have been offensive, it made sense. He wanted a strong feeling of open space in his office, and recognized that anyone overly familiar with small spaces might not be able to create that.

After leaving the Gehry office, I established our own practice in 1991. Chiat/Day had taught us numerous things about how an office should work. As our studio worked on new office designs for them and other creative companies, we questioned what is normal, challenged assumptions and focused on 'why?'. Since the making of any kind of design product is a political act, our studio decided to address what we thought were the most serious malfunctions in our modern lifestyle: fragmentation of community, detachment and alienation, purposelessness, entropy and the absence of meaning in work. There are limits to what design can do, but we believe that the environment plays an enormous role in facilitating human relations. It shapes behavior: both for the good and for the bad. From that time, our work has focused on building creative communities through an intense consultation and collaboration process with our clients. The goal is to create environments, or stage sets, which succeed in making people feel connected, supported and engaged in today's new world.

Every project became a unique exploration about a better community: how people can feel they belong to something meaningful. How they can understand the system they work in, and what their unique role could be. How they could feel proud of their organization or school. How they could take ownership of the enterprise. Every move as a designer is thus informed by how it contributes to enriching and strengthening an organizational culture that cares for its people. Creativity will flourish within communities that genuinely support their people. We wanted our designs to be judged by how they re-interpreted and re-energized a humanistic concept of use, as well as the elegance of design resolution.

The concepts and case studies that follow this Intermezzo are important to highlight strategies that we arrived at during the early phases of our studio work. Before addressing that, it's important to describe the fundamental lessons we learned from working with creative companies.

1 LESSONS FROM THE CITY: LANDMARKS AND DESTINATIONS

When working with large organizations and large workplaces in the 1990's, we realized that the old office model not only failed, but failed in providing any template to support a new workplace concept. Searching for reference points, we naturally appropriated the city model. People intuitively knew how cities worked and how to use them. They understood the basic concepts of movement and circulation, they were familiar with environmental cues, and landmarks. Their mental map was inscribed with favored routes and destinations meaningful to them. They enjoyed the visual richness, and the energy and variety of the urban experience.

Of course, one of the obvious pitfalls of the large office is the 'sea of desks' syndrome. The people map needs spatial structuring. It needs landmarks to aid orientation and add visual richness. It needs meaningful destinations to help drive movement in

"The underlying reason we are driving communication technologies, legal frameworks, business models, organizational structures, innovation and enterprise so hard towards tools, frameworks and capabilities that amplify human talents for cooperation is because on the one hand we desperately seek meaning and identity in a world that forces us to quest for meaning and identity, and secondly, we as a species are designed to work in aggregates. Social isolation effectively dismantles us as individuals."

ALAN MOORE – NO STRAIGHT LINES

a manner not unlike shopping mall planning, which strategically places anchor tenants at opposite ends. We needed to evolve a formula for smart office planning with clear hierarchical circulation, like a city.

As a goal, smart circulation must address both clear orientation and the need to drive movement across the organization. A healthy workplace is one that supports and encourages movement energy, both for the physical fitness of employees and to optimize opportunities for serendipitous interactions.

"Every move as a designer is informed by how it contributes to enriching and strengthening an organizational culture that cares for its people."

CLIVE WILKINSON

Visible energy in the workplace is of course seductive, and fuels positive work energy levels. It is worth noting that quiet restaurants are seldom successful, whereas noisy restaurants where you cannot hear yourself speak, are very often successful. It would seem counterintuitive, but the reality is that we are all drawn to energy, as it energizes us too. Indeed, walking meetings in the modern workplace have become an important factor in new office design.

In considering departmental planning, we have discovered that a perfect colocation of adjacencies does not make perfect sense. If everyone who needed to be near everyone with whom they interacted was accommodated for the shortest possible connecting times or distances, there would be little movement energy around an office. The workplace theorist, Franklin Becker, coined the term 'functional inconvenience' to address planning to maximize physical movement and interactions, rather than short connections.

An essential factor which rounds out this component is the role of destinations. Any organizational plan needs careful definition and distribution of 'meaningful destinations' in order to drive productive movement. This can mean ensuring that employees engage more fully with the whole workplace community and its amenities. Enhanced engagement is a consequence when the employee is invited into the whole community space, in order to feel like a valuable member of the community.

2 CULTURE AND THE OFFICE AS BRAND AMBASSADOR

All projects begin with the challenge of accommodating the corporate brand with the internal organizational culture, which is usually completely different. Brand as an idea and an identity system contains inevitable ambiguities. For most corporations, the brand is the external face to the public, most often identified with the primary product or service. Since it has generally been crafted around the customer experience, it is also limited by that experience. For employees of the organization, brand necessarily comes to mean something much more complex: the company's mission and soul. Those brand values should ideally represent values that inspire employee attachment and loyalty.

The public relationships of the new office are similarly important. Historically, clients or visitors enjoyed a controlled experience of the office. Meeting facilities were generally front of house, so the experience went no further than the reception area and the meeting room. For security or confidentiality reasons, this pattern was commonplace. In the new office, management has begun to see definite advantages in offering a much richer experience for clients and visitors. We hear clients saying, "If people see how well organized, smart and dynamic we are, they will want to do business with us, and they will want to visit us for meetings (saving us time)". The office environment is now seen as a tool for marketing, and a physical brand expression. Not coincidentally, this feeds back into staff attraction and retention. The new knowledge workers do have a choice, and they will rate the coolness factor of the company they choose to work for.

Since the 1950's, branding has been through an evolution when an ad would tell you how good a product was, to the 1960's when they would tell you how a product made you feel, through to the 1980's with brands like Apple or Benetton who would ignore the product and address the world with moral and ethical values. By the first decade of 21st century, people demanded a new authenticity and wanted their brand or product to display a sense of integrity. Organizations entered an era where defining and representing who they were and what they offered became paramount in serving a society that could block or shut out messaging that did not appeal.

The office as an expression of an evolved corporate brand is essential, particularly for knowledge workers. It is as important that the physical space has a sense of centre or heart, as it is for a company to have a sense of centre and heart. This is often achieved by

Slinky space planning of TBWA\Chiat\Day,
Los Angeles. Neighborhoods can retain fluid
boundaries while also promoting a sense of
group belonging.

57

adoption of urban planning tactics: a centrally configured semi-public area, a 'main street' or 'square', an atrium space. The type of space is less important than the sense of centre and personality that is conveyed. There should be a definite relationship between this space and the company's brand, so that this becomes the 'company's centre'. The public brand is elusive from an insider perspective. The brand meaning to employees is entirely different and made up out of numerous social, ethical and philosophical viewpoints, often encapsulated in the company's 'mission'.

This community brand is the one to identify, understand and embrace in developing work environments for a very human employee population. It carries the symbol of community and is vitally important to fostering engagement and attachment in people. The sense of belonging is intangible but highly valuable in any successful company. It carries the intangible and primordial value of belonging to a family.

3 DISRUPTION AND 'SLINKY' PLANNING

In the 1980's, a ruling paradigm for designers was that the client users needed to be comfortable. Ergonomic seating, lots of space to spread out, good lighting and carpet everywhere. A comfortable employee was a happy employee. It took insightful leaders to realize this was a major distraction from the business prerogative of effectiveness and productivity. Too much comfort was going to put people to sleep. Ad agencies like Chiat/Day were pushing to disrupt industry norms and produce a completely new kind of public discourse around life style and the material world. Comfort was the enemy.

The business tool of disruption visioning was developed to help advertising clients move into a new frame of mind and move beyond the deeply ingrained brand messages from the immediate past. The disruption workshop process relied on three steps: the first session examines current conventions and seeks to describe all factors contributing to 'where we are now', including benchmarking against competitors in the industry. The second session, called 'blue sky' seeks to leave all previous ideas behind and devote all energy to questions of 'what if?' This session was crucial to describing a new future that all could buy into. The third and final session focused on achieving a synthesis: on merging

"I don't want my people comfortable, I want them provoked."

JAY CHIAT

the vision and current realities to craft an inspiring and effective path forward.

For designers, there were two lessons in this. We needed to rethink much of our own design ideology, and we needed to consider how this kind of creative strategy could be folded into our workplace design product. The work environment needed to be provocative. It needed to mirror the kind of behavior expected of creative employees. It's axiomatic that we live in congruity with our environments. We craft homes and hospitality spaces for relaxation. We build sports venues with energetic architecture. We build museums and libraries as contemplative environments.

Restaurants are shaped for vibrant socializing. A creative workplace needs to be creative and unexpected, even surprising. And that experience needs to be almost cinematic: it must unfold as the users move through it. Hence, a further observation we made was about the fluidity of workspace. Due to technological changes, the business world was undergoing dramatic evolution, which impacted the workplace. Exponential growth and retraction could occur overnight. The new workplace needed to be highly flexible, and yet truly flexible space tended to suffer from a chaotic lack of structure.

The perfect example of this was the offices of *Wired* magazine in San Francisco in the late 1990's. Desks were ad hoc doors on trestle supports – equipment, cables and paper were strewn around, and finding anything became impossible. To ameliorate this, we conjectured that a visible order could assist with orientation and structure without necessarily losing any flexibility. If departments could be color coded (for instance) and allowed to have their own identity – they could also be allowed to flow into each other like osmosis (see diagram). We called this semi-structured open system space 'slinky planning' after the flexible coiled child's toy. The workspace physical boundaries should allow groups to expand and contract while still enjoying a sense of place – or belonging – within a defined work neighborhood.

4 CHOICE, DIVERSITY AND SERENDIPITY

One early observation of the business environment in the late 20th century office was the simplicity of its tools. Every office had a maximum of four types of space. There were enclosed offices, meeting rooms, corridors, and open cubicles. Each of these categories was brutally similar, perhaps for democratic reasons. Every office looked like every other office, every meeting room looked like every other meeting room. The corridors were conceived for maximum efficiency, like race tracks where horses were replaced by people. If management personnel were solely motivated by efficient movement and democratic frugality, they would be in pig heaven.

This environment was, however, utterly dysfunctional for the new types of office community. Collaboration was either non-existent or occurred like speed dating in closed meeting rooms, contact with other colleagues was severely curtailed. Silos were rampant – no one knew where the office began or ended, no one knew who worked on what. When we were working on programming one of the largest global agencies in New York City, our clients and our team were bemused to discover an entire department of 80 people, in the same building, that no one knew existed, or indeed what part they played in the larger corporate machine.

Things were very different in the smaller companies. When we observed the work environment of smaller creative organizations, we noticed that young people would interact in the most unlikely settings. We recognized that the new office badly needed a range and diversity of different work-settings distributed throughout the office to promote formal and informal interaction, with a variety of furnishings and equipment. It was acceptable to contract the private space of the workstation, if you were offering a richer kind of public shared space. These space types could also contribute to this sense of the city: they could become like street porches, or cafes, or parks, or clubs. They could contribute the two key aspects of urban design: a legible public image, and a diverse mix of cross-promoting uses. And as an added bonus, people could feel some ownership in this new 'public space'.

In our early efforts to understand the large workplace, we reviewed a study

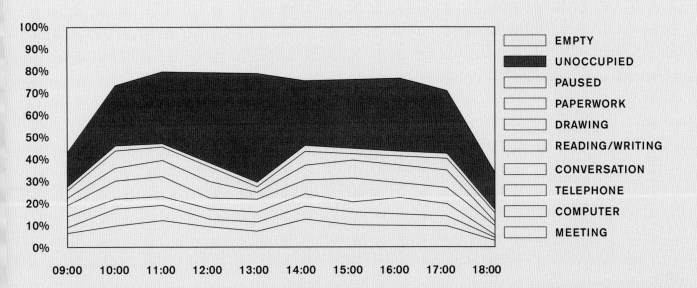

100% EMPTY
90% UNOCCUPIED
80% PAUSED
70% PAPERWORK
60% DRAWING
50% READING/WRITING
40% CONVERSATION
30% TELEPHONE
20% COMPUTER
10% MEETING
0%

09:00 10:00 11:00 12:00 13:00 14:00 15:00 16:00 17:00 18:00

TOP Diagram from a DEGW study: a day in the life of a typical office worker, highlighting time away from the desk. The diagram helped us to communicate the need to have the office design respond directly to staff movement and the opportunities for serendipitous meeting and work away from the desk.

BELOW Chess players at the Szechenyi Baths in Budapest.

> **"Man evolved to feel strongly about few people, short distances, and relatively brief intervals of time; and these are still the dimensions of life that are important to him."**
>
> MALCOLM GLADWELL – BLINK

undertaken around 1995 by the global workplace consultants DEGW. The study measured time usage in a typical office worker's day, from 9.00am to 5.00pm. The demarcation between common types of work was unremarkable. Various segments spent on computer work, writing, talking on the telephone, in meetings, etc. were as expected. However, one area stood out dramatically: the worker's time spent in the office but not in any routine work function, and not at the workstation or desk. What were people occupied with during this time? We felt that this pointed to a work category too important not to address directly in design strategy.

The new office needed space to support work away from the desk and casual meeting/interaction with others to take place productively. It needed to encourage serendipity in encounters, or unstructured collaboration, as this was increasingly becoming a potent venue of knowledge sharing in the new workplace. Business leaders also took this message seriously. As Laurie Coots, Chief Marketing Officer of Chiat/Day, said: "we cannot make people creative, but we can create the conditions that encourage creativity".

5 INTUITIVE CIRCULATION AND FLOW

My personal environmental education was helped by a strange experience when I moved to Sydney, Australia in 1989 for six months, following 12 years of living in London. I had just moved into an apartment and needed to make dinner for some friends. With little time to spare, I went to the local supermarket to get products for the meal. Following an initial disorientation, I quickly realized that I had no knowledge of this supermarket and could not find anything. All the products were different from the ones on supermarket shelves in the U.K – different labels, different names. I could not navigate intuitively and had to painstakingly read all the labels. It took twice as long to complete my shopping, and several months to acquire an intuitive map of the Australian supermarket.

The logistics of structuring large companies are similar to the structuring of cities, which provide a legible order which in turn leads to intuitive navigation. In order to communicate well, collaborate well, and move effectively around a company, you need a legible order: a pattern of movement (streets or paths), destination points (nodes), distinct work zones (neighborhoods or districts), recognizable physical elements (landmarks). These elements are notably similar to the abstracted elements of the city taught in schools.

In his influential work published in 1960, *The Image of the City*, the urban planner and author Kevin Lynch describes the attributes affording legibility to the city as "paths, edges, nodes, districts and landmarks". He saw these elements as profoundly valuable to facilitate an understanding of, and orientation in, the city. In an analogy to the animal kingdom, he suggests that strong familiarity with one's surroundings is paramount to maintaining security, survival of the species and the ability to fully exploit opportunities within one's surroundings.

Of these elements, paths are perhaps the most important. We experience the city in motion moving through it, along its paths (or streets), and all other attributes are perceived as distributed along these paths. We understand the limits of areas or neighborhoods by their edges, which could be waterfront, or railway tracks or blank walls, but essentially edges that limit our movement. We experience the different parts of the city as districts (or neighborhoods) underscored by their unique qualities. Different parts of the city have different defining features, such as their age, scale or use of buildings, a shifted street pattern, a central commercial area, or other defining features. We routinely travel to and from nodes, which may be transport junctions, public facilities or use destinations. We orientate ourselves intuitively using landmarks, which can vary from the scale of tall buildings to the intimate scale of door knobs: their defining characteristic being distinctness and unique character. Landmarks may be topographical peculiarities, or any kind of man-made structure or signboard. Those most familiar with the city will subconsciously navigate using these landmarks, some of which may be unique to their perceptions. We absorb and reconstitute three dimensional maps of our surroundings, so the shape of space and coloration of enclosing walls may tell us exactly where we are without knowing the name of the street or any conventional announcement of place. Here we are like bees in a hive: creatures attuned to their environment through an almost electrical field of floating information. However, Kevin Lynch's attributes are primarily limited to the issue of legibility of the city. In order to embrace the full complexity of the large office (small city), we need to examine all of its attributes.

6 NEIGHBORHOODS AND ORGANIZATIONAL LEARNING

Large workplaces have a need for identifiable neighborhoods to mitigate their scale and to create places for effective organizational learning. Within accessible structures, and appropriately scaled employee communities, learning occurs most powerfully at the team level. Research data supports the finding that people learn most from those in closest proximity. In addition, most learning occurs in practical application within the team area, and not in classrooms or training rooms. The neighborhood idea extends the zone of accessible relationships and secure environments, increasing opportunities for learning from more people, and other teams within the neighborhood.

The idea of neighborhoods in the workplace became hip currency in the 1990s, although few people knew quite what to do with them. Was it a sentimental notion, or did it have real value? Whatever the case, the fact remained that conjugating the structure of an office into manageable coherent units made sense. They worked on several levels: they facilitated orientation within the office

Flexible neighborhood planning of TBWA\Chiat\Day, Los Angeles, 1998.

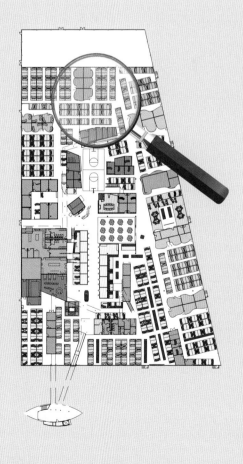

> ## "How big can we get before we get bad?"
>
> JAY CHIAT, CHIAT/DAY

7 HUMAN SCALE AND THE WORKSTATION

Having designed several workplace projects for large companies, we undertook some smaller ones. A difference became immediately apparent. Small companies operate like extended families. Whether they number 5 people or 50 people, the crucial difference is that everyone knows everyone else – more or less. This familiarity means several things. People have a sense of belonging to the larger group. The relationships with most of their colleagues developed over time which mean that they feel comfortable and secure around them. Many obstacles of work are avoided as they know their colleagues' strengths and weaknesses, how best to communicate with them and therefore how best to collaborate. They have a sense of ownership of their work and their company, leading frequently to good job satisfaction.

In these positive circumstances, the design configuration of the workplace is less critical. For one thing, the small scale means that the ability to orientate oneself and utilize office facilities is reduced. People have a great capacity to work around specific obstacles when other conditions are generally positive. They will not even perceive them as such. Smaller offices therefore have greater freedoms and rely on different social and business relationships. This may be analogous to community life in small towns or villages, which functions very differently to life in large cities.

Large workplaces, like cities, have very different structural challenges. There is a saying that there is no place in which you can be more lonely and isolated than in a city. Since cities by their nature are populated by hordes of strangers, this is not really surprising. All these strangers are similarly challenged, similarly insecure in the city, and generally deal with their needs by restricting their social groups, disengaging from public life and erecting barriers to connecting with strangers.

Something similar is also true for large workplaces. When you start employment in a large company in an office of 1,000 people, you hardly feel like your presence can make an impact. You are more likely to feel yourself invisible: a very small cog in a very big wheel. Just as in the city, you can experience isolation and alienation very quickly. To begin to transform that, you need bridges to connect to others. Corporate management usually addresses this by inserting newcomers into a group. The group or team thus begins to form the building block for the physical structure of the company. Questions of ownership in both the company and the work, however,

and gave legibility to corporate structure, they scaled down community groups allowing people to belong to a smaller community – and feel a stronger attachment to the larger group simultaneously.

Validation of this idea came from sources like the Fred Rogers children's TV show of the 1960's and 70's, *Mr. Rogers' Neighborhood*, which celebrated the small neighborhood community and its cohesive values. People have a social need to feel part of a group or tribe engaged in productive activity or play and the structure and physical boundaries of a neighborhood can embody this. For us, neighborhoods became the social building blocks of larger organizations. While each neighborhood requires physical boundaries, these boundaries must also be porous and allow groups to expand and contract without creating disconnected siloes.

Neighborhood structuring resembles landscape design: any form of visual boundary can work. As such, this can be an area to exercise design freedom.

In planning new urban neighborhoods in the 1980's, the new urbanist theorists promoted a neighborhood scale that is a quarter mile from centre to edge: the distance that is the equivalent of a five minute walk at a leisurely pace. Of course, the office scale is very different, but each typology relies on a pre-determined scale for community cohesion. The numerical size is important. Referencing the anthropologist Robin Dunbar's ratios, a neighborhood should never exceed 150 people, and is ideally considerably smaller: from 50 – 100 people. The magic ceiling of 150 represents the maximum number of relationships individual people can typically memorize, accept and support. Each organization needs to assess the size that works best for their unique community.

become tenuous. It is quite simply very hard to believe that you will make an impact, or make a difference in any meaningful way. These last points are crucial to security, job satisfaction and personal attachment to work: people do not work for money alone, unless they are desperate.

Reducing our design considerations to the scale of the individual worker, we needed to reappraise the workstation solution for the new ways of working. As the basic building block of the office, no other component wielded so much influence on the life of a worker. Workers were issued with a startling array of desking solutions that often had little to do with their work, and a lot to do with furniture companies pushing product. The one common factor was that they mostly looked like cubicles and reminded one of chicken battery farming. Cubicles had been the disruptive invention of the 1960's. They essentially offered an enclosed office to all workers (very democratic) but improved efficiency by shrinking its footprint and increasing density, removing the wasteful ceiling, and slicing off its walls at 6 ft to allow some fresh air to

the ardent and grateful worker within. The system was a packaging solution, and hugely popular with management. Its advent into the market came at a time when people were still frequently imitating machines in their routine work processes, so the deprivations of the cubicle were not as negative as they later became. By the end of the 20th century, however, work in most developed countries had transformed.

When the proliferation of personal computers began, with the attendant explosion of the internet, a whole host of changes were thrust upon the world. Routine task work was either rapidly processed by these new machines, or increasingly outsourced to developing countries where work could be executed at a fraction of the cost. In order to maintain its position, the developed world was driven into nurturing a 'knowledge economy', which we can also call an 'idea economy'. All commerce relies on the growth of new products and new markets, and conceiving products has become a key strength of the developed world.

The new generation of workers now needed suitable conditions to envision

Small companies operate as extended families.

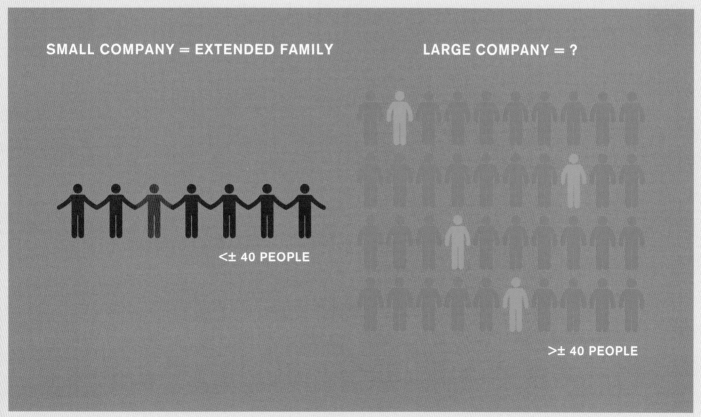

SMALL COMPANY = EXTENDED FAMILY   LARGE COMPANY = ?

<± 40 PEOPLE

>± 40 PEOPLE

WHAT DID WE LEARN?

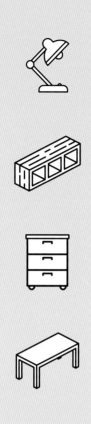

Physical components of a good workstation: light, a tackable surface, storage space, and a flat surface to work on. Put the ingredients in a blender to make a workstation.

the future and collaborate in developing new products for a new world. This meant new types of office equipment, and new furniture that would support new ways of working. At the same time, corporate managers were looking to maximize density to drive down overhead costs. Flexibility was again key. During the preceding years of convulsive change, many companies had experienced debilitating costs in internal restructuring, which were fundamentally unproductive.

As to the desk, we had to rethink it from scratch. We looked at its requirements in their most basic form. We need light, we need a tackable surface, we need personal storage, and we need a table to layout stuff. This is really not much, and certainly a lot less than the often unnecessarily elaborate products of

the furniture manufacturers. Where market products do not exist, it makes sense to make your own. For TBWA/Chiat/Day's new Los Angeles headquarters we did just that.

With the client's collaboration we designed and prototyped a new product which was called The Nest (see photographs on page 86), in reference to a new way of looking at the worker's desk. In partnership with the client, we applied for and received two patents on the design, and then shopped the product back to the furniture industry. Steelcase purchased the rights to manufacture, and used the TBWA/Chiat/Day project which needed 500 desks as a beta-testing site. The product was very successful and won a Chicago Neocon Gold Design Award in 1999. However, the production tooling had been a rapid process, leading to inefficient manufacturing, and the product was not ultimately cost effective. It sold, as Steelcase said, to 'price insensitive clients'.

Moving into the next era of office design, the market is seeing increasing openness and simplicity in new products. People are putting faith in a new open architecture, which opens communication between people. The desk is becoming smaller and more table-like, but space saving here is being offset by another new significant offering to the users: diversity and variety of worksettings.

IN SUMMARY

If one is to draw conclusions from the story related thus far, the first impression might be to observe that the office is an invention that has struggled to present a consistently successful design proposition. A large part of the complexity derives from the fact that humans are unusually adaptable and multiple forms of the office have relied on their acquiescence. Emerging from the agricultural economy, the early industrialists exploited the unskilled laborers. The division of labor process, coupled with Taylorist control, suppressed learning and education, ensuring the working classes would remain docile, subservient and disadvantaged. In spite of the efforts of trade unions, this dehumanizing pattern was only finally untangled by the emergence of the digital economy that largely displaced routine work.

One of the great lessons of the last 100 years was the destructive impact of technological progress. In World War I, for the first time in warfare, the leadership of the warring nations lost control of technology: of their weapons of mass destruction, so great was their destructive power. The killing fields of Europe and Russia witnessed casualties in the area of 40 million, for a war that lacked even a good reason for its occurrence. Perhaps the one beneficial impact of the conflict, coupled with the convulsions of World War II, was the ensuing universal distrust of the old guards of global and national leaderships, which lead to new, more democratic, power structures in the mid-century.

Our modern age thus bears the contradictory traces of cultural disruptions, of nationalistic conflicts, of a new global inter-connectedness and interdependence. These forces have shaped the modern city and in turn, shaped the modern workplace. Though many organizations still inhabit a 19ᵗʰ century mindset about the office and work, we see the new workplace as an evolving microcosm of the city, since it has become a complex organism which mirrors both the city's shaping forces and its visual and psychological effects. And we see the manipulations of history on the thinking worker, from the early bourgeoise urban dweller to the homogenized white collar worker, to the knowledge worker of today, and the myriad invented heroes of modern entertainment. A mythology surrounds these heroes of the modern world because we intentionally created this mythology to help make sense of our world.

The workplace of today is a kaleidoscopic reflection of all the intrusions into its reality. We stand on the edge of a new era of mobility and micro-electronics, of the internet of things (IoT) support systems, of artificial intelligence (AI) and virtual reality (VR). Far from suggesting that AI (in particular) will destroy human jobs, we believe that humanity will use the new technology as a springboard for inventing a world of new vocations, just as it has done many times before. And we trust that this new world will become more human-focused, ecologically supportive, socially effective and community oriented.

65

Part Two

Where Are We Going?

"Every social space has a history, one invariably grounded in nature, in natural conditions that are at once primordial and unique in the sense that they are always and everywhere endowed with specific characteristics (site, climate, etc.)"

HENRI LEFEBVRE – THE PRODUCTION OF SPACE

Setting the Stage

"The departure point for this history of space is not to be found in geographical descriptions of natural space, but rather in the study of natural rhythms, and of the modification of those rhythms and their inscription in space by means of human actions, especially work-related actions."

68

As designers, we cannot write the play, or the story of human life, we can only set the stage. Every community will produce its own unique stories. By listening to the community and observing the context, by choreographing the use, by leveraging familiar domestic and urban imagery, by responding to shared archetypes of community and human settlement, and to the extent that design is a collaborative effort, we can help create the conditions within which great drama happens.

Every complex community is necessarily layered with multiple requirements. In a search for simplicity and clarity, good design should address universal concepts of human habitation. By this we mean those concepts that work as 'archetypes' of community forming: the essential constituents of the community organism without which the community will struggle to sustain itself. Some of these may appear capricious or whimsical, like the idea of serious play. However, in a world where creative thinking is essential to survival, serious play is the gym workout for maintaining creative health.

How these ideas may be folded into the triad of a community vision, a strategic brief and a design process is illustrated through the examples of the project case studies, which are extracted from the project portfolio of our design studio, Clive Wilkinson architects. Clearly, no project is ever focused on a singular thing, so these examples invariably overlap with other concerns.

Our design process since the last century, has evolved a number of design concepts that resonate with the idea of supporting and reinforcing a creative community, independent of what that community

actually does. The role of design in shaping these working environments is different to the various social, economic and political drivers as it endeavors to reconcile and synthesize all possible forces upon the design challenge and emerge with a spatial solution that brings clarity, intelligence and a concept of beauty into play.

In every case, these design solutions come out of deep conversations with the larger team of players. The client's vision and the company's background, the other team members who often provide conceptual break-throughs, the physical and geographic context, the social and political milieu at the time, and so on. These conversations provide the unique narrative basis that once extended into a design which responds to the multiple layers of need and use, ensure the unique character of each project. They are all different, since the human and physical context is always different. In the preceding section, we review lessons learned from the early client projects. In this section, we develop and evolve those lessons into more integrated and persuasive concepts that look to the future.

Beyond the influences of project teams and professional colleagues, a vast library of books constantly advocate for specialized approaches to the subject of organizational communities. In the course of writing this book, I referred to over 100 such books and endeavored to fold in many lessons from these diverse sources. As such, this book is a synthesis of practice experience with related theoretical explorations. The first books to seduce me in my architectural education were Christopher Alexander's *A Pattern Language*, and Jane Jacobs *Life and Death of Great American Cities*.

The *Pattern Language* introduced a completely radical idea of utilizing an extensive matrix of clearly defined performance criteria to test and validate an architectural proposition. Critics at the time dismissed the notion, proposing that a great work of architecture was so much more than the sum of its parts. However, their critiques failed to address the fact that most buildings would benefit immeasurably by considering a much greater set of human performance issues in order to become better buildings. Our design approach henceforth took the view that all inputs were good, and that great architecture will rise to celebrate human complexity – just as the great Gothic cathedrals celebrated in their adornment the entire knowledge of humanity at the time: they were quite literally encyclopedias cast in stone to illuminate a largely illiterate feudal audience.

Jan Gehl's book about using public space, *Life Between Buildings* awoke me to negative space. This discovery opened up a strange and disturbing realization, that architects focus on the wrong thing: the solid building as an object. But we don't experience objects in any useful way other than aesthetic and symbolic. Life in the city is a meandering poem of streets carved like canyons, with shops and businesses like some floral embellishment. Almost any walk in a city like London leaves you with messages of both intense hard-faced urbanity and a strangely orchestrated rolling landscape, which the green street trees reinforce. Nature and the garden entered the European city from around 1700 with the first monarchist properties that were given over for the public pleasure – perhaps to recover the dream of living in harmony with the natural world. It is a common observation that the older cities of the world remain magical and intensely human as their street planning was predicated on the traffic of horse, cart and pedestrian.

Much of our early work in designing large workplace communities included a search for common threads that would communicate with people outside of the design sphere. For this we looked to sociological, artistic and historical sources. We experimented with thematic language, and inexpensive construction materials and techniques since project budgets were always tight. We borrowed from numerous sources as all architects do. We also experimented with incomplete or open-ended design work that emphasizes process over product. Our space planning consistently needed to maximize flexibility in order to allow our clients the ability to rapidly redeploy the business organization to meet new challenges. Hence, learning alongside our clients, we evolved these following concepts which have played a major role in our design endeavor of shaping successful and sustainable work communities.

69

"We may see ourselves as living late in the history of consumer society, but the most sophisticated contemporary economy stands to be perceived by subsequent generations as no less primitive than we judge Europe to have been in the Dark Ages."

ALAIN DE BOTTON – THE PLEASURES AND SORROWS OF WORK

The City as Shared Memory

The search for a common language to structure community space.

Communities gather around sets of shared interests, trade relationships and the potential for realizing mutual goals. Communication relies on languages that operate at different levels, ranging from body language and spoken tongue, to 'environmental clothing' and tribal branding. Tribal messaging is inherent in the clothing people elect to wear, and in the decorated or embellished spaces they occupy. In this sense, all man-made environments speak. Everything human speaks.

Shared memory is a powerful tool for enhanced communication. We are attuned to the fabric and processes of cities and towns. We navigate these places instinctually, using public pathways called streets, avenues and sidewalks. Since everything plays a part in this complex picture, we do not need to constantly 'read' the environment. It simply becomes familiar and intuitive, and we behave as if we own it. When considering large workplace design, there is no single encyclopedia of ideas more relevant to solving design problems since most physical problems of human habitation have already been resolved in the city.

The medieval city, which became the Elizabethan city of the illustration, addressed and formalized all the needs and concerns that shape community. What we now refer to as neighborhoods, town halls and main street were embedded in the Medieval city, which evolved gradually over hundreds of years in response to local needs, desires and forces. Context and topography played an intrinsic role in their formation and ensured an intimate relationship with the surrounding land. Important public functions, like the civic and religious structures, generally took on more prominence and became landmarks aiding orientation, as well as civic identity and meaning.

From 1500, the private ownership of land was an incipient factor in shaping cities where the wealthy and privileged ensured their property rights through legislation – and brought vanity into the urban scene with their decorous edifices. Cities do indeed inscribe and reflect wealth, power and hierarchies, in their form and structure in an ebb and flow with economic prosperity. Private interests and land ownership would in fact henceforth stall regeneration, as Sir Christopher Wren discovered to his chagrin. His ambitious plans to improve, rationalize and consolidate the urban plan of London following the great fire of 1666, and which the king supported, were thwarted due to landowners' rights. Old London's

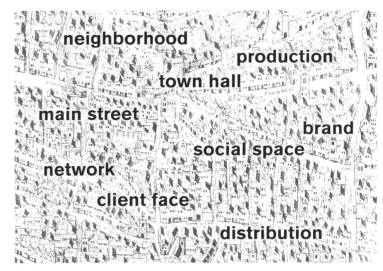

Map of London, c. 1550-59.

extensive maze of lanes, courts and passages are a testament to the resilience of title boundaries that go back centuries.

In the same way that the city gradually evolved from the grips of aristocracy, heraldry, excessive wealth and privilege, to one based on trade, merchants and professions, so hierarchy in the workplace has diminished. A clear understanding has emerged that the flat organization is a far better apparatus with which to face the future. To quote Peter Drucker: "It is a sound, structural principle to have the fewest layers, that is, to have an organization that is as 'flat' as possible – if only because, as information theory tells us, 'every relay doubles the noise and cuts the message in half'."

The first two case studies offer two perspectives on the city as a well of design ideas and inspiration. The ad agency TBWA\Chiat\Day promoted the idea of a village constructed inside a building. Santa Monica College Centre for Media and Design, with the KCRW radio station, took this one step further to shape new and existing buildings around an idea of urban space, and then further shaped internal planning as if the outdoor urban space had seamlessly penetrated it.

LOCATION Los Angeles, California, United States
COMPLETED December 1998
FLOOR AREA 120,000 square feet
POPULATION 500 growing to 900

TBWA\Chiat\Day 'Advertising City'

72

The headquarters of ad agency TBWA\Chiat\Day was our first exploration of the office as a microcosm of the city and also the project that launched our studio in doing global work. The building subject for renovation was a huge warehouse where the entire 500-person agency could be situated on one floor, in one space. For this reason it offered the starting point for a large distributed 'village' layout. The iconographic language used spoke to memories of the city for community orientation, rootedness and resonance.

They had been our first client in 1992 when we designed and completed their offices on the third floor of the Frank Gehry binocular building. Ad agencies are peculiar beasts in the workplace world. They care more about their physical space than almost any other kind of company, for the good reason that advertising lives or dies on the effectiveness of creative ideas, which work place design can either help, support and enable, or resist and disable.

Chiat/Day (the agency's corporate name before 1995) had moved offices every five years. Each of the iterations had pushed their workplace culture in a new direction. In 1995, as a response in part to growth and density challenges, they renovated their binocular building in Venice to install the first real 'virtual office': no paper, no offices, no designated workstations. Their visionary founder, Jay Chiat, was always 10 years ahead of the times. While the Chiat/Day virtual office attracted worldwide attention, it fell short of providing a functional environment. The rest of the

world was still transacting business via paper, so being the only electronic one was a major challenge. Every document that entered the office needed scanning since filing had been consigned to the trash bin. Space was tight and employees scrambled every morning to find a spot to work. Being dispersed throughout the office, no one knew where anyone was. While teamwork improved in the face of adversity, dysfunctional aspects drove down morale. Some group leaders were forced to use the trunks of their cars as filing cabinets.

Through the course of these struggles, the agency was bought out by the TBWA network, and management determined that a new work environment was needed. TBWA\Chiat\Day had outgrown their existing premises and planned to relocate to the Playa Vista area of Los Angeles. Few large office space opportunities existed in 1996 for large organizations in Los Angeles, and the agency's management jumped at the empty warehouse in the Playa Vista industrial area.

The vision for their new headquarters called for the creation of an internal 'village' where the company could be brought together in one space. The ambitious program and the scale of the warehouse offered the chance of developing this small city environment with multiple levels, green park space and an irregular 'skyline'. Traditional urban planning concepts of Downtown, Main Street, neighborhoods, parks, alleys, civic functions, building facades and street furniture – and a range of diverse structures accommodating meeting spaces, with tents for project rooms

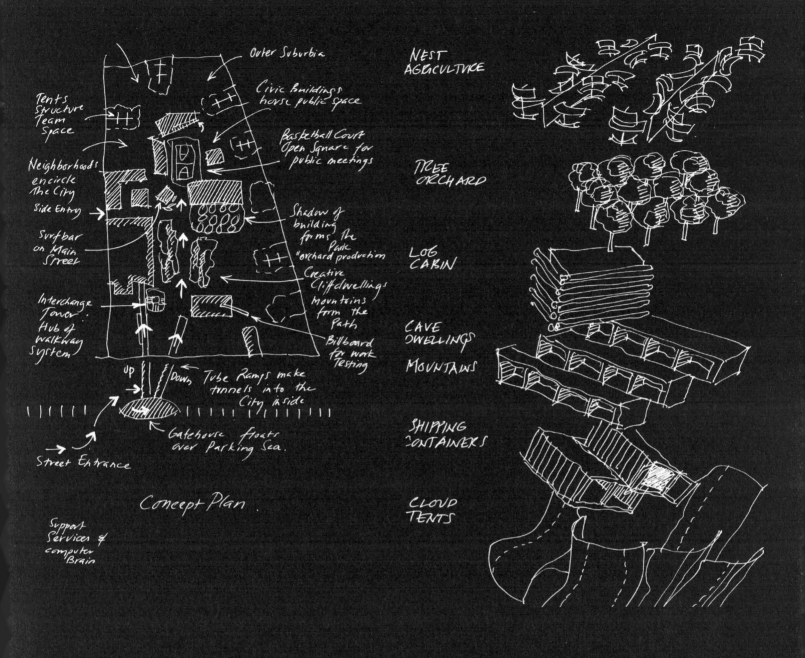

Outer Suburbia

NEST AGRICULTURE

Civic Buildings house public space

Tents Structure Team space

Basketball Court Open Square for public meetings

TREE ORCHARD

Neighborhoods encircle The City
Side Entry

Shadow of building forms the Park "orchard production

LOG CABIN

Surfbar on Main Street

Creative Cliff dwellings mountains from the Path

CAVE DWELLINGS

MOUNTAINS

Interchange Tower: Hub of walkway System

Billboard for work Testing

Up Down Tube Ramps make tunnels into the City inside

SHIPPING CONTAINERS

Gatehouse floats over Parking Sea.

Street Entrance

Concept Plan.

CLOUD TENTS

Support Services & computer Brain

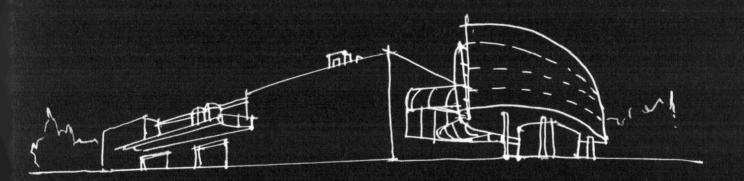

ABOVE **Sketches for the 'City' components.**

BELOW **Early sketch for the new Gatehouse.**

– all became planning elements necessary to humanize the raw industrial space. The various departments and service facilities were to be connected through Main Street which bisects the ground floor, and bridges and ramps that connect mezzanines in the high warehouse space.

On the exterior, a sculptural metal-clad Gatehouse pavilion was proposed to accommodate the agency's main entrance and provide an identifying landmark. Today cities are generally entered via the capsule-like travel of airplanes. The warehouse site provided the opportunity to offer a capsulized entry in the form of a gatehouse. This structure accommodates a reception area and gallery for displaying the agency's work and is connected to the main warehouse by two pedestrian bridges, one leading to the ground floor and one to the second level inside. We raised the Gatehouse up off the ground to free the surface for the required parking and connected it to the building with long enclosed tubes to simulate entering a plane at the airport. The message was clear that by entering TBWA\Chiat\Day you were traveling somewhere different.

The agency's philosophy of creativity defining the core of their business led to the placement of the creative department in the centre. Lee Clow, the creative director, described his creative staff as "anti-social, paranoid, visionary hermits" who should be living in caves, but caves as in the Greek island of Santorini, with a great view out over the ocean. This lead to the design of the Cliff Dwellings either side of Main Street where creative teams operate in mechanistic 'cave' structures – protected on their sides but open and accessible to the whole agency. At three stories high, these structures lend a sense of urban scale to the whole agency.

The need to articulate diversity in the distribution of functions led to the adoption of different methods for making space. Cliff Dwellings became steel structures to minimize head clearances, wood framing was cost effective for most build-out, and temporary structures were best formed in fabric tents, allowing easy replacement and reminding people of shrouded buildings under construction (a city is always under construction). Shipping containers provided the first model for the Cliff Dwellings, but these were substituted for custom steelwork since the client thought the metal containers could be too confining.

The work station was a critical building block for the agency. In the 1990's there was literally no desking product on the US marketplace that was not a mass-produced cubicle. In the absence of finding anything suitable, we proposed to custom design the workstations. The desktop form was curved based on the sweep of an arm – 'everything within reach'. The desks were intended to be almost portable – moved and grouped freely – allowing teams to configure in different ways. Clusters of these workstations, like mechanical orchards, encircle the city centre, and accommodate the project teams in 'office' neighborhoods, interspersed with project dens in flexible, open tent structures. With adjustable shielding screens, the workstations were cozy settings that were called 'Nests'. We patented the design and sold the rights to Steelcase who manufactured them for the open market. The product was recognized with a Neocon Gold design award in 1999.

Due to the urban character of the interior, the project became known as 'Advertising City' and set a new benchmark in office design for the way it merged lifestyle and recreation opportunities within an open architecture. Possibly the strangest thing about TBWA\Chiat\Day and its success is that, with the exception of skylights, there are almost no windows to the outside world – which you barely realise. It has become a world unto itself and has remained fully operational and largely unaltered for over 20 years, in spite of a doubling in population density. Very recent changes have been driven by the need to add further density and contract individual workspace, since a major market shift has occurred since 1998.

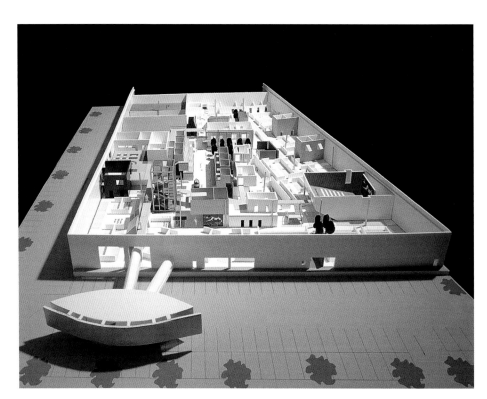

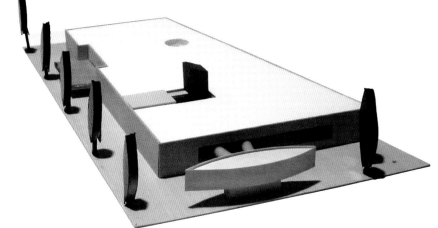

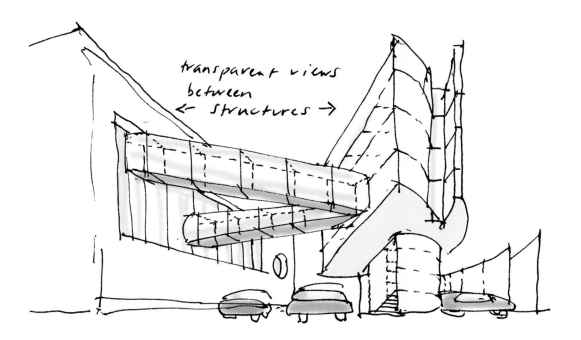

transparent views between
← structures →

ABOVE First physical model of the internal village.

MIDDLE Initial concept model that we used to sell the client on the new Gatehouse.

BELOW Sketch for the Gatehouse.

NEXT PAGE On the exterior, a metal-clad Gatehouse pavilion was proposed to accommodate the agency's main entrance and to provide an identifying landmark. The Gatehouse was raised off the ground to free the surface for parking and was connected to the building with long, enclosed tubes to simulate the experience of getting on a plane.

THE CITY AS SHARED MEMORY

78

ABOVE You enter the agency via entrance tunnels – long, enclosed tubes intentionally void of windows to intensify the sensation of entering another world. Off in the distance is Main Street, which is where the angle of the path changes.

OPPOSITE PAGE The first view you have upon entering the warehouse via the upper tunnel is of the workspace. We have always considered that a visual connection to the purpose of a space will connect users with its intent and meaning. When you enter a building, it should reveal its purpose.

LONGITUDINAL SECTION

CROSS SECTION

Expansion
10,000 SQF

Basketball court

Broadcast building

VBE edit suite

Container bar

Side entry

Central services

Cliff dwellings

Elevator tower

Main street

Tent structure projections

Executive stations

War room tent

Art studio

Central park

Open office neighborhood

Creative studio

GROUND FLOOR

Gatehouse

ABOVE Sections of the warehouse emphasize the horizontal length of the building.

BELOW Floor plan of the warehouse and Gatehouse.

THE THEATRE OF WORK

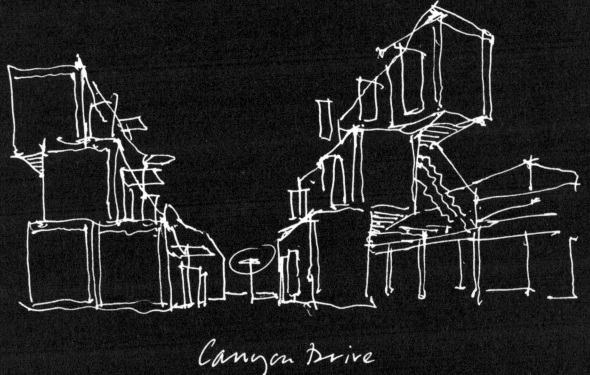

Canyon Drive

shutter
parts

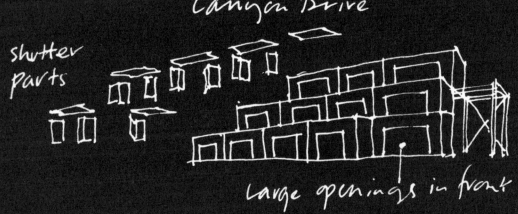

Large openings in front

TEWA GROSVENOR — CLIFF DWELLINGS

Sketch for the Cliff Dwellings facing each other across Main Street. We had originally developed a single line of Cliff Dwellings that overlooked the office, but this created an unfortunate hierarchy. So we broke the form into two and made one half face the other instead. This move underscored the prominence of Main Street, symbolically placing creativity at the core of the agency.

Shaped by the split composition of the Cliff Dwellings, with teams of art directors and copywriters on either side, the central axis of Main Street organizes the village layout of the warehouse and shared spaces that run along the path, such as the Central Park, the main wooden conference room structure, the shipping container boardroom, and the Basketball Court.

ABOVE **Central Park acts as the lungs of the agency.**

MIDDLE LEFT **Main Conference Room.**

MIDDLE RIGHT **At the end of Main Street is the Basketball Court, a powerful statement of the time that the function of recreation or leisure should be folded into a creative workspace. Staff could play in small, informal games during the day, and in more competitive inter-team games at night. With a large video projection system housed in the adjacent shipping container meeting room, the Basketball Court is a highly versatile space with the ability to host all-hands meetings and agency gatherings.**

BELOW **The Surf Bar and Cliff Dwellings.**

OPPOSITE PAGE **A closer look at the Cliff Dwellings. Two-person rooms for art directors and copywriters. No doors.**

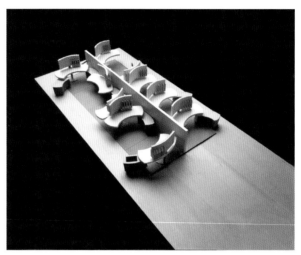

86

ABOVE LEFT The custom-designed
Nest workstations were a critical
building block. In the absence of
finding anything suitable in the furniture marketplace, we proposed
designing the desks in-house. The
desktop form was curved, based on
the sweep of an arm – 'everything
within reach'. The workstations
were intended to be almost portable – moved and grouped freely
– allowing teams to configure in
different ways.

ABOVE RIGHT With the custom
workstations, collaboration can
now occur at the desk.

MIDDLE Model highlighting
flexibility in the workstation
configurations.

BELOW Neighborhood with workstations and a (temporary) project
tent in the distance.

87

ABOVE **TBWA\Chiat\Day, Los Angeles, 2016. 18 years later, and the space looks almost unchanged.**

BELOW The essence of the TBWA\Chiat\Day plan is the urban framework, which permits efficient flow and connection between different parts of the agency, and the hierarchy of street, alley and circulation pathways. In 2008, 10 years later, we applied the same urban strategy to planning the Santa Monica College Center for Media and Design.

LOCATION Santa Monica, California, United States
COMPLETED August 2018
FLOOR AREA 115,000 square feet (50,000 SF Renovation +
30,000 SF Addition + 35,000 SF KCRW Media Centre)
POPULATION 2,500 (max) [1,300 Building D +
700 Building C + 500 Building B]

Santa Monica College Centre for Media and Design & KCRW Media Centre

The Santa Monica College's new Centre for Media and Design allowed us another opportunity to configure building interiors using urban planning strategies. But this time, we could extend the paradigm to create new buildings from scratch to simulate a truly urban proposition flowing through both interior and exterior spaces. We began with a large asphalt parking lot with a single school building, like an island within it, and ended up with an integrated four building campus with a new town square.

To create an integrated urban proposition, we needed to knit together the new and old structures. The existing Academy of Entertainment Technology building was modernist in form with a buff brick embellishing much of the exterior. We determined to re-use the brick so that new and old would merge together. The existing building had expressed large block like forms – we repeated this motif in the new. As a wayfinding device, we introduced a counterpoint of a yellow fibre-cement board band that tied the structures together, and acted as a canopy on the square. The square itself was furnished with a raised area to act as a stage, so communal events could happen with ease.

The client's functional brief evolved from a need to promote a modest extension and new building for the radio station, to the goal of creating a sophisticated satellite Media Centre for the college. In the summer of 2008,

Clive Wilkinson Architects was selected to implement a master plan for the site, including a new headquarters for their world-renowned KCRW Radio Station. The programmatic mixture of educational facilities and professional offices posed an opportunity to explore uniting the two ventures. We came to the realize, through a series of investigative workshops, that the various media programs all shared the common theme of 'storytelling'. We therefore began thinking of the new campus within a narrative for a progressive sequence of learning.

The success of a college education is increasingly gauged by a single criterion: how well does it really prepare students for the workplace? In addition to instilling academic fundamentals, colleges are expected more than ever to produce fully skilled graduates capable of entering the modern workplace with little on-the-job training. However, few institutions are truly committed to bridging the gap between education and work. The new Centre for Media and Design is an experiment in co-locating a media education program and a professional broadcasting organization to maximize the collateral benefits between them.

As described by one of our team leaders, Ed Ogosta: "We set to work on creating an architecture that acts as the narrative vehicle, binding the campus into a sequence of experiences that present education as a

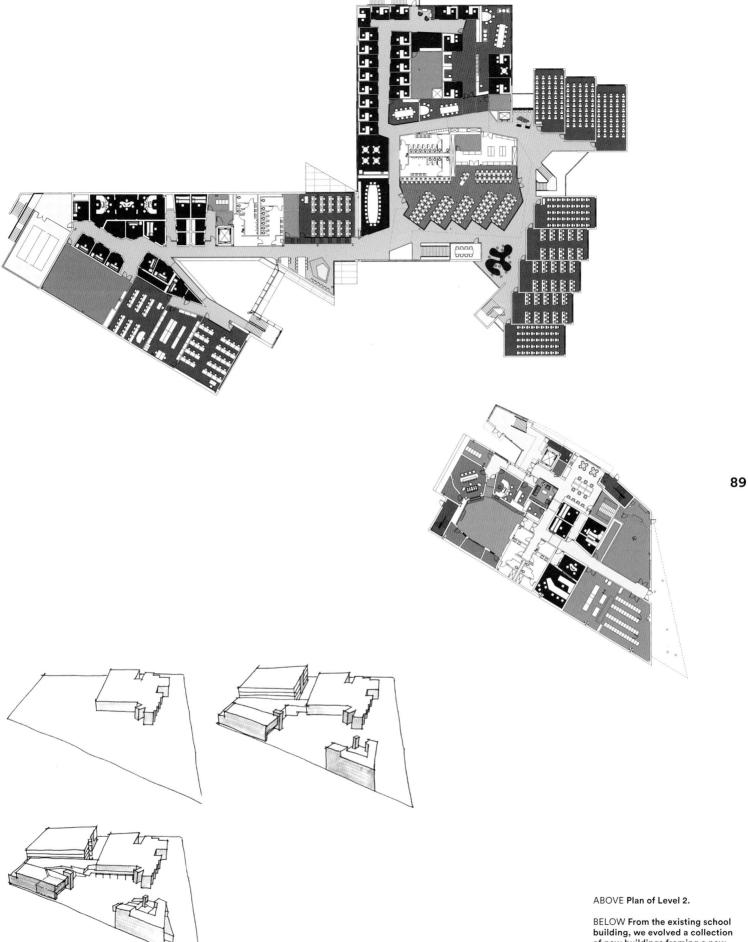

89

ABOVE **Plan of Level 2.**

BELOW **From the existing school building, we evolved a collection of new buildings framing a new urban courtyard and community structure.**

THE CITY AS SHARED MEMORY

progressive cycle. The campus story starts from the first day of college, through to the professional workplace. Three campus buildings, each opening onto a central orienting courtyard, embody this cycle of education as follows:

Existing Media Technology building: arrival point and incubator for ideas.

This building, slated for a complete interior redesign, consists of instructional classrooms and offices deployed along a main path, indicated by a yellow folding ribbon. Interior glass walls maxmize transparency into classroom spaces, thereby exhibiting ideas-in-formation.

New Media Technology addition: experimentation and discovery.

The ribbon continues into this building, where students can explore and test their ideas in professional-grade production spaces. A film studio, screening room, student radio station, newspaper lab, control rooms, and editing work-bays give students the tools to realize and exhibit their work.

New KCRW building: maturity and real-world application.

KCRW is a professional centre for the convergence of media and is the logical endpoint for this narrative sequence of learning. Characterized by a similar internal path and open, visible workspaces, KCRW will share resources with SMC to encourage reciprocal education.

Courtyard: creative arena.

The glue between these experiences is the courtyard, which enables all programs to publicly converge into a single creative community, via a café, supportive landscaping and event infrastructure."

The fully renovated existing faculty building, replete with classrooms, student lounges and faculty offices operates as an arrival point for new media students, as an instructional facility and an incubator of new ideas. The New Media Technology addition, housing well-equipped production facilities and editing suites, will continue the story with an emphasis on experimentation and discovery.

Aerial view of the campus.

Finally, the new KCRW building will act as the endpoint for the narrative sequence, where ideas have matured and find their places in a real-world application. Connecting these experiences is the hard-paved arena of the central courtyard where converging building entrances, a café, supportive landscaping and event infrastructure will enable all programs to converge into a single creative community.

By co-locating the nascent realm of academia with the applied realm of the professional workplace, a new kind of community arises: one that approaches work not unlike a medieval guild, albeit with digital tools. Our architecture provides an armature for this guild-like hybrid. Openness, transparency, spaces for interaction, flexible workspace and places for exhibition are the architectural means we employed for breaking down barriers between school and office. The new campus is thus an experiment in synergies: diverse disciplines will converge within a village-like clustering, learning, experimenting and working together to illuminate the stories of our world.

90

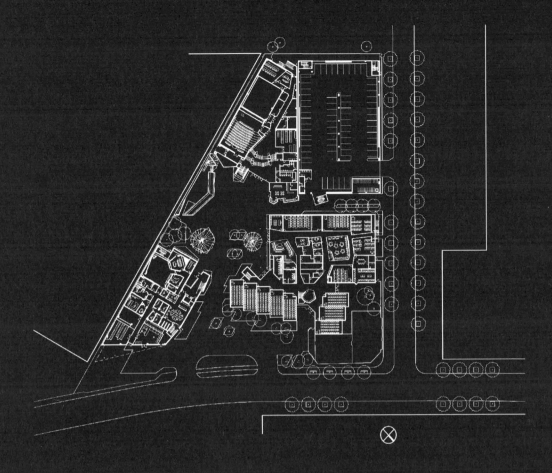

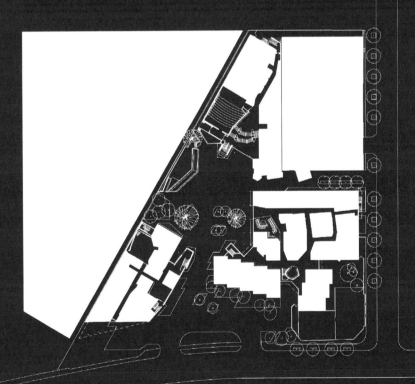

ABOVE Site plan and figure-ground plan highlighting the urban character of the campus.

NEXT PAGE View of the new Media Technology building from the courtyard.

THE CITY AS SHARED MEMORY

OPPOSITE PAGE ABOVE Atrium in the new Media Technology addition.

OPPOSITE PAGE BELOW The extension building accommodates a wide variety of hands-on production facilities, including a screening room.

ABOVE View of the two-story atrium and the central courtyard.

BELOW New seven-level parking structure.

NEXT PAGE View from Stewart Street. The new KCRW Media Center is on the left, and the renovated and expanded Media Technology building is on the right.

THE CITY AS SHARED MEMORY

98

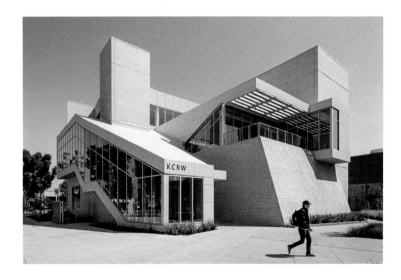

ABOVE **Stairwell in the KCRW building.**

BELOW **View of the central courtyard at dusk.**

CENTRE **View of the sculptural, two-story atrium in the renovated and expanded Media Technology building.**

OPPOSITE PAGE ABOVE **Link between the existing and new Media Technology buildings, connecting old and new.**

OPPOSITE PAGE BELOW **The new, three-story KCRW Media Center marks the first time the beloved radio station will operate from their own facility.**

Workspace in the new KCRW Media Center is framed by a large cut-out in the building mass. A wide variety of production facilities, such as broadcasting studios, control rooms and editing bays, are positioned along the perimeter, allowing staff to oscillate between collaborative work and focused individual work.

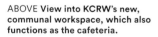

102

ABOVE **View into KCRW's new, communal workspace, which also functions as the cafeteria.**

CENTRE **Mezzanine viewing gallery overlooking the performance studio, which will allow listeners and the greater community more opportunities to interact closely with the station.**

OPPOSITE PAGE ABOVE **View of the control room looking into the performance studio.**

OPPOSITE PAGE BELOW **Music Director Jason Bentley in the performance studio.**

The Culture Model

How culture shapes both brand and the total environment.

Each age considers itself on the edge of a precipice. The future is unknown, and in order to move forward, there's a collective projection, a kind of whirlwind of notions and ideas that are pushed out there. But no certainty exists that any of them will stick. What characterizes an age therefore may be far more about what this uncertainty suggests, than the meagre cultural accomplishments of the time. We know, for instance, that the 1950's were consumed with paranoia about the bomb, about the Cold War, even as we closely consider the sophisticated modern furnishings of the time. We know that the 'flower power' era ten years later was mostly a collective reaction to America's involvement in Vietnam, though we dig the inspiring pop music that epitomized that time. What makes culture itself interesting is mostly what rises above the psychological traumas: it is those signs of a powerful and sentient humanity that make being alive and human worthwhile.

Nothing has more influence on the design of man-made environments than the Culture Model, and in office design, nothing is less talked about. The developed world has been content to indiscriminately promote Western hegemony and sell its products across the globe for several centuries. The result is a kind of offensive cultural imperialism. However, some recent globalization tendencies have attempted to redress the imbalance and have been focused on merging cultures in an effort to promote 'inclusion' and acceptance. Arguably, some globalization tendencies have had the reverse effect.

Culture ascribes meanings and value reflexively to any given things, consciously or unconsciously, within global societies and tribes. The culture of any tribe is inextricable from its unique identity and value system, inscribed in these things. The strength and stability of culture derives from the fact that it is group based and that the individual will hold onto certain basic assumptions in order to ratify his or her membership of the group. According to the MIT management guru Edgar H. Schein, organizational culture can be analysed at several levels: (1) visible artifacts, (2) espoused beliefs, values, rules, and behavioral norms, and (3) tacit, taken for granted, basic underlying assumptions. This last item is what makes culture both powerful and difficult to change, since assumptions below the surface can be so well concealed.

In working with new clients, there is always a period when the espoused beliefs and values are discussed and debated, and often the workplace transformation is embedded within a cultural transformation. Our role becomes clearer with addressing visible artifacts, where design can play a role, but mining the underlying assumptions and their interrelationships is most challenging. Frequently, people are unaware of the constraining impact of their own assumptions. This is where a change management process pays big dividends: leadership and the design team can collaborate to instigate a broad iterative conversation about organizational change and new desirable behaviors.

Historically, every culture has evolved to fill a need for a group identity and a moral code with which to guide their actions to ensure survival. Regional and local cultures will respond differently when presented with the same challenges. This inevitable 'difference' gives places and people their distinctness, which a globalizing world is threatening to homogenize.

When you walk the streets of a venerable city like Rome or Moscow, you find yourself marvelling at the embellishment of the architecture. The styles vary across each city, and date back hundreds, if not thousands, of years. Across successive periods, the language of architecture reached a refined level of articulation. The

"We may see ourselves as living late in the history of consumer society, but the most sophisticated contemporary economy stands to be perceived by subsequent generations as no less primitive than we judge Europe to have been in the Dark Ages."

ALAIN DE BOTTON – THE PLEASURES AND SORROWS OF WORK

Models of culture: maturity/immaturity. It is worthwhile to compare the youth of today to the youth of two centuries ago. We are drawn to messages in the painting of Marie Antionette.

106

Victorian era when the forward thrust of industry dislodged the old patrician order and brought the nouveau riche to the table, with their singular detachment from any tradition. Architectural style became a comodification of the styles of any previous era.

The first glimpses of modernity that saw light with another recourse to the examples of nature became Art Nouveau at the end of the 19th century. The Great War of 1914-1918 lead to mass disillusionment with the ruling powers and indeed anything that represented the class that had lead the world into that cataclysmic hell. Primary forms were resurrected again, representing the New. Malevich and De Styl, Paul Klee and colleagues of the Bauhaus produced seductive artistic templates for a new world, rejecting the romantic attempt to to turn back the clock. Manifestos and pronoucements of a new era prevailed, where craft and the machine age could make peace.

These preoccupations have always represented statements about culture and society and are fueled by how they live within society. However, perhaps it is not the iconic moments of architecture, but rather the common works of all these ages that most persuasively articulate their respective societies, in part because they dominate the urban landscape. They make up the majority of the building fabric and project the most truthful image of their age. When you move through a relatively new American city, you become painfully aware of the weakness of a cultural image. You can travel for hours through a landscape so weak in human communication that we have forgotten any sense of obligation to project a modest level of civility. It is as if you have walked into a cocktail party of elderly people where they all had forgotten to dress in anything other than their underwear.

architects or masterbuilders were communicating, consciously or unconsciously, the values, styles and affectations of their age. They endeavored to represent what a building should mean to its users and its public.

We now enjoy that legacy. Where these building works were most successful was when their authors were invested, proud and inspired by the age in which they lived. The more we learn about the architectural language, the more we understand how fluent were these authors, the more we discover the essence of identity and self image emblemmatic of their age. European cities remain compelling and seductive for this very reason: that we internalize languages of different eras almost to the point of hearing them speak. We call this silent communcation 'culture'.

Like many other cities around the world, European cities have enjoyed many consecutive centuries of this layering and embellishment of language. We can discern cycles of belief systems at work. We witnessed the descent of the Baroque into Rococco, where form became untethered from Euclidean order, resulting in an overly stylized return to emulating nature. We witnessed the ascendance of neoclassicism in a revolutionary guise with the work of Ettiene Louis Boulle and Claude Nicolas LeDoux at the time of the French Revolution, when elemental geometry and the perfect forms of cubes, spheres and cones dominated. We witnessed a chaotic

"The age demanded an image of its accelerated grimace."

EZRA POUND

Some years ago, I came across this painting of Marie Antionette, which conveys an image both playful and fanciful, not unlike the corresponding image of a young girl from our age. Both characters are making conscious statements about their culture and about their 'tribe'. Both strike poses which celebrate the human body and fashionable clothing, and also make reference to nature. But what is truly unusual about the 18th century version? Marie Antionette has grey hair. Whether oiled and powdered, or a wig, she is underscoring her role in society by adopting grey hair, almost certainly because it was a conspicuous sign of power. In 1780, power resided in rich elderly people, who had grey hair – and that was 'cool'.

A second unusual thing is projected through the classical composition. The age of Marie Antoinette was arguably one of western culture's high points. A masterful consistency of medium, message, ornament and hierarchical order is projected. Whereas the girl on the right projects a naïve image, toy-like accessories and a child-like innocence amounting to a celebration of immaturity.

These contrasting images communicate the empirical truth of their times: Marie Antoinette inhabits a historical era wherein culture had become refined to the point of constriction: it was becoming a closed system, within which designers and artists were constrained by the rules. The girl of today is able to constantly reinvent herself and shape-shift. She inhabits an immature era which is reflexively in the process of creative projections. It is valuable to understand that this is a freedom in which we can and should revel. Whatever we conjecture as truths for our age will become redundant a short time later. The truth is a state of flux.

What one observes with human dress can be transposed to the architectural environment. The palaces of the 18th century showcased a kind of cultural saturation. Classical architectural style would be draped with late Baroque stylization and references to the natural world, all reigned into the service of creating masterworks. The eye is rewarded with rich detail but little is left to intellectual appreciation.

An environment that is an example of an elevated 'mature' culture should be compared to the relatively immature culture of today. St Petersburg reminds us of a similarly gilded effect we somewhat accidentally created within a culture both immature and childlike. When we took on the project to create a headquarters building for the Disney Store we developed a hexagonal plastic furnishing system to allow them to store all the toy products in development. The 'gilded' interior was capable of constant reconfiguration since each module could be relocated. It became hence an open or 'immature' system with superficial parallels to the glorious Age of Enlightenment.

The Grand Church of the Winter Palace in St. Petersburg, Russia (right), juxtaposed with The Disney Store Headquarters in Pasadena, California (left).

LOCATION Pasadena, California, United States
COMPLETED March 2007
FLOOR AREA 81,000 square feet
POPULATION 230

The Disney Store Headquarters

108

Disney is a compelling case for cultural investigation. The brand started by Walt Disney has achieved a massive level of cultural penetration across the world, shaping both adult and childhood fantasies and aspirations within its value system. The Disney project is itself in constant evolution with new market driven products and our role became developing a platform that encouraged open collaboration and rapid prototyping for their Disney Store merchandise division, at the time managed under license by The Children's Place organization.

Working within three contiguous old industrial buildings, our design solution for the Disney Store Headquarters in downtown Pasadena evolved from the desire to create a functional yet playful environment that accords with the Disney image. Workplace strategists DEGW developed an organizational plan with our studio, which was articulated with colorful modular and flexible systems that blurred the boundaries between architecture and furniture. The historically significant 1927 Royal Laundry Building is wood framed and composed of three parts, within a brick walled structure which inspired the creation of brick-like elements for the interior. These modular elements allude to the playful block building habits of children.

The existing building envelope was maintained by retaining its integrity, while inserting strategic architectural objects in the space. The two major portions of the building are anchored by two main conference rooms. The first, known as the 'Block Conference Room' is formed on two sides by removable foam block walls. When these foam modules are disassembled for company-wide meetings of up to 200 people, they become the seating system. On most days, they are vertically stacked in a brick pattern to form the walls for a 20-person meeting room. The red, orange, yellow and ochre color palette was inspired by the existing brick wall colors. This color palette is echoed in the modular Vitra Storage Wall furniture system, which extends throughout the workspace.

The second main element was a conference room, formed by a purpose-designed modular honeycomb structure and is located in the atrium portion of the building. Originally conceived as a flexible means of managing the Disney sample product display, it became the centrepiece of the space. Approximately 500 modular honeycombs units, 24 inches wide by 17 inches deep and fabricated in rotation-molded plastic, form a dramatic two-story open conference room. The organic configuration of the undulating honeycomb units capture the light from the clerestory windows creating a warm glow throughout the space. One major benefit in using a movable storage system as a major architectural element is its portability. Disney can reconfigure their spatial divisions with ease, and also take the product with them when they move.

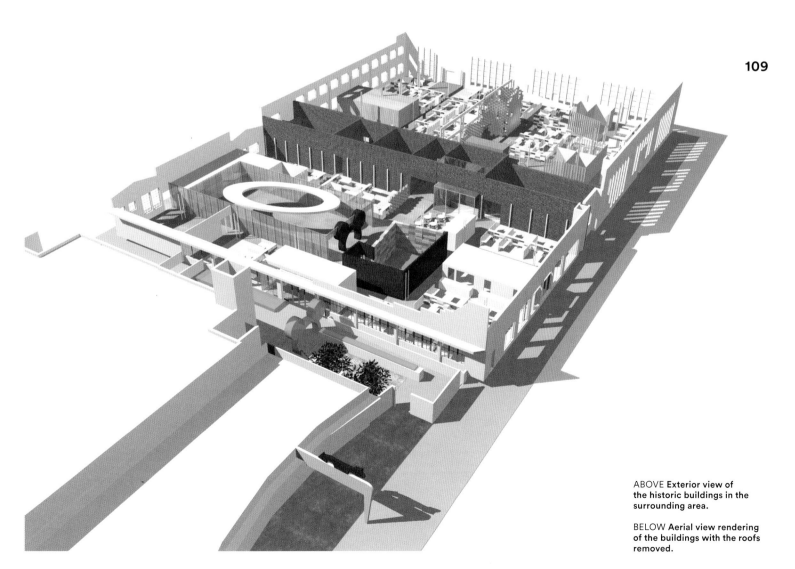

ABOVE **Exterior view of the historic buildings in the surrounding area.**

BELOW **Aerial view rendering of the buildings with the roofs removed.**

THE CULTURE MODEL

ABOVE The modular honeycomb conference room, conceived as a flexible means of managing the display of sample products. Our honeycomb system was subsequently licensed to Belgian furniture manufacturer Quinze & Milan for the commercial market.

BELOW The 'Block' conference room, deconstructed for a 200-person staff meeting (left) and constructed (right).

OPPOSITE PAGE View into the two-story workspace.

NEXT PAGE The central atrium of The Disney Store Headquarters was shaped by our proprietary hexagonal storage system. The honeycombs were designed to store toys in prototyping, which would otherwise be littering the office. The Vitra workstation system created a strong, secondary architectural framework to the space.

111

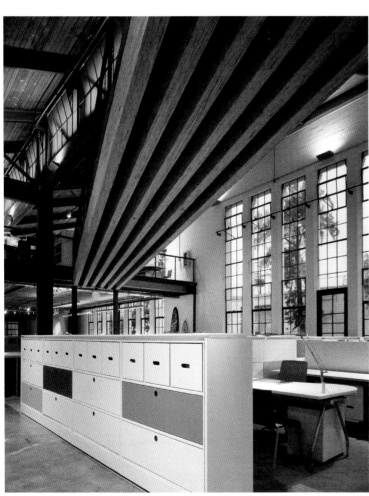

OPPOSITE PAGE **Highly flexible meeting/prototyping space. All of the seating blocks are removable and reconfigurable.**

ABOVE **Marketing department.**

BELOW **View into workspace under the bridge.**

OPPOSITE PAGE **Pantry lounge.**

ABOVE **In addition to providing an internal landscaped courtyard and new skylights throughout, the building connects occupants to the exterior with a new landscaped courtyard at the front entrance, which includes an ivy topiary of 'Mickey Mouse ears'.**

BELOW **Outdoor courtyard.**

THE CULTURE MODEL

LOCATION Irvine, California, United States
COMPLETED September 2001
FLOOR AREA 100,000 square foot
POPULATION 375

Foote Cone & Belding Worldwide

118

Culture seen through the lens of marketing is a kaleidoscopic consumer paradise. Our project for Foote, Cone & Belding (FCB) was an exercise in attempting to use the eclectic business of an ad agency as the basis for a narrative design. The work of an agency is to build engagement and attachment to the cultural brands of their clients, the accumulative imagery of which is almost schizophrenic and vastly diverse in scope. We were interested in stretching the concept of a highly varied internal landscape, informed by a narrative that was in parallel with the work of our client. We called this an 'episodic architecture' in which the environment changed and evolved with minimal reference to the adjacent architectural landscape. This offered a rich dense series of spaces as eclectic as the businesses they house, eschewing the typical architectural drive for consistency.

The leaders of FCB were enthralled by our recently completed TBWA\Chiat\Day project and wanted to challenge preconceptions of how an office space could be shaped and how it could serve to inspire their staff into a new way of embracing creativity. The client brief emphasized open communication, collaborative work, and the removal of obstacles to fast business flow. This project allowed us to peel away old status-based planning ideas which prioritized executive areas. We opened up private offices, distributed teams in neighborhoods and improved visual contact in work spaces.

The site was a former home of a heart valve manufacturing business and a good candidate for recycling into a new creative use. However, separation walls between office and manufacturing needed to be torn down, and the sense of warehouse openness needed to be carried through from the manufacturing area into the sterile two-story lab portion. The divide between the two areas was dramatic, and this led to our conceiving of the relationship as land to sea, and our strategy of inserting double height warehouse-like space in the office side as creating a harbor in the land, with structures like you might find on a dockside. Two floating structures were inserted in the warehouse to accommodate rooms needed to support the adjacent open work areas. They were linked with a jetty-like bridge, which terminates 'at sea', close to the rear staff entrance.

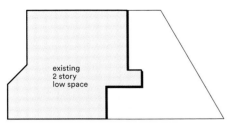

Existing office warehouse configuration

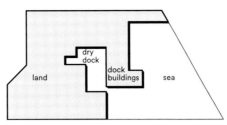

Open space penetrates closed space

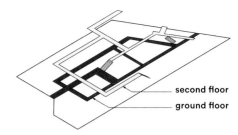

Circulation

second floor
ground floor

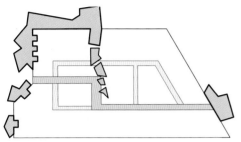

Landscaping

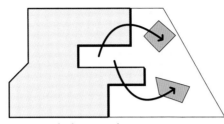

Remove and relocate workspace

Maximized contact

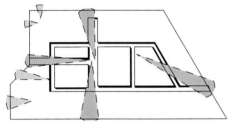

Circulation and view paths

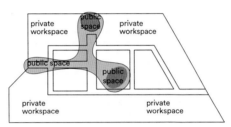

Public and private

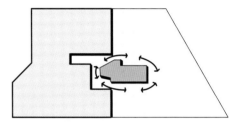

Circulation creates city centre

119

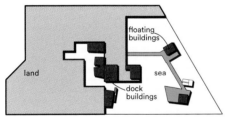

Port activity

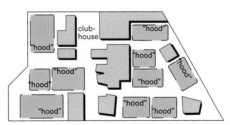

Neighborhoods

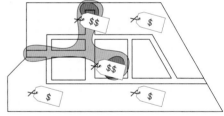

Financial strategy

OPPOSITE PAGE **Early concept model** promotes the land/sea separation idea between two halves of the warehouse.

ABOVE **Matrix of overlapping** themes and constraints.

BELOW **Large scale physical** models were used extensively to develop the design and allow an understanding of the spatial conditions. No one ever liked the dice rooms.

Beyond the romantic metaphor of a harbor side, the business organism of FCB needed to be accommodated. Their operational needs called for new offices without doors, a rational workstation solution, an editing suite and support services. From the front entrance a wide street leads you past a two-story red display wall through office area to the 'dry dock'. Here public meeting rooms are housed in steel faced structures and the raised Boardroom offers a grotto like enclosure through its 20-foot-high walls of hanging surfboards (142 white boards shaped by a local surf shop). Leading off this space is the lounge/caféteria zone with an 18-foot wide glazed overhead door opening to the outdoor courtyard.

Continuing up the main red staircase, which penetrates an existing concrete wall, you arrive at the mezzanine overlooking the creative warehouse area. Conference rooms frame a wide view over the agency, with the pale trapezoidal shapes of green and blue work desks spreading below you. The open meeting area of ping and pong sits astride the caution-striped offices of the agency's leaders. From the mezzanine, the steel and wood jetty carry you past the floating wood conference room to the rear entry. Here, sails of tent fabric rise from the ground and the boat structure, housing five separate informal meeting spaces and softening acoustical noise. The surrounding neighborhoods are structured by simple spine walls, carrying power and telephone cabling with a locally manufactured custom workstation.

FCB leadership was at first energized by their new offices but we soon noted a cultural dysfunction. The client had assumed the edgy culture of Chiat/Day in Venice California could be effectively transplanted to the more conservative Orange County community. Feedback from staff and visitors reinforced the perception that the FCB staffers found adaptation difficult, and there has been significant churn in the building.

120

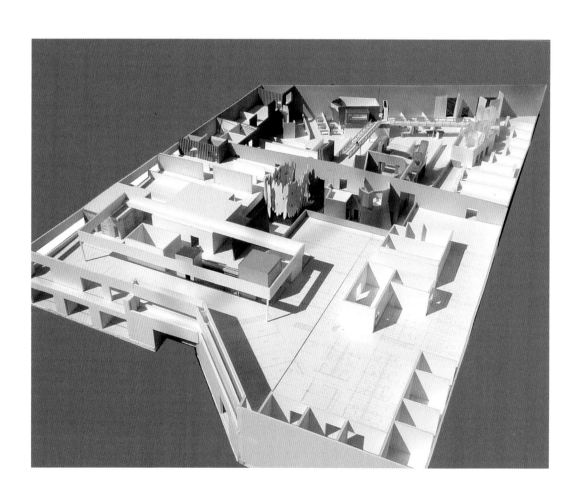

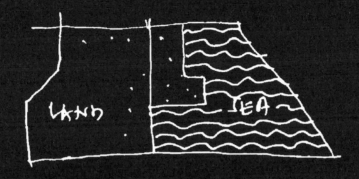

LAND · · · SEA

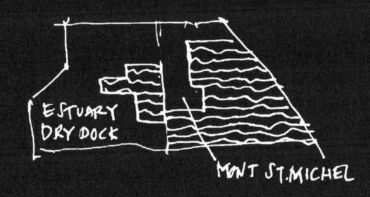

ESTUARY
DRY DOCK

MONT ST.MICHEL

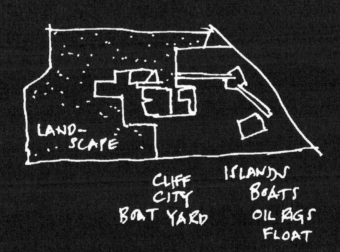

LAND-
SCAPE

CLIFF   ISLANDS
CITY   BOATS
BOAT YARD   OIL RIGS
               FLOAT

ABOVE AND OPPOSITE PAGE
Extending the land/sea metaphor,
peninsulas and islands are positioned to dramatize the space.

THE CULTURE MODEL

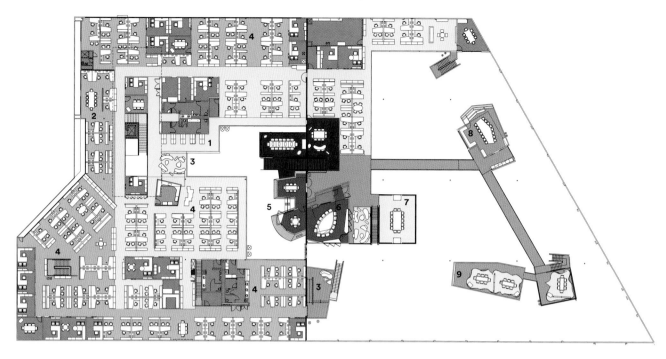

MEZZANINE FLOOR PLAN

1. Library
2. Open meeting area
3. Informal meeting area
4. Open workstations
5. Dry dock meeting rooms
6. Main conference room
7. Ping & pong meeting platform
8. Island #1 Conference room
9. Island #2 Project tents

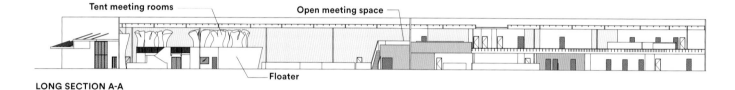

LONG SECTION A-A

Tent meeting rooms — Open meeting space — Floater

122

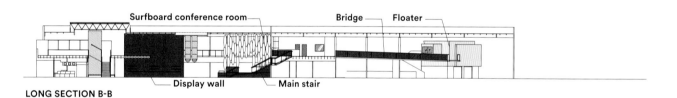

LONG SECTION B-B

Surfboard conference room — Bridge — Floater — Display wall — Main stair

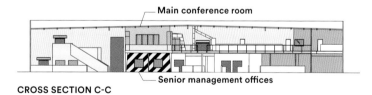

CROSS SECTION C-C

Main conference room — Senior management offices

CROSS SECTION D-D

Surfboard conference room — Drydock meeting rooms — Caféteria

TOP Mezzanine level floor plan highlights the open area with bridges and islands.

ABOVE Sections through the space.

ABOVE The board room and adjacent meeting structures.

BELOW Reception area with Kawasaki bike. As seemingly eccentric as the vignettes may appear, they are a deliberate attempt to reflect the wide diversity in creative work that happens in an ad agency. A consistent architectural signature would be inappropriate in this context and would fail to communicate the city-like diversity and texture that our client wanted: an open-ended architecture of unfolding episodes.

THE CULTURE MODEL

OPPOSITE PAGE The board room formed with 150 surfboards hanging on stainless steel cable, with a suspended glass ceiling to assist in reflecting sound.

ABOVE Entering through the two-story area, we cut away the floor slab to open up the promenade through the agency and leading to the board room and red staircase.

THE CULTURE MODEL

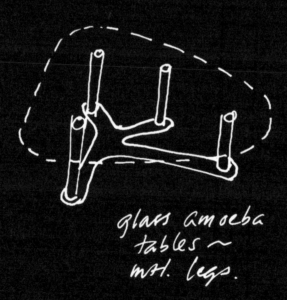

glass amoeba
tables ~
mtl. legs.

Since the area had been farmland
in very recent times, we designed
custom furniture which involved
shaggy sheep chairs and sofas.

ABOVE **Ping and pong meeting room.**

BELOW AND OPPOSITE PAGE
Sheep furniture in the café.

THE CULTURE MODEL

128

ABOVE The executive office.

BELOW The café opens to the outside via a garage door.

OPPOSITE PAGE ABOVE Bridge over the workspace with two-person custom plywood and plastic laminate desks.

OPPOSITE PAGE BELOW The tent meeting spaces.

THE CULTURE MODEL

Disrupt and Play

Knowledge work is stimulated in an environment of controlled discord.

The idea of provocation, disturbance, disruption and disconnection are critical components of challenging hidden assumptions and changing current ways of thinking. Since the world is changing so rapidly, it should be obvious that organizations need to be in a constant state of evolution to meet shifting market conditions – quite simply to survive. Beginning in the 1990's, many businesses understood the need to disrupt corporate thinking which historically relied on predictable and linear market behavior, whereas markets themselves were being constantly disrupted by new technological innovations. It was not enough to 'keep up' – you needed to get ahead and stay ahead. Your people needed to think in a non-linear fashion and get creative.

Creativity is a notoriously unmanageable process, as it relies on breakthrough thinking which itself cannot be guided or controlled. Generally speaking, whoever thinks that they can sit down at a desk and be creative is probably blissfully unaware that they may be regurgitating old thoughts and practices and repeating past activities. The creative breakthrough is the thing you don't know until you stumble upon it and it can happen anywhere. For one thing, creative work is necessarily wasteful. The favorite tech term of 'fail early, fail fast' is an acknowledgement that only through rapid prototyping of ideas can one learn what works and doesn't work and move forward to potentially creative solutions. Planning for productive waste is therefore important.

The creative breakthrough thought seldom happens at the desk. It may happen in a subway train, in the shower before breakfast, or the moment before you go to sleep – and then of course you forget the thought. In other words, it happens most

SANTA **SATAN**

The smallest difference between images can mean completely divergent things.

when there is a phase change. Your surroundings have shifted from the routine norm of work. Most creative shifts occur when combinations of unlikely bedfellows come about. The smartphone merged mobile audio player, computer and phone to create an indispensable device.

Play was once an integral part of adult life, and largely inseparable from the play of children. People in medieval times quite literally participated in the same stories, myths and make-believe charades as their children. Simulating other characters and other worlds played a big part in the regular collective festivities in which they indulged – in parts of Europe there were as many as 115 festivals every year. The rise of Protestantism and later, capitalism, put an end to most of those forms of communal pleasure. The industrial revolution had no place for anything that was not put into the service of industrial productivity. As Johan Huizunga noted in his influential book *Homo Ludens*: "Modern work is desperately serious. When utility rules, adults lose something essential in the capacity to think; they lose the free curiosity that occurs in the open, felt fingering space of play".

Modern thought has prioritized a return to play, in particular serious play which emphasizes simulation and experimentation to create paths to innovative work. Instilling curiosity and a maker-mindset in employees is now regarded as critical to a creative community. To quote the father of modern management, Peter Drucker, "The new venture therefore needs to start out with the assumption that its product or service may find customers in markets no one thought of, for uses no one envisaged

"Imagination is the primary activity of the soul."

JAMES HILMAN

> "If an office does not incorporate play in some form, it communicates that there is "no place for play" or in other words, no place for testing ideas."

CLIVE WILKINSON

when the product or service was designed, and that it will be bought by customers outside its field of vision and even unknown to the new venture".

In workplace strategy, 'disruption' is referenced in the context of breaking with norms, and repositioning corporate identities. However, its primary value is in business transformation – in shedding old linear practices and adopting new networked systems. We first encountered disruption as an actual visioning strategy through working with advertising agencies like TBWA\Chiat\Day. They had formulated a disruption methodology that consisted of three one-day client workshops, structured in a logical sequence of steps.

The first session was called 'Convention' and required the client participants to define who their company was, where it was in the world, benchmarking itself, defining its product offering and marketplace, and coming to agreement on identifying the conventions that contain or restrict their thought processes. This session must examine the relationship between company and customer, or consumer, and what new connections are possible which in turn could lead to restructuring the company. The outcome is a list of conventions to disrupt.

The second day session was called 'Disruption' and focused on breaking convention and producing 'blue sky' thinking: dreaming about where the company could go in the future and how it could embrace a changing world. The workshop participants are pushed to discussion on radical views on transforming conventions and how the company might evolve in the future.

The last session is called 'Vision', or 'Synthesis', and aims to unify convention with blue sky ideas to produce an inspiring, logical and actionable vision for the future of the brand and the community. As with the earlier sessions, a voting system is employed in order to ensure buy-in from all participants. The results of the disruption process, ideally, provide an excellent basis for a design vision – and we have used this interrogation process with many clients.

Two of our projects highlight different aspects of disruption and play, and both disrupted workplace conventions and created radical new work environments. Pallotta TeamWorks was a visionary company that hosted major charity fund raising events. To meet an impossible budget, we had to truly think different, and investigate alternative strategies which drove a space solution we could not have been imagined at the outset. Britain's top-rated ad agency, Mother, had a unique view on shared workspace – and had progressively grown the simple kitchen table that they started with, to the point when we were designing a 200-person table.

LOCATION Los Angeles, California, United States
COMPLETED March 2002
FLOOR AREA 47,000 square feet
POPULATION 300

Pallotta TeamWorks Headquarters

A growing US charity event company, Pallotta TeamWorks, introduced themselves with a challenging proposition: to create an inspiring new headquarters for them in a raw warehouse with a shoestring budget. It soon became clear that their budget was not adequate for even a bare bones workplace, indeed there was not enough money to provide an electrical infrastructure or air conditioning, an essential in the climate of the San Fernando Valley. Pallotta was focused on reinventing charity fund-raising with its large-scale outdoor charity events. We realized it needed to think like frugal campers in order to find a way to occupy the building.

Since we couldn't air-condition the space, we asked ourselves 'why do we have to air condition the whole building? What if we just conditioned the places where people worked and left the rest of the space unconditioned?' We pitched an idea to create air-conditioned tents for work neighborhoods, and leave the remaining 60 percent of the space unconditioned.

The concept of 'breathing islands' was developed. Air conditioning was limited to those areas where staff spend the most time working, with circulation areas treated as streets or pathways, with no direct conditioning. We placed the air conditioning units on top of columns so no new roof strengthening was needed and hung the custom-made tents from the same columns. We used shipping containers as offices, and to anchor the tents, so there was minimal wastage.

Taking cues from the mobile 'tent cities' created by the client to shelter charity event participants each night, the tented islands thus act as giant air diffusers, minimizing the volume of conditioned air required for comfortable working. The tents also provide intimate and distinct work neighborhoods, distributing air and reflecting diffused light. Suspended from the existing roof column grid, they stretch in different directions according to programmatic needs of the workspaces. Their corners are anchored down by prefabricated shipping containers, which, at an average cost of $3,400 each, were the least costly way to house private offices and support facilities. The resulting project generated considerable savings in use over conventional office build-outs, and reinforced the client's message of promoting responsible, sustainable ways of living on this planet.

Everything on the project began with the question "why do we need to do this?" With the reception desk, there was much debate about what it means to have a person sitting behind a big counter addressing you. Dan Pallotta wanted it to feel like there was no barrier, like the receptionist could be right next to you, not across from you. Then the idea of Buckminster Fuller's world map projection came up, which is delightful in having no political boundaries. We were struck by its triangular geometry, and then realized we could just fold map sections down to create legs for a full table, and it would still be the most geometrically true representation of the earth. This became the first thing you encountered in entering Pallotta TeamWorks, supplemented by a few stools that you and the receptionist could use.

Color on the project was deliberately used to choreograph views and distinguish

133

more public and neighborhood zones. Set against the crisp white of the tents is a palette of 14 tonally varying blues used at the four corners of each neighborhood. The blues reference the hue variety that is seen in the skies which are so much part of the landscape of the charity events, together with the dramatic white tent landscape. It was a tragedy that this great company was subsequently brought down in a political and fiscal controversy that is still splitting the philanthropy business.

134

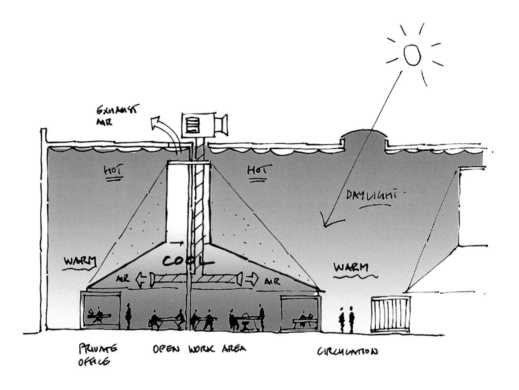

ABOVE Financial constraints led to an economical concept of locating the client's work areas in air-conditioned 'breathing islands' loosely enclosed in tents, within the unconditioned warehouse. To further save money, shipping containers acted as both private offices and the corner anchors for the tent structures.

BELOW Physical model of the tent neighborhoods.

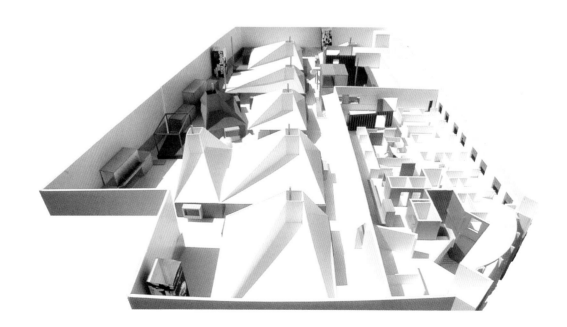

THE THEATRE OF WORK

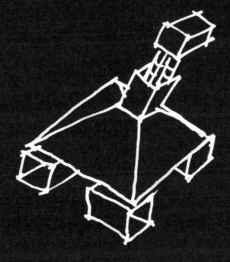

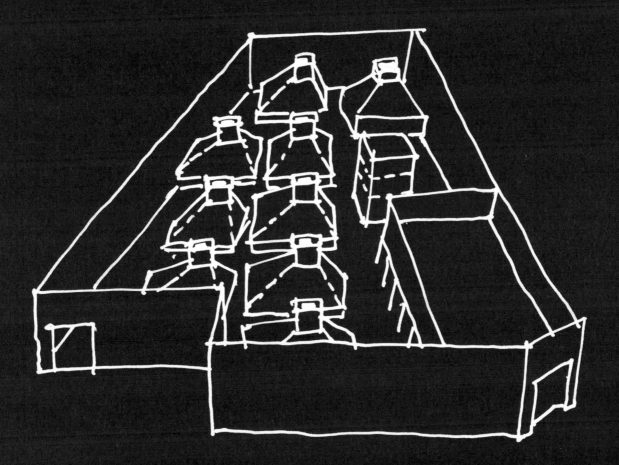

Initial sketch of tents and the inspiration of Christo's 1991 Japan and California Umbrellas.

136

The central hub of the community was a container 6-pack of meeting spaces, which incorporated a fountain and reflecting pond. The uppermost meeting space was accessed via a bridge from the mezzanine. The visible AC ducts serve the enclosed rooms.

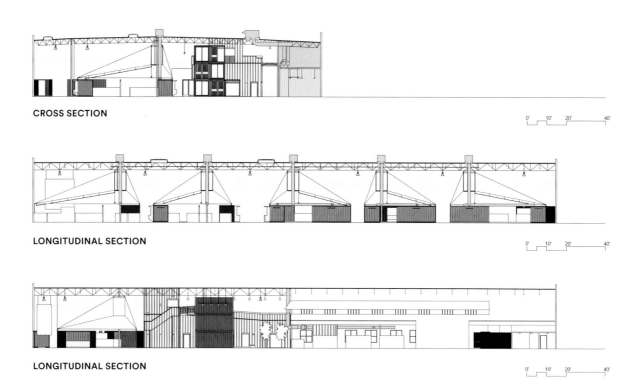

CROSS SECTION

0'   10'   20'   40'

LONGITUDINAL SECTION

0'   10'   20'   40'

LONGITUDINAL SECTION

0'   10'   20'   40'

THE THEATRE OF WORK

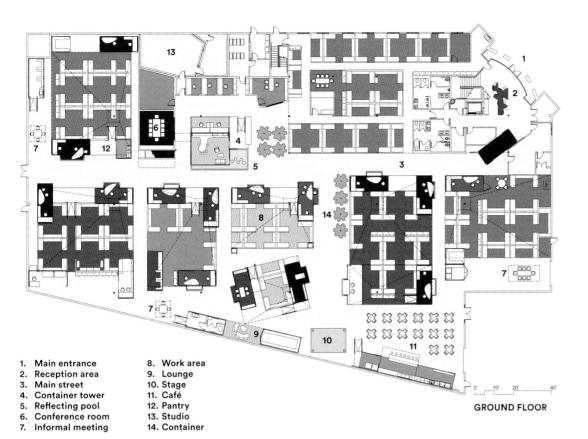

1. Main entrance
2. Reception area
3. Main street
4. Container tower
5. Reflecting pool
6. Conference room
7. Informal meeting
8. Work area
9. Lounge
10. Stage
11. Café
12. Pantry
13. Studio
14. Container

GROUND FLOOR

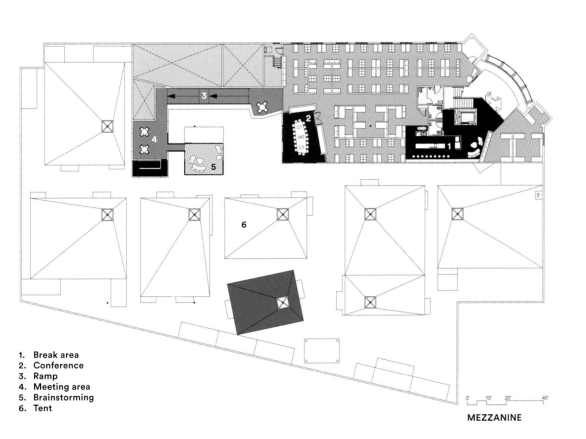

1. Break area
2. Conference
3. Ramp
4. Meeting area
5. Brainstorming
6. Tent

MEZZANINE

OPPOSITE PAGE ABOVE **Calming** effects of water and raw wood framing.

THIS PAGE AND OPPOSITE PAGE BELOW **Floor plans and sections.**

View from the mezzanine over the tent landscape.

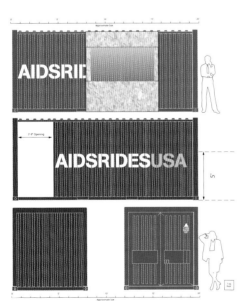

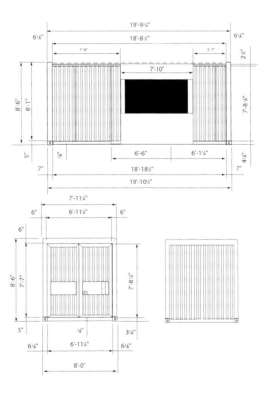

OPPOSITE PAGE Shipping containers are just too tight to make good spaces to work in, so we cut openings on one side and made plywood porches with seats for visitors. Furniture was all re-used from their previous offices. To the right is the three-story meeting tower we made to connect to the mezzanine office area and to impart a sense of urban scale.

ABOVE The main circulation axis was called Main Street, and was populated with shipping containers and the raw wood structure that enveloped the production rooms and extended the mezzanine. The metaphor of tents and shipping containers resonated with the event production company as this was their basic kit for their three-day AidsRides and Breast Cancer Marches.

ABOVE The reception desk was formed from Buckminster Fuller's world map projection. No political boundaries, no front and back, no obstacle between guest and host, a space for gathering and welcoming outsiders.

BELOW The container café.

OPPOSITE PAGE The shipping container offices with plywood porch extensions to relieve the tight spaces.

LOCATION London, United Kingdom
COMPLETED February 2004
FLOOR AREA 42,000 square feet
POPULATION 200

Mother London

146

Our client, Mother, had broken into the UK advertising scene with a disruptive and humorous approach to selling products and services. Their attitude towards workspace was equally dismissive about traditional norms.

We started working with ad agency Mother in 2002. In the previous six years, Mother had grown from a six-person boutique ad agency working out of a kitchen into Britain's top-rated agency. Their radical approach to the advertising business and contemporary culture was translated into their work environment. A flat organization with no space privileges, everyone at Mother worked around a single large worktable. As the company grew, the table grew. When Clive Wilkinson Architects was awarded the project over British competitors, Mother tripled their space size by leasing three floors in the Tea Building warehouse, in Shoreditch, London.

Our design for their new office explored how one could reduce the furniture junk of an office down to simple but unexpected design solutions, both playful and disruptive. The desired flexibility would be achieved via a massive desk – where people moved when necessary, not the furniture. The desk became a road wrapping around the space. It was made of concrete because it's a good material for a road. The road ran straight down to the ground floor entrance as a concrete staircase to ensure everyone could get to their working area quickly.

Early on, Mother had discovered the collaboration bonding that occurs when people work in close proximity, and also how that broke down when people hived off to work more individually. Their main founder, Robert Saville, was a firm believer in removing all barriers, and especially doors, throughout the agency. At one point, he admitted that if he could have his way, there'd be no doors on the toilets.

The business of advertising is ephemeral, but the client was inspired by a site-poured concrete table that would be ridiculously permanent. It is still in use, and has worked as mediator, connector, provocateur, interpreter and therapist to this creative community. In order to achieve a strong connection to the Loading Bay Lobby two floors below, we built a new concrete staircase the width of a small road cutting through the building to connect the three floors. This 14 ft wide staircase would turn into the Agency's cast-in-place concrete worktable and circuit the third-floor room like a racetrack. At 250 feet long it became perhaps the world's largest table, broken in sections for circulation, with a maximum capacity of 200 people.

All surfaces were painted white, with a white epoxy floor, to achieve a neutral art studio space. To mitigate sound in the hard factory space, and integrate lighting with an acoustic solution, we designed 7-foot-long lampshades padded with 75mm of acoustic foam. The 50 individual light fixtures were then covered with 50 different patterns of Marimekko fabric. We reached out to Marimekko and they allowed us to visit them in Helsinki, Finland, and select from archive stock in their factory, dating from 1954 – 2004, achieving the effect of a large art installation. On other floors, customized plastic refrigeration curtains were used to subdivide spaces for different disciplines and subsidiary companies.

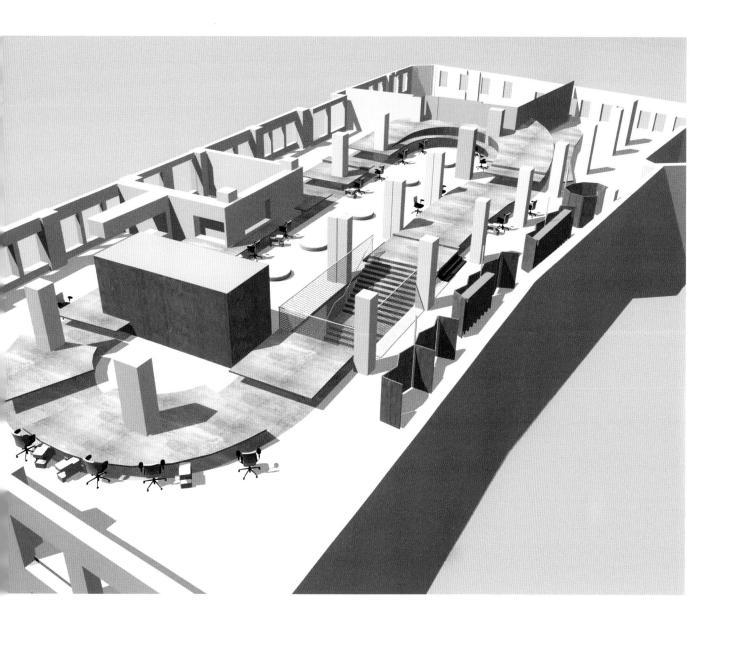

ABOVE **Drawing for the 'concrete race track' at third floor.**

BELOW **Early renderings show how the ground floor lobby would be connected to the main work floor.**

Mother Ramp

148

In considering the formal possibilities, we recalled the 1925 Giacomo
Matte-Trucco race track for Fiat
Lingotto in Turin on the roof of their
factory building. Something highly
provocative about the notion of
'heavy concrete', and 'racetrack',
and 'factory' seemed both so right
and so wrong for an ephemeral
business like advertising.

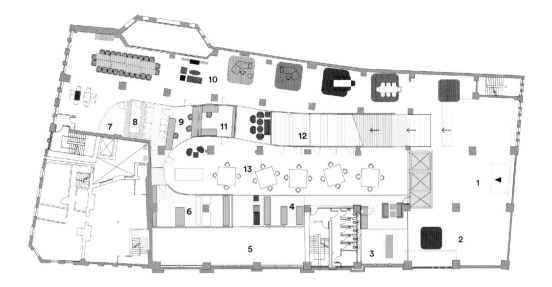

SECOND FLOOR
1. Entry lobby
2. Café
3. Coffee bar
4. Shipping/courier area
5. Play area
6. Portfolio storage
7. Storage
8. Office supplies
9. IT room
10. 'The Living Room'
11. Info centre
12. File folder storage
13. Studio

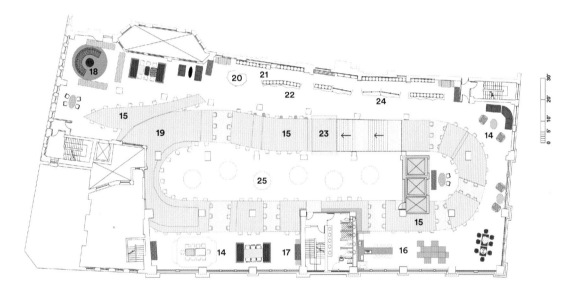

THIRD FLOOR
14. Break-out spaces
15. Table
16. Coffee bar
17. Printer/fax
18. 'The War Room'
19. Sloping table
20. Phone booth
21. Personal lockers
22. Display walls
23. Landing
24. Laptop/mobile phone issue
25. Ottomans

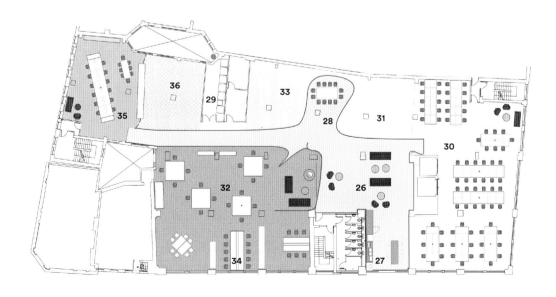

FOURTH FLOOR
26. Reception
27. Coffee bar
28. Shared meeting space
29. IT room
30. Subsidiary company #1
31. Expansion space #1
32. Subsidiary company #2
33. Expansion space #2
34. Freelancer's table
35. Subsidiary company #3
36. Expansion space #3

DISRUPT AND PLAY

OPPOSITE PAGE ABOVE **Open
seating allows easy break out from
the table work space.**

OPPOSITE PAGE BELOW **The
250 foot x 14 foot concrete table
at Mother London, 2004. You
may have grown up playing in the
street. Here, the table became a
street you work on.**

ABOVE **Concrete is folded up from
the ground floor to the second floor
and then wrapped around the floor
as an oval track.**

BELOW **Table cants to take the
curve.**

The second floor has quiet spaces for collaboration. Everything is visibly open but with modest visual and acoustic screening provided by plastic industrial curtains that we had customized for Mother, on curving steel tracks. The industrial simplicity allowed the furnishings to be eccentric.

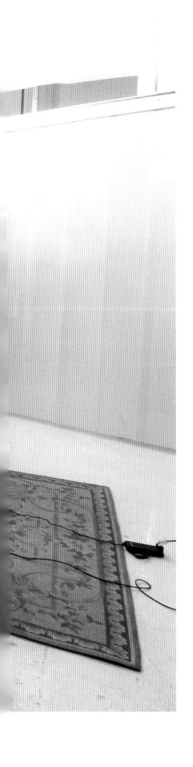

OPPOSITE PAGE We solved light and acoustics for the workspace in one simple light fixture element. As the space was full of hard surfaces, we needed an absorbent material that could control sound. We proposed wrapping the basic fluorescent light fixtures with 75mm acoustic foam on plywood frames, and covering them with decorative fabric.

ABOVE Formerly a truck loading bay, the ground floor of Mother acts as reception and is given over to communal use, mainly as a lunchtime catering offering. We provided minimal elements like the glass entry cube and the stainless steel bar. The red tables were Ilse Crawford's design.

BELOW Little had changed at Mother eight years later in 2012.

DISRUPT AND PLAY

Choice and Diversity

Work happens in many different ways. The workplace must support that.

Work happens in many different ways, and any new workplace must support that fact. The organization of work process has suffered from a kind of management straightjacket since 1800's. Staff would be organized in rows, as in the military, and the gun would be replaced with a desk. Management would be positioned in an all-seeing command centre, to observe compliance with the production process.

Routine work was apparently well served by this ordered environment, but the electronic age changed all that. Computers progressively took over routine work, freeing up people for new kinds of jobs. Non-routine manual work was on the increase. The new types of work needed more strategic supportive settings. Both collaborative work and individual work became specialized, and a host of workplace furniture options begins to flood the market. The new office becomes a place that may ideally offer both the comforts of a boutique hotel as well the versatility of a domestic environment. Mobile technology fuels this change, since there is no more need to be tethered to a big computer CPU and electric/data cabling.

In 2006, we started working with Nokia on transforming their Helsinki headquarters. Nokia is a very proud old Finnish company and they felt that their democratic but somewhat rigid way of working only needed superficial updating. We endeavored to persuade them to offer a variety of choice in work settings for their staff and were unsuccessful until we came upon a big advertisement for one of their new smart phones. The ad slogan read: "Not One Thing, But Many" referring to all the different capabilities of their phone. We simply

"Not One Thing, But Many."

NOKIA SMARTPHONE AD, 2006

reminded them that they should do as they advertise. "Not One Thing, But Many" led to a much richer work environment that enabled their mobile staff to be more effective.

Choice in the new workplace is essential to support the variety of different ways that people work, and which may change during the course of a typical day. By offering choice, leadership is also sending a message that they respect and value their employees and see the need to support them. Of course a further benefit of providing a range of work setting typologies is the physical movement generated thereby. More people moving around the office and using its amenities is both physically healthy and opportune for chance encounters with others.

Diversity works in a similar way by offering visual and functional variety, and a stimulating environment. We look at the ambitious mobile working project for Macquarie Bank in Sydney in 2006-9 and compare that to the equally mobile and forward thinking Publicis ad agency project in New York City eight years later.

157

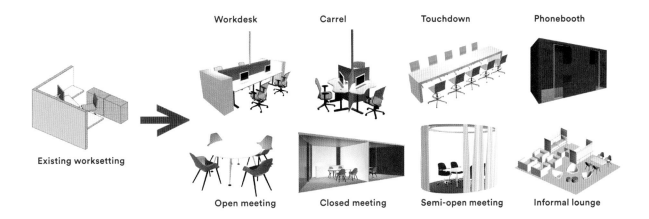

Workdesk   Carrel   Touchdown   Phonebooth

Existing worksetting

Open meeting   Closed meeting   Semi-open meeting   Informal lounge

CHOICE AND DIVERSITY

LOCATION Sydney, Australia
COMPLETED October 2009
FLOOR AREA 330,000 square feet
POPULATION 3,000

Macquarie Group
One Shelley Street

158

One Shelley Street represented our biggest opportunity to participate in the transformation of a corporate culture. The brief, as agreed to by the executive, was to move the investment bankers from traditional designated desk layouts in typical office space to a highly mobile and varied working format. A wide range of work settings were developed, and supplemented by a destination-driven concept that encouraged people to use the whole building. Diverse work plazas on every floor were themed differently to offer choice and variety, to drive vertical movement between floors and ensure that a high level of community cohesion was achieved. In helping to sell the idea of personal mobility, we used the phrase "you are giving up a desk, but will own the whole office".

The One Shelley Street project thus became an effort to reframe the requirements and performance of the 21st century office. We proposed a radical, large-scale workplace design that leveraged mobility, transparency, multiple tailor-made work settings, destination work plazas, follow-me technology, and carbon neutral systems. The result was part space-station, part cathedral, and part vertical Greek village.

The project accommodated a large population of 3,000 employees with associated restaurant, health club and café spaces in a new building in Sydney, Australia. Working with Woods Bagot as executive architect, and Fitzpatrick + Partners, architect for the base building, Clive Wilkinson Architects implemented a complex design solution that

embellishes the building's 10-story atrium with 26 cantilevered meeting pods. The office workspace utilizes the innovative 'activity based working' solution (ABW), initially developed by Dutch consultants Veldhoen + Company, and now widely adopted as an effective alternative to traditional fixed office planning. Deployed here for Macquarie Bank, ABW allows a dynamic and flexible collaboration platform for their financial business.

Rethinking the traditional corporate office, where typically the public accessed

areas are restricted to the ground level, we developed a strategy to open up the building vertically, activating the atrium and bringing transparency and user interaction to the heart of Macquarie. The typical guest relations meeting spaces are distributed across the Atrium, allowing guests a strong visual connection with the workplace activity. These cantilevered pods form the 'Meeting Tree' and are accessed primarily via an open staircase which provides an animated vertical connection and links them all together. The visible energy of people circulating and interacting in the highly transparent atrium underscores the revitalized corporate brand as a forward thinking and highly collaborative company.

The Shelley Street atrium evolution arguably began 200 years earlier. The Paris arcades of 1800 borrowed and adapted the new greenhouse glass structures, made possible by the new industrial production of iron. In 1850 Joseph Paxton, himself a gardener, proposed and built in nine months his design for the 1851 Great Exhibition: the Crystal Palace. It was the first palatial structure entirely made of glass and itself a movable building, since it was moved after the 1851 event in Hyde Park, London to Sydenham Hill.

The ABW system is structured in neighborhoods of approximately 100 people, which provide the employees with a variety of work settings. Since these specifically address the variety of daily tasks performed, productivity is enhanced. As everyone is mobile, flexibility and collaboration are increased. Through this open architecture and flexible technology, tools are provided that enable and empower the employees to work wherever and whenever they want, essentially creating one fluid work environment. This initiates an experience where empowerment leads to employees identifying with their environment, thus creating the feel of a greater community, which promotes collaboration and further empowers the employees. The business benefit of mobile working is the ability to ensure that the space operates with a higher intensity of usage (approximately 80%) rather than the typical 40% efficiency in traditional offices. The energy level in the office is correspondingly richer.

The Main Street on Level 1 offers communal spaces that are highly conducive to corporate and philanthropic events and includes a café and dining areas. Within the office floors 'plazas' were modeled after collaboration typologies – the Dining Room, Garden, Tree House, Playroom, and Coffee House, where cross-pollination among business groups is encouraged through spontaneous encounters. The interior staircase, linking

OPPOSITE PAGE Sketch from a client presentation. Workshops with the client lead us to characterize the merchant bankers as Samurai in their fast-moving and uncompromising deal-making capabilities.

ABOVE Container shipping in the adjacent Darling Harbor influenced the atrium design.

MIDDLE Building exterior.

BELOW A Parisian arcade. In an earlier example of the atrium typology, the Paris arcades of 1800 borrowed and adapted the new greenhouse glass structures, made possible by the new industrial production of iron. The Crystal Palace of 1851 was to extend this idea into the pantheon of large commercial structures.

the various neighborhoods, has reduced the use of the elevators by 50%. A business benefit of ABW is the elimination of 'churn' – the cost of moving groups and redefining spaces. A large percentage of furniture was adapted and re-used, but most significantly, ABW working allows a huge saving in resource efficiency, real estate and operating costs – benefiting clients, investors, shareholders and the environment.

By October 2009 all of the 3,000 employees had moved into the new building.

Although activity-based work environments were not yet the norm, the acceptance level among Macquarie employees rose beyond initial anticipation. Nearly 55% change their workspaces each day, and 77% were in favor of the freedom to do so. Opening to considerable media exposure, One Shelley St positioned itself as a model for the new global sustainable office building and was promoted as a trailblazer for the new connected and creative office building.

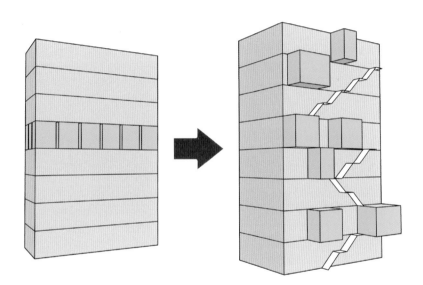

ABOVE The rationale for distributing the traditional guest relations suite over 10 floors.

RIGHT Architectural study model. Reconceiving the guest experience from an isolated guest relations floor, to a central experience within the new atrium.

OPPOSITE PAGE The early atrium sketch that proposed installing a gantry structure at the top of the atrium and prefabricating moveable meeting pods attached to the gantry. If you needed a 10-person meeting on Level 3, you pressed the right button and the required pod was delivered to your floor. Macquarie loved the idea but decided that meeting rooms were the one thing they did not need to be movable! The image of the pod system, however, remained in the final design.

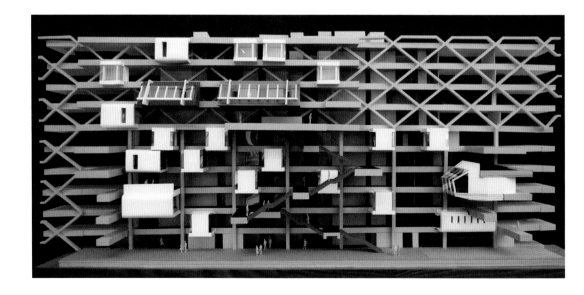

THE THEATRE OF WORK

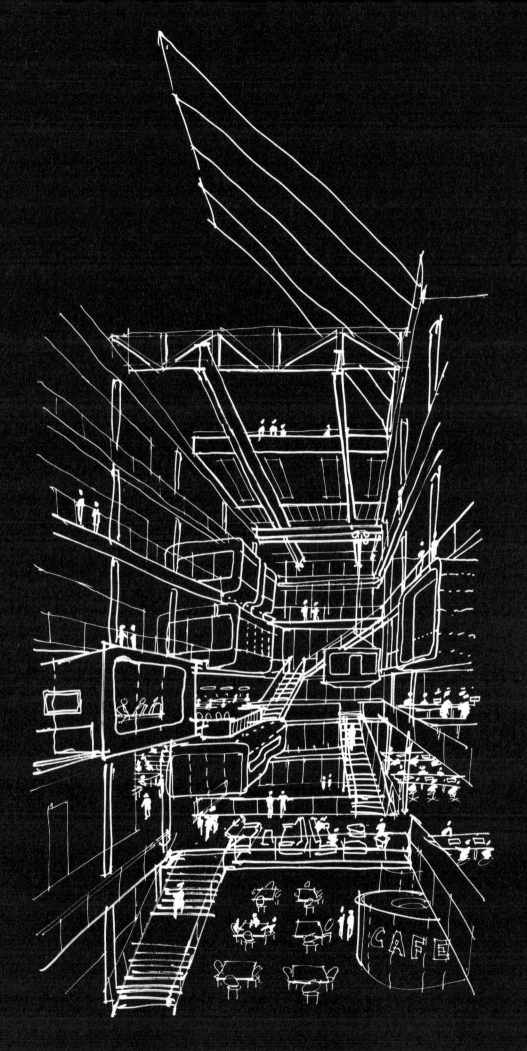

CHOICE AND DIVERSITY

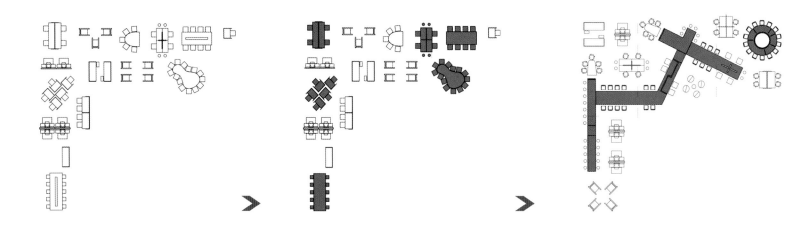

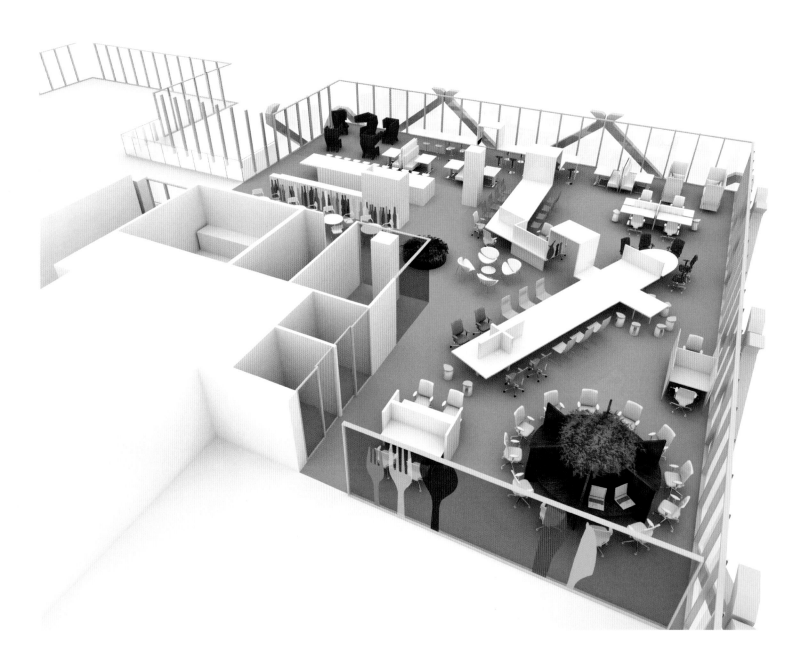

THE THEATRE OF WORK

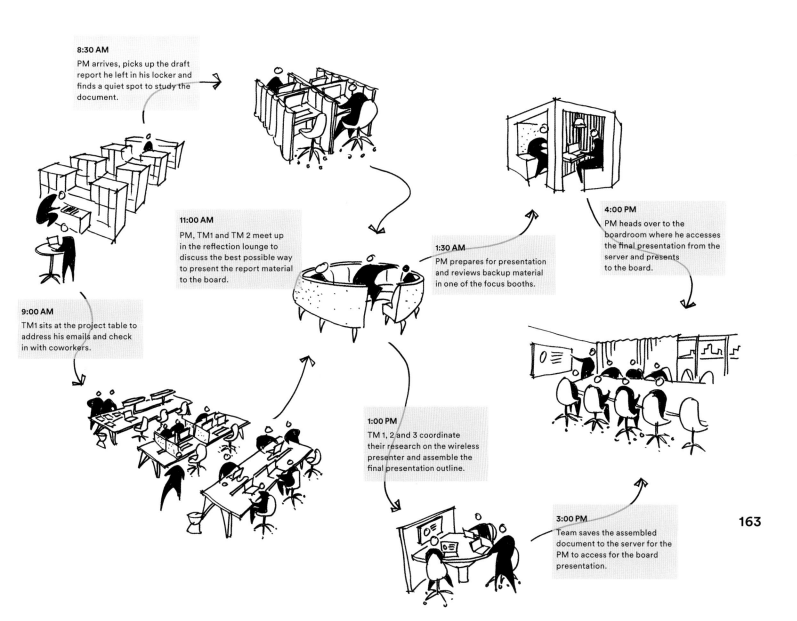

8:30 AM
PM arrives, picks up the draft report he left in his locker and finds a quiet spot to study the document.

11:00 AM
PM, TM1 and TM 2 meet up in the reflection lounge to discuss the best possible way to present the report material to the board.

9:00 AM
TM1 sits at the project table to address his emails and check in with coworkers.

1:30 AM
PM prepares for presentation and reviews backup material in one of the focus booths.

4:00 PM
PM heads over to the boardroom where he accesses the final presentation from the server and presents to the board.

1:00 PM
TM 1, 2 and 3 coordinate their research on the wireless presenter and assemble the final presentation outline.

3:00 PM
Team saves the assembled document to the server for the PM to access for the board presentation.

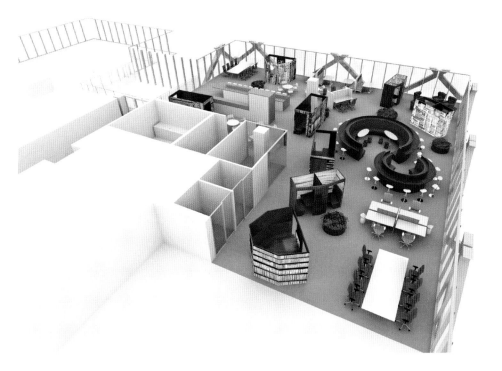

OPPOSITE PAGE ABOVE **The plazas were programmed to utilize exactly the same work-setting formula as a typical 100-person neighborhood, and therefore ensure that the way the plaza worked was identical in workplace efficiency. Design creativity occurred in the way in which this formula was interpreted and adapted to each theme.**

OPPOSITE PAGE BELOW AND BELOW **The Library Plaza. In addition to specific collaborative settings, themed 'plazas' are stacked vertically on each floor. The plazas are based on archetypes of human interaction, and they give a unique character to each floor with special collaborative settings and gathering spaces – formal and informal.**

ABOVE **Study of a day in the life of an ABW team illustrates the range of work settings put to use and serves to validate the concept.**

CHOICE AND DIVERSITY

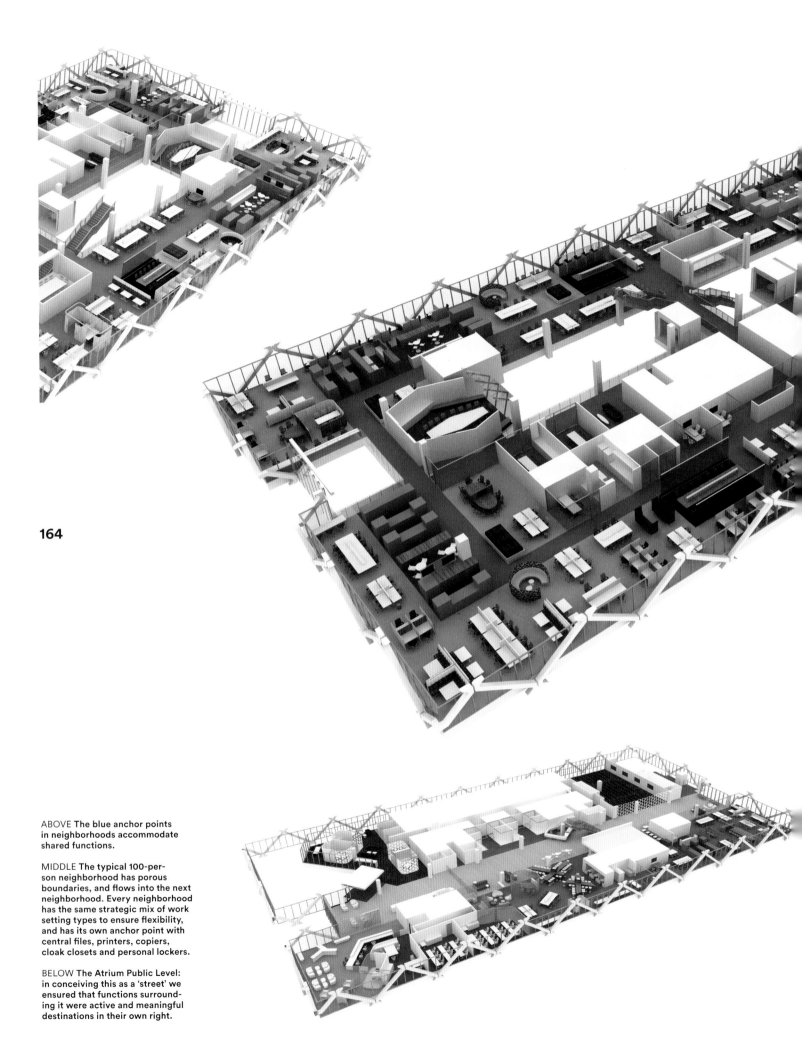

164

ABOVE The blue anchor points
in neighborhoods accommodate
shared functions.

MIDDLE The typical 100-per-
son neighborhood has porous
boundaries, and flows into the next
neighborhood. Every neighborhood
has the same strategic mix of work
setting types to ensure flexibility,
and has its own anchor point with
central files, printers, copiers,
cloak closets and personal lockers.

BELOW The Atrium Public Level:
in conceiving this as a 'street' we
ensured that functions surrounding it were active and meaningful
destinations in their own right.

ABOVE **Treehouse Plaza.**

BELOW **The Main Boardroom.**

NEXT PAGE **View down the atrium.**

CHOICE AND DIVERSITY

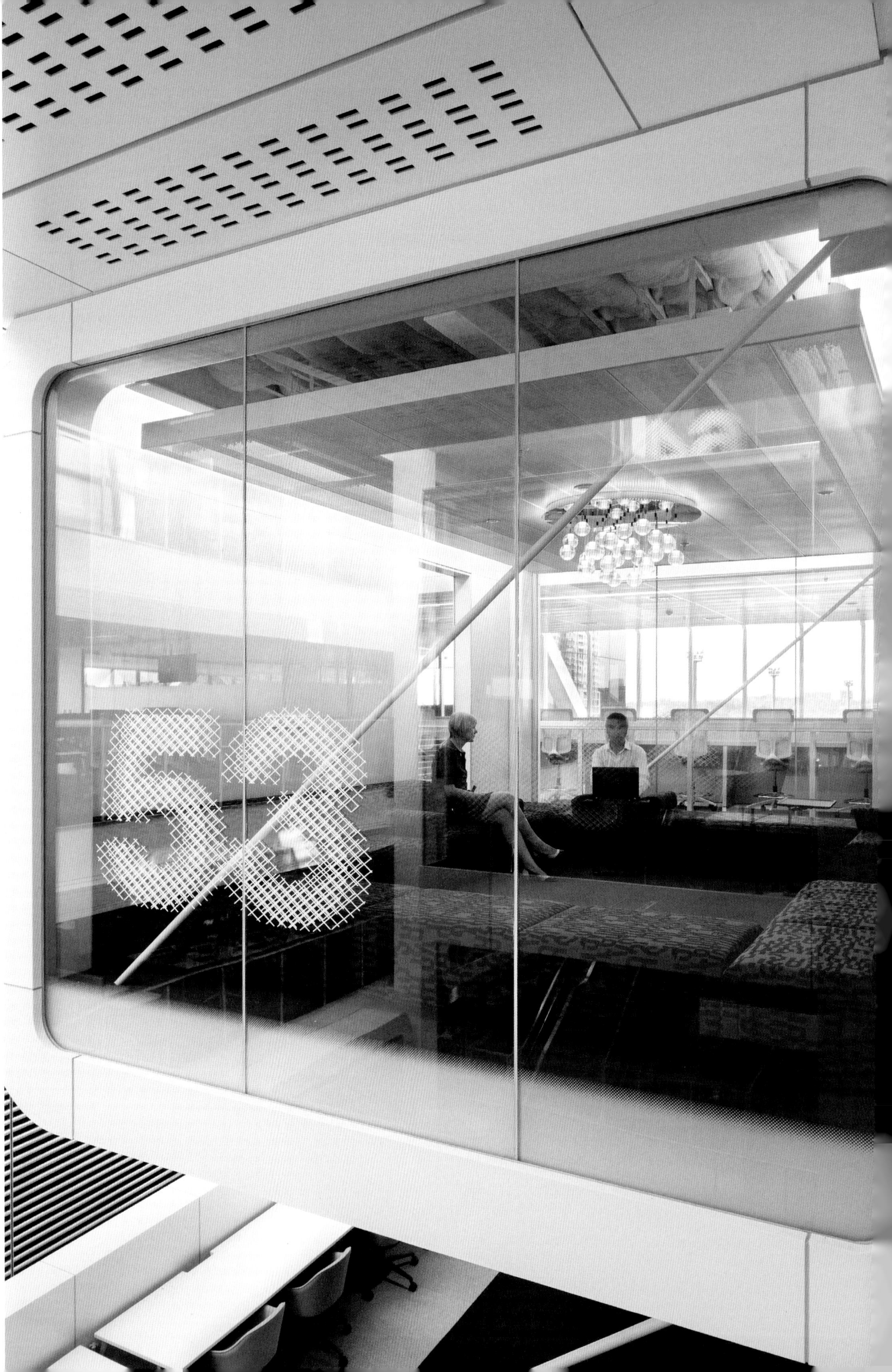
53

OPPOSITE PAGE **A meeting pod in Moroccan meeting configuration.**

ABOVE **Open working environments on the atrium edge.**

BELOW **The atrium public level.**

CHOICE AND DIVERSITY

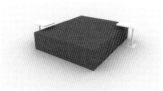

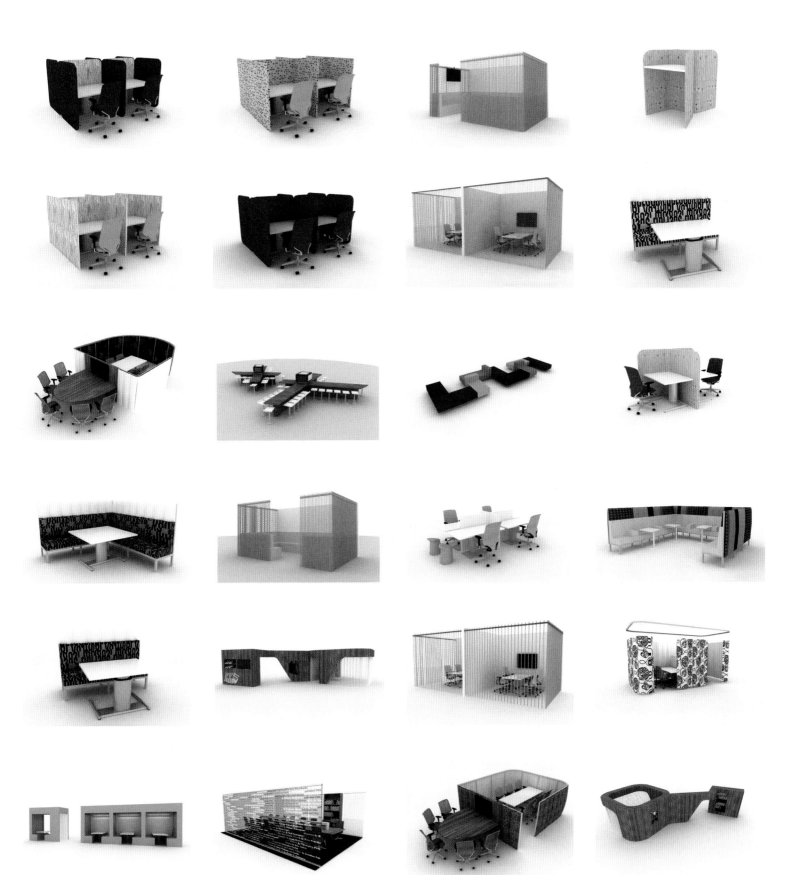

Custom furniture created for the activity based working areas.

OPPOSITE PAGE **Café on the Atrium Street.**

ABOVE **A high level meeting room.**

BELOW **The Library Plaza with quiet work cell.**

CHOICE AND DIVERSITY

OPPOSITE PAGE View down the Atrium.

ABOVE AND BELOW Following completion of the building, Will Walker, Head of Business Services Division, commented: "The building has gone above and beyond our original objectives. We have created a space that speaks volumes about Macquarie, our culture and the environment in which a project like this is possible. People outside of Macquarie often ask 'How do you get an organization to buy into a building like this?' But our culture is centreed upon freedom within boundaries and this approach allows us to push the envelope whilst managing risk. That is the real success factor here."

CHOICE AND DIVERSITY

ABOVE Seventh floor café space.

BELOW Interior of the Skybox Meeting Room.

OPPOSITE PAGE The Skybox Meeting Room – since a vertical monitor screen would be too publicly exposed, the glass topped table accommodates built-in horizontal screens which are invisible when turned off.

THE THEATRE OF WORK

LOCATION New York, New York, United States
COMPLETED January 2014
FLOOR AREA 190,000 square feet
POPULATION 1,200

Publicis North American Headquarters

178

In 2013, global advertising agency, Publicis, commissioned us to design their new North America headquarters in New York City. Located adjacent to Times Square, the leased space spans eight contiguous floors in a conventional mid-town office building, providing an opportunity to unite their three remote offices scattered across Manhattan.

Twenty years elapsed from our first ad agency project for Chiat/Day in Los Angeles, and the media world had been turned upside down in the interim. Our explorations with Publicis hinged on finding an approach that would support their business transformation to develop content for and engage in a new media world. The new media was pervasive, multi-platformed, and changing constantly. Publicis would embrace mobility and variety in 'work platforms' distributed in an organically shaped and connected interior. Designated seating was out. Employees could choose where and how they would work every day, with a suite of options across the floors.

Our workshops revealed needs for event hosting, multi-use space and pragmatic team-oriented bench desking. To foster their collaborative culture, the agency was engaged in an iterative dialogue to establish destinations on each of the eight floors. Spaces such as the plaza, pub, multi-use space, and home

BELOW **Comparative diagrams for activity based working at Publicis. With unassigned seats, the mobile workspace can respond to typical vacancy rates and offer a greater variety of worksettings while saving space and carbon footprint.**

OPPOSITE PAGE **Images for the Tree – sliced across seven floors (eighth floor added later).**

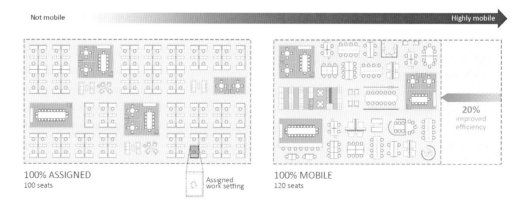

Not mobile   Highly mobile

100% ASSIGNED
100 seats

Assigned
work setting

100% MOBILE
120 seats

20%
improved
efficiency

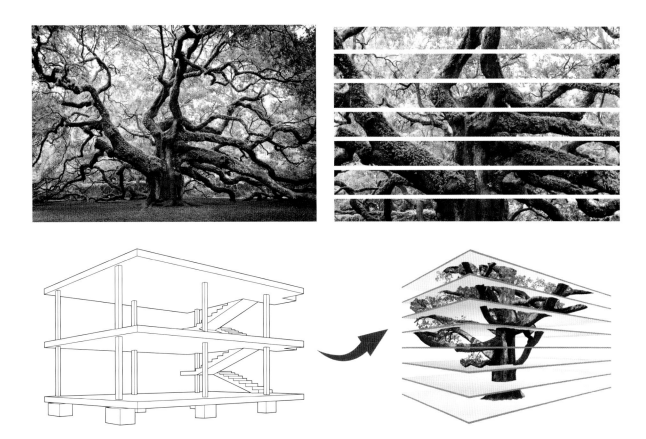

room provide opportunities to bring the Publicis community together, encourage spontaneous interactions, and cultivate knowledge sharing through an events program.

The building itself presented a problem: it was generic and lacking character, with an oversized central core. In an effort to express a strong creative identity for Publicis, we proposed reconceiving the traditional mold of the skyscraper by dematerializing the building core. This works to create continuity on all floors, connecting their employees as one community. To eliminate silos and encourage movement, we proposed cutting large atria and adding a staircase to connect the floors. The concept of a tree extending through all eight floors informs the architectural language of the space, from fragmentation of the building core to branch-like ceiling elements.

A beneficial effect of this 'organic order' of tree trunk and branches was its predisposition to change. The project was built in phases to work around three floors that were occupied by Publicis people. Over the two-year construction duration, agency growth drove the need for adding a whole floor. Due to the flexible design language, this was easily accommodated without conveying any sense that it was different from the other floors.

By breaking down the borders of a traditional office and desk ownership, users can leverage the diversity of collaborative activity within their neighborhoods. Each neighborhood (or business group) is designed to be self-sustaining with all of the tools necessary to support daily tasks. This open, interactive and collaborative environment will challenge Publicis to remain a premier creative agency and will allow them to expand intelligently in the future.

Early on, the agency embraced Activity Based Working (ABW) for their new space. This method of mobile working empowers users by supporting varying work styles with a wide range of settings. With ABW, employees are not assigned desks; instead, they share all of the desks, team work settings, meeting rooms, and other office areas. This style of working decreases daily desk vacancies, saving on costs and allowing for a more flexible utilization of office space while creating a highly collaborative working environment.

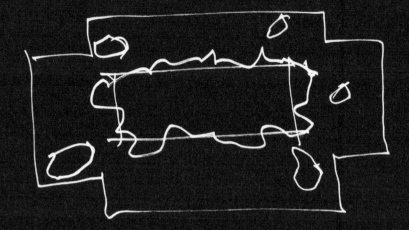

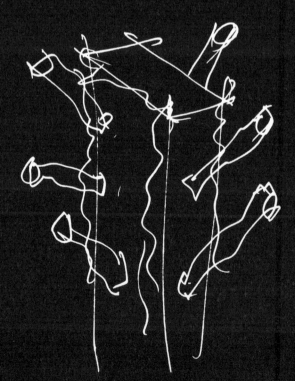

Sketches for dematerializing the building core. To produce a plan that would optimize connection to windows and views and improve the building core with its linear circulation, we proposed a concept of tree trunk and branches. The core was the organic tree trunk, and branches allowed some special enclosures against the windows.

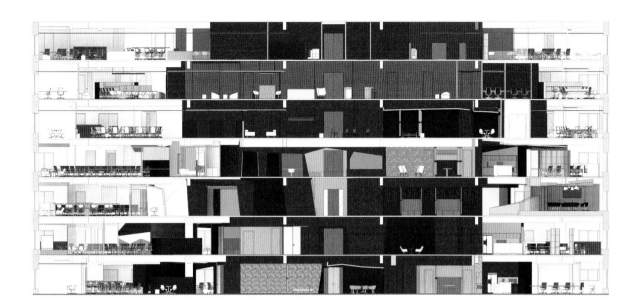

 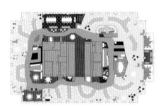 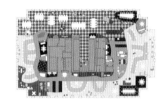 

  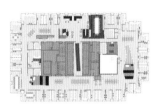 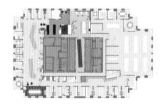

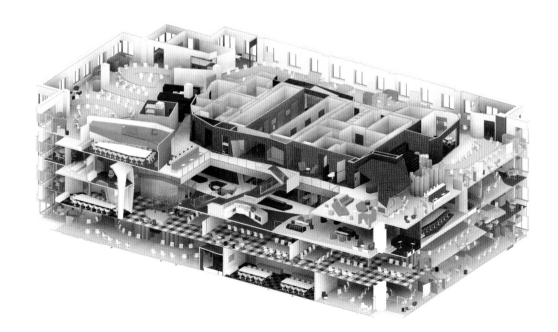

ABOVE **Section through the first seven floors.**

MIDDLE **Eight floor plans.**

BELOW **Unique collaboration spaces support a variety of work.**

CHOICE AND DIVERSITY

The Publicis central atrium houses many overlapping functions. Here the need for exhibition space intersects with meeting space so rooms can become display surfaces.

ABOVE **Unique collaboration spaces support a variety of work.**

MIDDLE **Multi-purpose space.**

OPPOSITE PAGE ABOVE **Typical work desks.**

OPPOSITE PAGE BELOW **Connecting staircase and adjacent meeting room.**

CHOICE AND DIVERSITY

186

The Publicis entrance hall
stretches through four floors.

189

OPPOSITE PAGE ABOVE **Work nook.**

OPPOSITE PAGE BELOW **Unique collaboration spaces support a variety of work.**

CENTRE **Guest reception is merged with barista bar.**

ABOVE **Typical large conference room.**

Flow, Fluidity and Transparency

Transparency is simultaneously spatial, social and ethical.

Since our earliest workplace projects, the concept of 'transparency' has been elevated to a critical position in workplace theory. In part, this is due to the multiple meanings that the word bears. Transparency can be as simple as offering a view through or into something or some place. This kind of transparency tells you what is within, and is spatial in nature. It can also imply accessibility in the sense of understanding how a subject community or environment is working, which is social in nature. This kind of transparency allows you to understand how a process or event is working. Finally, it can have an ethical dimension, imply accountability: following the notion that any system or corporate body that operates in the public eye is committed to upholding high standards and being righteous and accountable.

In the case of workplace communities, all three qualities can come together – the spatial, the social and the ethical – offering complete and comprehensible disclosure of the workings of the business. As such it promotes the employee's understanding of how the business works and therefore how his or her role and contribution can be manifested within it.

What is called transparency can also be considered 'open architecture'. The 'open office' with its perceived distractions, has been criticized for failing to address the needs of users – in particular, failing to shield employees from distractions and noise. To quote Ethan Bernstein in the *Harvard Business Review*: "For all that transparency does to drive out wasteful practices and promote collaboration and

"The (stage) set is the geometry of the eventual play, so that a wrong set makes many scenes impossible to play, and even destroys many scenes for the actors."

PETER BROOK – THE EMPTY SPACE

shared learning, too much of it can trigger distortions of fact and counterproductive inhibitions. Wide open workspaces can leave employees feeling exposed and vulnerable". He goes on to state that by balancing transparency and privacy, organizations can encourage just the right amount of 'deviance' to foster innovative behavior and boost productivity. Inclusion of zones of privacy are necessary to help shield concentrated work processes.

Openness certainly has innumerable benefits in facilitating participatory cultures, accelerating innovation and speed to market. Its by-product is organizational and social cohesion. The sensitivities, particularly with concentrated work, that are challenged in these new environments can and should be dealt with through good design. Materials and space can be strategically designed, to solve most of the perceived problems, without regressing to a closed and siloed architecture. In the words of author and educator, Alan Moore, "openness is resilience".

In parallel with transparency, flow is a crucial condition with two distinct but reciprocal characteristics. Flow within the space of an office speaks to open communication and mobility, and is vital to effective collaboration and knowledge sharing. Flow within work itself is another crucial component: it retains the seductive promise of stimulating or lubricating productivity and the thought process, bringing new insights into being. Since we are now powerfully

"Speed of connection, frequency of interaction, speed to market – all are dependent on flow and transparency."

CLIVE WILKINSON

focused on the creative pathway, it is valuable to address flow within the activity of work. The psychologist and author, Mihaly Csikszentmihalyi, expounded his Flow theory to explain an optimum creative process in his book *Creativity*. Through numerous interviews with creative people, Csikszentmihalyi extrapolated the core conditions of the experience. His conclusions can be paraphrased as follows:

> There are clear goals every step of the way. In flow, we always know what needs to be done.
>
> There is immediate feedback to one's actions. We know how well we are doing, just as a musician hears the note he has played.
>
> There is balance between chalenges and skills. Our abilities are well matched to opportunities for action.
>
> Action and awareness are merged. Our concentration is focused on what we do.
>
> Distractions are excluded from consciousness. We are aware only of what is relevant here and now.
>
> There is no worry of failure. We are too involved to be concerned with failure.
>
> Self-consciousness disapears. The self expands through acts of self-forgetfulness.
>
> The sense of time becomes distorted. Clock time no longer marks experienced time.
>
> The activity becomes autotelic – an end in itself. What we do is worth doing for its own sake.

This process is clearly an idealized one that could be extremely valuable for businesses in the future. If management were able to create the conditions to support this process widely, they would be well equipped to challenge their markets. Transparency in its many forms promises to remove barriers to flow, but what of the typical day in the life of an office worker?

As already noted in Part One, we reviewed the study by global workplace strategists, DEGW, that illustrated how much of a typical worker's day was spent in various activities. Each task was identified and mapped on the eight-hour day chart. The shocking revelation of the study was the extent of time a worker spent away from his or her desk, in no designated activity. This lead to studies that verified that a worker's desk was empty for approximately 40% of the day and it signaled a level of real estate waste that had not previously been understood.

Considering the new mobility, our studio began to relook at how unpopular corridor space could be reprogrammed, reconfigured, opened up and redesigned to capture its innate ability to manage flow and host serendipitous meetings, as well as individual work away from the desk. Our projects for Macquarie, London and Microsoft, Vancouver both propose robust and fluid circulation systems that can host serendipitous events, as the pulsing heart of a company, wherein most in-office communication takes place.

LOCATION London, United Kingdom
COMPLETED March 2011
FLOOR AREA 217,500 square feet
POPULATION 2,000

Macquarie Group Ropemaker Place

Privacy and exclusivity have long been coveted within banking institutions. Your money is safe where no one can see it, or get to it. This was our second project for the Macquarie Group who were keen to reverse public perceptions and create a culture of transparency albeit within an appropriate corporate governance and compliance framework. The need to do this effectively was even more compelling following the global banking crisis of 2009. Hence, Macquarie's new headquarters at Ropemaker Place in the City of London was designed to be a model for a new transparency in banking services, revolving around an open atrium and a dramatic connecting staircase that invited movement through their workplace. The financial services institution thus took a radical approach to showcasing and connecting its separate divisions with this new London workspace.

Having been fragmented in different buildings across the city, Macquarie leased six contiguous floors in a new LEED Platinum/ BREAAM rated building to unify its company. In an effort to facilitate a clear and open connection between corporate divisions, the project team worked with the client to carve out a new vertical opening in the form of a six story atrium. This effort was the more remarkable as Macquarie would need to pay market leasing rate on the floor area that was sacrificed to enable this moment of spatial generosity.

The new office environment would have a strong emphasis on collaboration, transparency and client service. Like a vertical 'high street', the new atrium accommodates

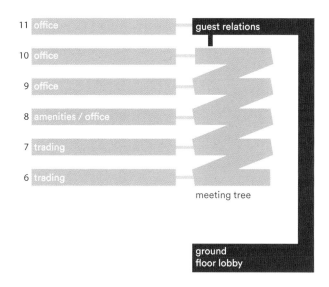

193

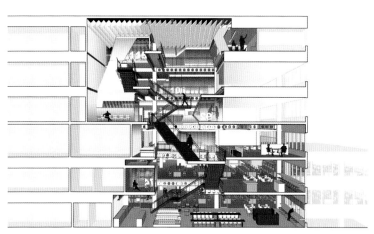

Cross section through the atrium, highlighting the organic path of the staircase.

key communal functions as genuine destinations, which together create a village of opportunities for the workers. Destinations around the atrium are a mixture of 'meeting tree' rooms, staff pantries on every floor, open work areas and amenity spaces like the level 6 business lounge, the level 8 café, the engine room and the garden terrace. The bottom floor adjoined the trading floor with its high intensity activity.

While the atrium serves to connect the businesses, it also becomes a visual bridge into the workings of the bank for clients and visitors, who are greeted in the ground floor lobby and emerge, via elevators, on the level 11 guest relations area. From here, they can engage in confidential dealings in private rooms, use the conference or event spaces, or meet within the dramatic atrium volume, enjoying clear views into all the Macquarie workspace.

Several sustainable initiatives are achieved with the building, including significant decreases in energy consumption, waste and elevator usage, and net carbon footprint reduction, in line with BREAAM Excellent and LEED Platinum rating. Structural beams cut out of the atrium were reused to create bridges and cantilevered pods. Engineered cellular space that responds to proven space ratios reduces churn costs, and a computer-controlled daylight harvesting system with LED lighting provides significant energy savings. An emphasis on foot traffic using the atrium staircase has cut elevator usage by 75% while promoting employee health.

In its finished form, the visible energy of people circulating and interacting in the highly transparent atrium serves as a catalyst for drawing the different business units together and provides the synergy to collaborate with each other in new business ventures. It further underscores their brand as an agile, forward thinking and highly collaborative 21st century company.

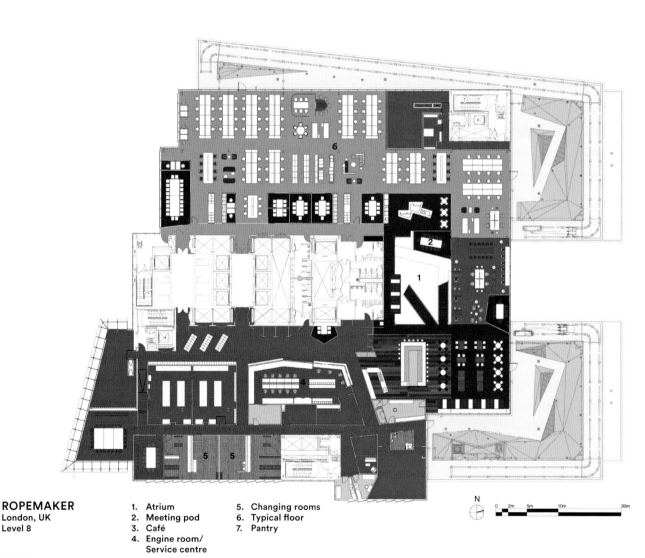

ROPEMAKER
London, UK
Level 8

1. Atrium
2. Meeting pod
3. Café
4. Engine room/ Service centre
5. Changing rooms
6. Typical floor
7. Pantry

N

0 2m 5m 10m 20m

Floor plan organization converges on the vertical circulation device of the atrium.

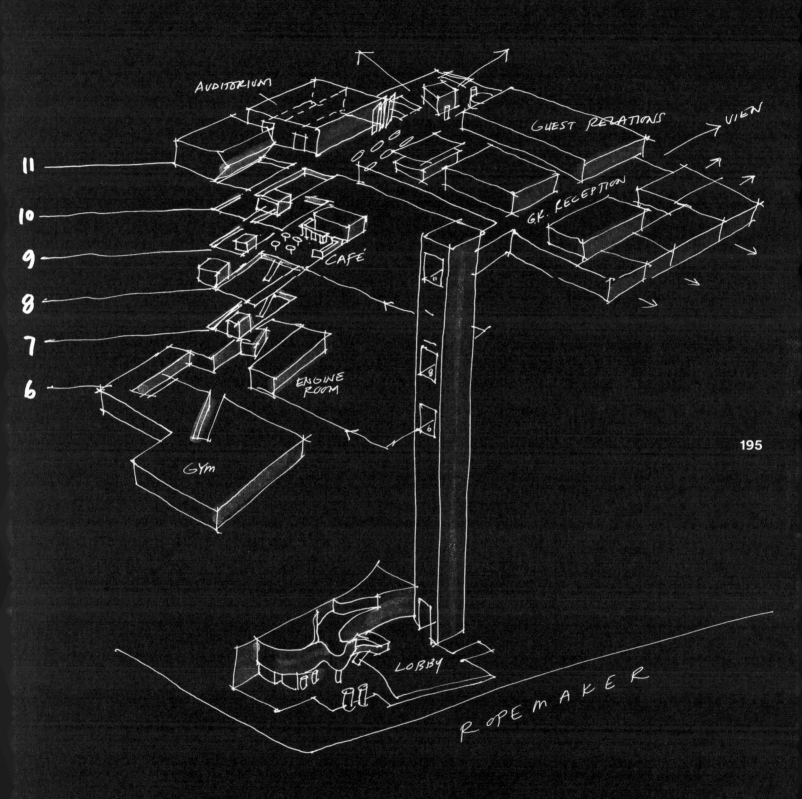

AUDITORIUM

GUEST RELATIONS

VIEW

11

10

9

CAFÉ

8

7

ENGINE ROOM

6

G.K. RECEPTION

GYM

195

LOBBY

ROPEMAKER

Concept sketch for stacking floors
and connecting via a new atrium.

ABOVE **The trading floor.**

BELOW RIGHT **Atrium sketch** showing the 'false skylight'.

OPPOSITE PAGE **In forming the** staircase we developed physical and computer models. Its organic configuration emerged from connecting different destinations. The use of a red color was part of a strategy to drive use of the stair, and underscore its essential role in the workspace. Lighting the treads individually furthered that goal.

THE THEATRE OF WORK

Communication between different business divisions was so important to Macquarie that we excavated a six-story atrium and inserted a connecting stair like a red umbilical cord.

THE THEATRE OF WORK

OPPOSITE PAGE **Horizontal views across the atrium reveal the different collaboration zones.**

ABOVE AND BELOW **Following completion of the project, we observed the atrium usage. On one occasion, we saw a group of about a dozen IT staffers walk up the stair from the bottom level to the meeting room at the top – a six full floors – as if they did that multiple times a day. Two lessons can be derived from this: if you make the connecting atrium attractive, people will use the stairs. People will also use the stairs when they are the first thing they see (rather than elevators).**

ABOVE **The pantry areas were intentionally designed in the round. All pantry equipment and refreshments are located on the island. People using it are invariably facing each other, increasing the likelihood of conversations occurring.**

OPPOSITE PAGE **Macquarie secured an exclusive ground floor lobby with direct rear access to the elevators. The ceiling is an extension of the 'false skylight' at the top of their atrium.**

FLOW, FLUIDITY AND TRANSPARENCY

LOCATION Vancouver, British Columbia, Canada
COMPLETED February 2016
FLOOR AREA 142,000 square feet
POPULATION 750

Microsoft Canada Excellence Centre

204

The ever-growing work force of the global tech-giant, Microsoft, prompted the software company to relocate and expand their Canadian headquarters, the Microsoft Canada Excellence Centre, MCEC, into two vast floor plates, adaptively reusing a department store building in downtown Vancouver. The solid façade of the building was reskinned with a new glass curtain wall, exposing the spectacular views of the city and the surrounding landscape. Up to this time, Microsoft had been fragmented into multiple offices with different business units across the city. Not only did these groups not communicate with one another, but they had varying security needs making some offices completely inaccessible.

Our firm began the project just as we were completing an extensive research project on their Seattle headquarters, wherein we were tasked at looking into future ways of working for the technology giant, including campus-wide planning strategies for greater connectivity between business groups. Their historic focus on concentrated work had given rise to a workplace standard that was almost completely cellular and siloed. In the 1980s Bill Gates had literally promised every developer a door, and this standard had marked the company ever since. A door is a powerful protector of concentration, and a powerful deterrent to collaboration. In the new knowledge economy, knowledge sharing is key and we worked to open up the landscape of the new MCEC, while at the same time protecting concentration space.

With the new program, we needed to accommodate two gaming companies and a software developer business unit. The masterplan needed to adapt for future flexibility so the business model could morph with anticipated future developments. Key to the success of such a large floor layout would be the circulation system, which wanted to both buffer business units acoustically but also allow visual connectivity. The employee workspace is supported with a wide variety of open and enclosed collaboration spaces to facilitate the various workflow demands.

The design team drew upon the local context: the distinct natural setting of both the company's Seattle headquarters as well as the natural landmarks of Canada's Lower Mainland to inform the architectural design. The pervasive use of wood elements, the airy branch-like ceiling structures and the more grounded, boulder-like enclosures are a deliberate visual reference to canopies and roots, respectively, of the giant tree specimens unique to the area. To capitalize on existing conditions, an existing void in the upper level's floor slab was utilized to introduce a communicating stair that spans and connects the two floors, as the trunk of a tree connects its disparate parts.

The expansive floorplates are further defined by neighborhoods of open work benches woven together with primary circulation paths that purposefully expand to incorporate open and semi-enclosed collaboration rooms. Moments of vibrant color punctuate these collaborative spaces as well as strategically located social gathering areas, such as the hubs for meeting and eating and multipurpose rooms. The new occupants have responded very positively to the design concept of simultaneously revealing the workings of the architecture and expressing an aspirational theme of working community within a naturalistic, wood-framed setting. In post occupancy focus groups, we learned that employees referred to it as Microsoft's coolest office.

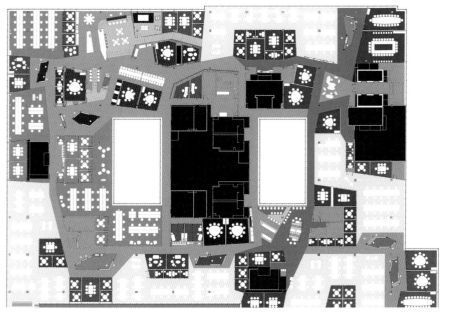

LEVEL 6

205

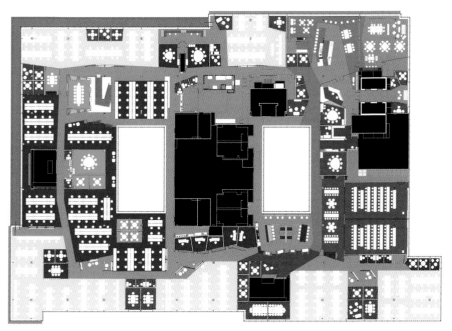

LEVEL 7

Floor plans with departmental layouts. The circulation loop is enlivened by organically responding to the adjacent program variety and view corridors, adding visual interest to moving through the large floor plates.

FLOW, FLUIDITY AND TRANSPARENCY

OPPOSITE PAGE **Main connecting
staircase looks into a meeting room.**

ABOVE **Community space at the
connecting atrium.**

BELOW **Connecting staircase
celebrating local wood.**

FLOW, FLUIDITY AND TRANSPARENCY

208

ABOVE The primary circulation is buffered from individual workspace through co-working and collaborative areas.

CENTRE Microsoft entrance area: both transparent and secure. Included throughout are amenity spaces, such as a distinctly unique reception area adjacent to a café with espresso bar for staff and visitors, a game room, and technology spaces including a well-equipped maker lab where employees can explore creative ideas for new projects.

NEXT PAGE Collaborative brainstorming areas give glimpses into the quiet work areas.

THE THEATRE OF WORK

OPPOSITE PAGE **Occupying the top two floors of the building, the new open workplace takes full advantage of the expansive views.**

ABOVE **Café spaces.**

FLOW, FLUIDITY AND TRANSPARENCY

The Learning Organization

In a rapidly changing world, continuous learning is essential to survival.

> "New insights fail to get put into practice because they conflict with deeply held internal images of how the world works, images that limit us to familiar ways of thinking and acting. That is why the discipline of managing mental models – surfacing, testing, and improving our internal pictures of how the world works – promises to be a major breakthrough for building learning organizations."

PETER M. SENGE – THE FIFTH DISCIPLINE

of large multi-national corporations. Fast moving startups that leveraged the promises of new technologies grabbed market share and disrupted entire product and service delivery platforms. Since the frames of reference were changing daily, and technological development was progressing relentlessly, it became critical for any player in the tech field to be in a constant state of learning. If you were not in the tech field, you were probably serving the tech field.

Knowledge sharing has been an industry buzz word for more than two decades, with simplistic models of how to encourage the process or optimize its benefits within large organizations. Everyone knows this is the answer – but few have any idea how to foster it on a more profound level. For organizational learning to take place, individual learning must precede it. Without that, no organizational learning will take place. Individual learning can feed into group learning, and group learning can lead into organizational learning in the right circumstances.

With his book, *The Fifth Discipline*, Peter M. Senge provides a far richer and more apt perspective on the learning institution. Since learning is fundamentally personal, he posits five disciplines that begin with the self, but extend to organizational learning:

Systems Thinking
The importance of locating ever thing with a holistic, or systemic, point of view.

Personal Mastery
The personal commitment to lifelong learning, which again seeks objectivity in seeing the world. And organiztions must encourage the personal growth of their people.

Mental Models
Since we act on shared mental models, we can only truly innovate when we examine and challenge our own mental models. Learning conversations must balance advocacy with inquiry.

Shared Visions
People excel and learn when there is a genuine and meaningful shared vision.

Team Learning
This last discipline is key to

For much of the modern era, a learning organization was, quite literally, a school. While a master/apprentice relationship existed within the old medieval guild system, the primary role of the apprentice was to be productive and reward his or her master through his or her labor. The apprentice was primarily a servant. In the 20th century, with the exception of the effects of two cataclysmic world wars, long term relative stability in markets, manufacturing and the economy meant that work 'carried on as usual'. Job training happened before the job started and the job remained largely unchanged over a career, requiring a large proportion of repetitive tasks. Computers and the internet changed all that.

Since 1980, driven by the Arpanet innovation becoming the internet, and personal computerization becoming widespread, the pace of change created instability and disrupted the market dominance institutional innovation and effectiveness, since a team that is highly functioning, in a state of flow, exceeds that collective capacity of its members. "The practice of shared vision involves the skills of unearthing shared 'pictures of the future' that foster genuine commitment and enrollment rather than compliance." Peter M. Senge

The starting point for a learning organization is learning teams. Teams can become learning teams through learning from each other. Since the most effective learning relies on a repetitive process of practice and performance, it quickly becomes clear that the ability to simulate is essential. Prototyping and modelling concepts within what Senge calls 'practice fields' provide ways of testing and developing ideas and the simulation process can be applied to almost any industry and any problem. Group intelligence should grow through this. The opposite of this is 'groupthink', where a group has prioritized consensus over genuine learning. Experimentation may also happen in a virtual world, as a representation of the real world.

It is important to note that those companies that have persisted and thrived over long periods of time almost always centreed on a powerful sense of their community: that they were a community first and foremost rather than a financial construct. This organic and fluid sense of self allows the entity to adapt to changing circumstances and re-consider their mission accordingly. Nokia for decades produced a broad range of industrial products, including tools and rubber boots, until their small line of mobile phones suddenly became a huge hit, and dominated world mobile phone markets for many years. It was perhaps an over-reliance on their internal community that led to a failure to recognize and invest in applications, which in turn led to their downfall. While they have transitioned again, the community is now reappraising their next life. It is arguable that the early success of their phones and the pressure of global expansion was irreconcilable with their self-image as a diverse and proudly local Finnish company, fragmenting the community and consequently losing communal focus. Involuntary fragmentation is extremely dangerous as it works against the holistic systems thinking that is so important to successful companies.

The Google founders, Larry Page and Sergei Brin, realized the importance of continuous learning early on and effectively replicated the seminar system that they experienced at Stanford University in distributed informal open spaces called 'tech talks' within their workplace. In their first offices, these spaces were located adjacent to coffee areas so that people were exposed to this structured form of knowledge sharing while getting coffee and could choose to join the talk for as long or as short a period as suited them. In the early days for Google, this loose informal knowledge sharing not only pushed learning, but it created a platform for people to hang with their peers and engage in easy conversation, much of which was cross-disciplinary, and which could drift into engineering questions. This worked like a modest town square and sent a message to staff and visitors that Google was truly focused on learning and the future.

Ten years later, our client GLG had built its business model as the world's largest professional learning organization based on sharing the expertise of their members. With their 40,000 members, they offered clients highly informed specialist expertise – precisely what they could not find on the internet – through this global network of experts. If you wanted to buy the Trans-Siberia pipeline, they could connect you with experts in Houston, Hong Kong, Beijing, Moscow and Frankfurt who could rapidly inform your feasibility analysis.

In studying ways of working for their new headquarters, they embraced activity based working, becoming possibly the first North American office to do so. Their office configuration facilitated an exceptional level of connectedness and a generous provision for learning opportunities within their multi-purpose event space offering.

216

LOCATION New York, New York, United States
COMPLETED June 2014
FLOOR AREA 65,000 square feet
POPULATION 350

GLG Global Headquarters

As the world's largest membership for professional learning and expertise, GLG (formerly the Gerson Lehrman Group) offers a unique business proposition. Their goal is to transform the way the world's top professionals share knowledge and learn. GLG did not exactly practice what they preached when we first began working with them. Their Mid-Town Manhattan offices were traditional and fragmented with insufficient collaboration areas for an intrinsically collaborative company. Rapid expansion drove the need to move, but it took a six-month long journey to investigate how they were to work in the future.

We worked closely with the CEO Alexander Saint Armand and his leadership team in analyzing alternative ways of working. An iterative and engaged questioning process lead to their embracing activity based working (ABW), which led to their being one of the first installations of this workstyle in America. A number of change management steps were undertaken to school their staff in the behavior changes necessary to make this a success. These included focus group sessions, town hall presentations, and change management seminars with the original authors of the ABW workstyle, Veldhoen, who were brought in from Holland to engage with the staff.

As previously noted, traditional offices with designated desks have a surprisingly consistent daily desk vacancy rate of 40-60%. ABW transforms the occupancy ratio up to around 80% and in so doing, saves 20% on operational costs and 20% of the corporate carbon footprint: in other words, it is a highly sustainable solution. New technologies enable the behavior changes, and also entail lower paper usage and lower waste production. Small changes like removing waste bins from desk areas and locating them at anchor point hubs encourages changes in paper handling. If it requires effort to dispose of paper, less paper is used.

The new office space we landed on was adjacent to the New York Public Library and overlooking Grand Central Terminal, in one of New York's earliest skyscrapers from 1929, One Grand Central Place on 42nd Street. We combined two low-level deep plan floors and planned a highly collaborative workplace for their staff, specifically tailored to host client-facing teaching and learning events. Our first challenge was to perform strategic surgery, to adapt the third and fourth floors of the 1928 building to accommodate the new atrium. We raised the third floor roof up to fourth floor level, removing old windows with their brick surrounds, and created a new dynamic skylight.

Planning of the space for ABW was facilitated by the open, highly transparent, deep floor plan. From arrival via elevators, visitors experience a reception zone where a host greets you, in full view of the light-filled atrium. The atrium is furnished as an inviting lounge and work area, and is coupled with a brass-encased coffee bar which acts as a gathering point for employees. The central area of the floor is furnished with a wide variety of work settings, some of which double as café seating for lunchtimes. Along the perimeter of the floor, more typical high-density bench seating allows a combination of team and individual work, and benefits from good light

217

and views. While the foundation colors for the space are white, black and grey, a spectrum of red to orange tones, derived from the GLG brand color, are employed as well as the opposite light spectrum of green. Color translucency is emphasized by the colored glass meeting rooms, which further extend the sense of a rich and varied environment. The new office allows GLG to bring client conversations, roundtables, and public gatherings in-house, making the space a hub of global thought leadership and education.

The project was completed in June 2014 and attracted considerable media attention. It was featured in Bloomberg News, Fast Company, Inc., The Wall Street Journal and on various TV networks. High staff engagement and brand reinforcement are achieved through employee empowerment and meaningful leadership. GLG are experiencing rapid expansion and are rolling out both the ABW workstyle and this effective branded environment to all their global offices.

218

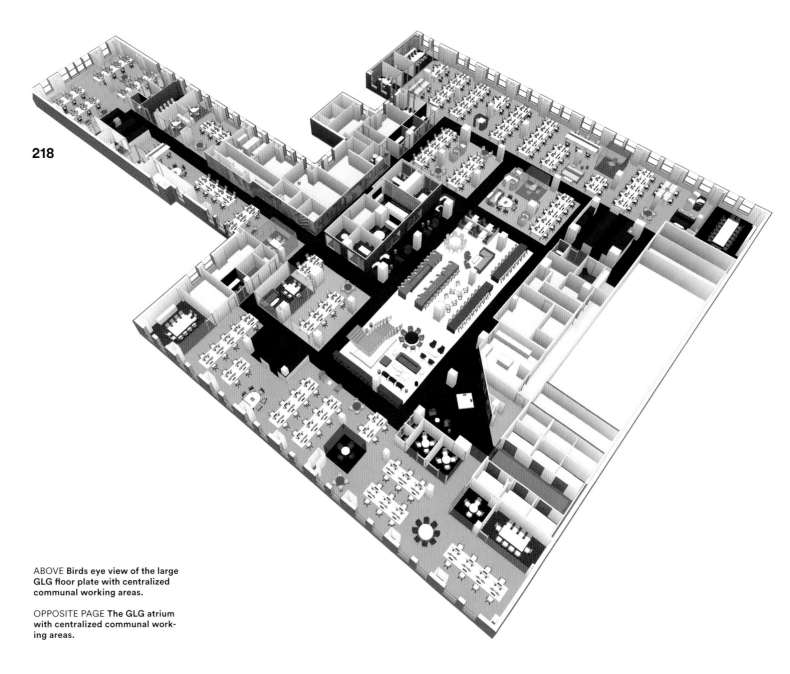

ABOVE **Birds eye view of the large GLG floor plate with centralized communal working areas.**

OPPOSITE PAGE **The GLG atrium with centralized communal working areas.**

The GLG atrium with centralized communal working areas. The reception desk is a minimal white pod to avoid creating a barrier between visitors and the staff hosts.

ABOVE Barista at the coffee bar: service runs from morning till early afternoon.

CENTRE Open but protected meeting places.

OPPOSITE PAGE ABOVE The café space with open and enclosed working area.

The angled skylight form was developed to control direct light and maximize horizontal distribution of light into the deep plan space, as well as accommodate mechanical shades and built in lighting. A new steel staircase was designed to offer a landing podium for town hall talks, and provide an easy, open connection between the floors.

LOCATION Mountain View, California, United States
COMPLETED March 2005
FLOOR AREA 180,000 SF Build-out; 500,000 SF Master Plan
POPULATION 1,000

Google Headquarters (Googleplex)

226

In June 2004, our studio won the invited Google design competition for their new headquarters based on a proposal for creating a diversified campus environment, using an existing office park in Mountain View, California. It's employee base were all high performing software engineers who had navigated their vaunted application process – at that time the company expended 56 hours researching and vetting every candidate. Continuous learning within the organization was a core part of their mission.

Our design scheme integrated highly focused software engineering workspace with learning, meeting, recreational and food facilities into the existing inner courtyards and building shell. The process was a learning experience for both our team and the client, as we were very fortunate to work directly with Google founders Larry Page and Sergey Brin. Their workspace benchmark was the traditional graduate rooms of Stanford University wherein much of their early thinking had germinated – ours was the office as an open village framework. The result merged highly focused, concentration space with highly social collaboration space, while taking a frugal and pragmatic approach to repurposing previous interior build out.

Faced with a daunting expansion curve, Google undertook a strategic reevaluation of its workplace processes. It assembled a large project team including workplace strategists DEGW and William McDonough, a cradle-to-cradle environmental visionary,

to set goals for the design of the 500,000 square foot campus in Silicon Valley. DEGW conducted interviews and observational research work, which established performance criteria for the design solution.

Through working with the founders, Page and Brin, we arrived at the idea of merging our workplace concepts with their spatial experience learned in educational environments. Within the loosely structured university system, there are resources available to allow the individual to focus, conceive, investigate, and execute the impossible – which is how Google launched its search business. In a university environment, you typically have the option of self-directed work, a selection of work styles or work environments, and independent study subject choices, either private or within a group. For example, a lesson learned from Stanford University was that coding engineers worked best in groups of three to four.

Facility performance became focused on satisfying four main criteria:

Concentration and collaboration utilizing a system of glass-enclosed three-person work rooms. These rooms were custom fabricated with absorbent tent ceilings to soften sound and deflect light into the deep floors. Services are integrated through a custom ceiling collar that distriutes supply and return air, sprinklers and artificial lighting.

Flexibility and adaptability which allowed rapid workgroup mobility and team reconfiguration.

Work/life balance through providing support services for people who work long hours. Several different food service cafés are provided and distributed micro kitchens are opened up to function as social hubs with lounge facilties, library areas and furnished open spaces to encourage spontanous meetings and gatherings.

Leveraged learning is a core company goal to maintain its innovation culture. Specific areas along public routes are furnished as tech talk zones where almost continuous seminars and knowledge sharing events would take place.

A typical university campus environment offers the concept of 'self-containment'. Within the immediate area, all of your basic work/life needs can be met – and the possibility of casual encounters with fellow students for collaboration or recreation is possible anytime during the day or night. At the university level, these opportunities support the goals of personal education, with a focus on each individual's interests, but when these interests become common to a community like Google, the results can be dramatic.

'Tech-talk' and formal lecture areas were provided where learning or teaching could occur in an organized fashion, but there were also common white boards located along the 'street' for the impromptu discussions on the problems of the day. The concept was continued through the design of 13 individual environments, which re-created environments usually found on a college campus, and were systematically integrated into the overall design of each building by the use of a thermal contour diagram: hot areas being more public and active zones, while cold being more secluded, quieter and private. These zones were defined by location along the primary and secondary circulation corridors.

The result of providing an environmental backbone support for the combination of independent study, along with the opportunity for community accomplishment offers the best of all possibilities: one which satisfies the needs of the individual as well as the collective, and results in the success of both. Following the participation of the environmental consultant, a sustainable energy-conserving environment was a high priority, and most building materials used were either cradle-to-cradle products, or contained high-recycled content. Doors culled from previous build outs were used on the two-story tower elements as design embellishment, and all open workstations were recycled product.

The project was fast tracked on a market rate budget for completion in March 2005 only nine months after we were awarded the project. A tight balance was achieved between the urgent need for workspace and the duration required for quality construction. Continuous research and testing during the project execution were concluded with the workplace strategists conducting post occupancy research to enhance Google's workspace learning as part of the company's continuously experimental culture. The founders had told us they would grow out of the building within two years. As it turned out, Google has continuously and successfully occupied the building to date with little changes, though it has indeed grown massively across multiple buildings.

227

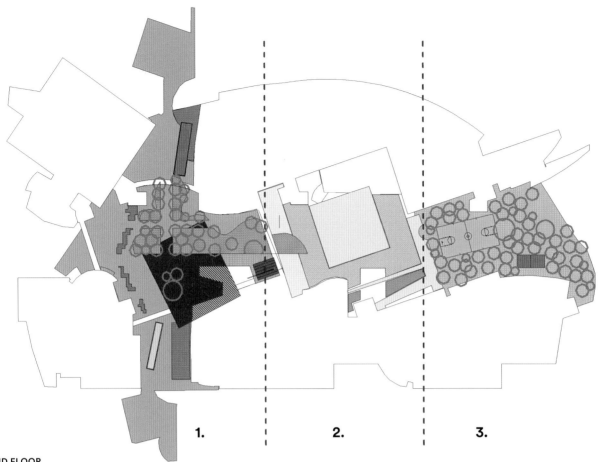

GROUND FLOOR

Landscape network:
• 3 unique environments
• enhance existing condition/potential
• exploit inside-outside relationships
• bring green into buildings by exploiting terraces and patios

1.   2.   3.

ABOVE AND OPPOSITE PAGE
ABOVE **We analyzed the existing Mountain View Campus, which Google had inherited from Sun Microsystems in 2003. This required an analytical study** of existing site conditions and opportunities of connecting the four buildings into one community. We looked for opportunities in the existing landscaping, hardscape, connectivity of the campus, division of outdoor activities (three unique environments) and inside/outside connections.

BELOW AND OPPOSITE PAGE
BELOW **Matrix of Constraints and Opportunities in the new campus:** we systematically extrapolated the multiple layers of constraints and opportunities that factored into the project, representing these in plan layers to ensure design performance on multiple levels.

CONSTRAINTS

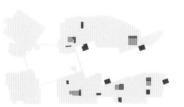

1. Existing infrastructure

2. Structural constraints

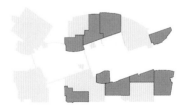

3. Fire compartmentation

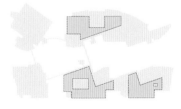

4. Oversized height zones

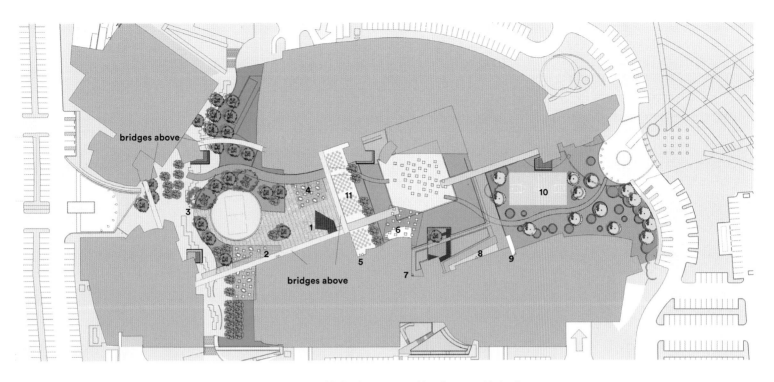

1. New entry canopy on new hardscape
2. New doors exiting on new hardscape terrace
3. Cuts in berm to improve access
4. New 'bakery' hardscape terrace

5. New doors; provide hardscape
6. New caféteria terrace
7. New door: provide hardscape
8. New door: provide hardscape

9. New door: provide hardscape
10. Proposed basketball court
11. New hardscape; giant chess boards

229

OPPORTUNITIES

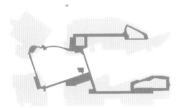

1. Primary circulation

2. Enclosed meeting spaces

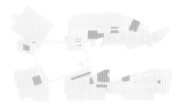

3. Network learning

4. Work/life balance

5. Nomadic work zones

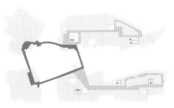

6. Lighting concept

7. Time use – early morning

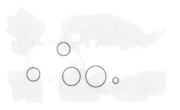

8. Time use – late evening

THE LEARNING ORGANIZATION

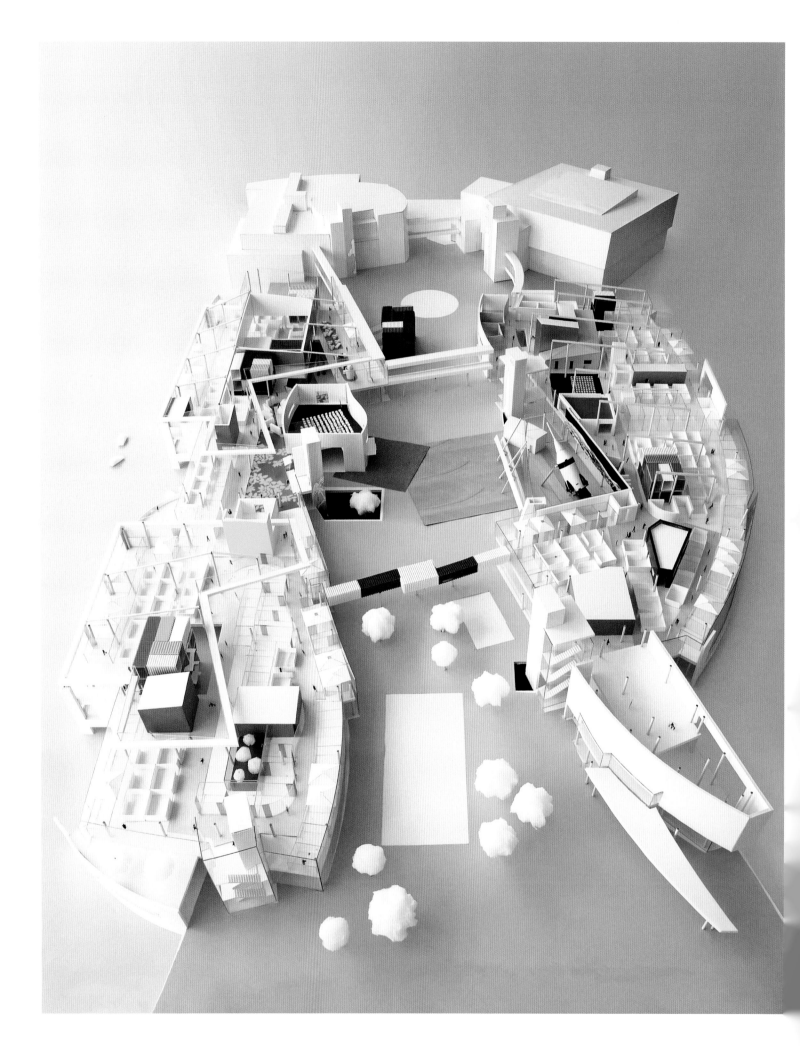

THE THEATRE OF WORK

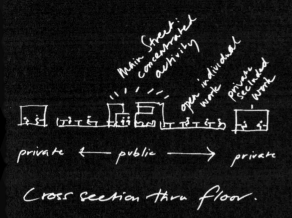

Main Street concentrated activity

open individual work

private secluded work

private ← → public ← → private

Cross section thru floor.

1. Promote communication and knowledge sharing through a plan that optimizes opportunities for interaction, formal and informal

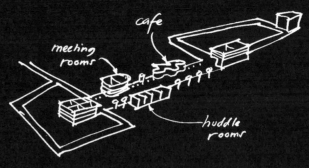

cafe

meeting rooms

huddle rooms

Structure a 'Main Street' with shared-use building blocks.

2. Create a heart or central focus to the space:
  • to improve orientation and circulation
  • to enchance a sense of community

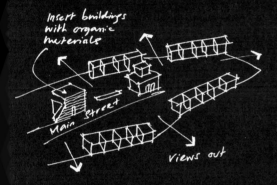

Insert buildings with organic materials

Main Street

Views out

3. Provide a strong connection to the outside world:
  • via transparency and opening views
  • by using natural, organic materials in the space

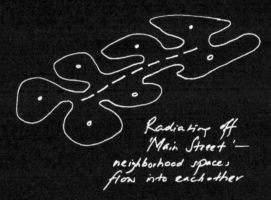

Radiating off 'Main Street' — neighborhood spaces flow into each other

231

4. Create a neighborhood feel:
  • promote a sense of team and space 'ownership': a family feel
  • configure neighborhoods for flexibility to accomodate growth and change

ADAPTABLE

INSPIRED

DIVERSE

WORK

Google

PLAY

NATURAL

INTELLIGENT

YOUTHFUL

5. Createa space that embodies Google brand and community identity

6. Establish a workstation strategy to allow flexibility and customization

OPPOSITE PAGE The original campus model that won the competition for our firm, showing the circulation, the neighborhood distribution and landmark elements. The red and white bridge was not implemented, nor were the various shipping container towers.

ABOVE Six primary concept directions agreed with Google.

Clubhouse
- active nomad work
- opportunity for chance encounters

Bakery Coffee Shop
- active nomad work
- opportunity for change and collaboration

Supper Club
- alternative dining setting for focused collaborative work

Conference
- focused space for larger collaborative groups
- white boards
- projection cabailities

Library
- quiet nomadic work
- visitor workspace

I-Bar
- active nomadic work
- visitor workspace

1	2	3	4	5	6

Hot

232

THE THEATRE OF WORK

Terrace
• quiet alternative for nomadic work
• visitor workspace

Open meeting
• quiet nomadic work
• visitor workspace
• impromtu team collabration

Open Huddle
• impromtu team collaboration

Closed Meeting
• foused space for collaboration
• white boards
• projection capabilities
• optional as war room

Huddle Room
• quiet nomadic work
• focused collaboration space
• white boards

Workstation
• quiet resident work
• furniture reconfigurable to meet team's needs

Workroom
• quiet resident work
• furniture reconfigurable to meet team's needs
• panelized framing systems to acommodate joining offices for bigger teams

7   8   9   10   11   12   13   Cold

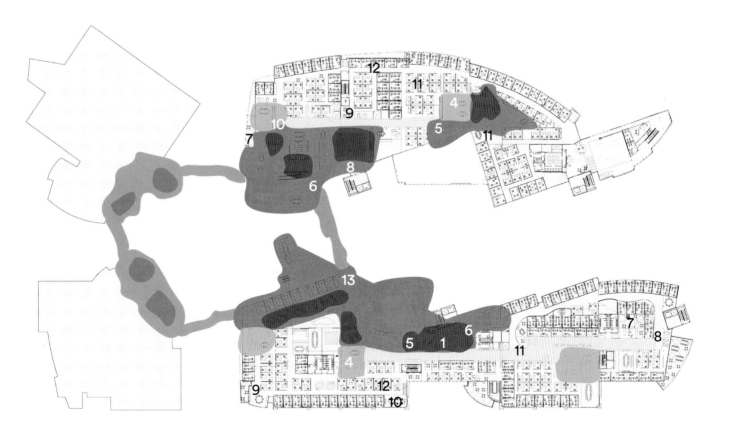

Thermal contour map highlighting the acoustic contours with quiet areas on the perimeter. The range of collaborative spaces is illustrated above.

THE LEARNING ORGANIZATION

Co-location of spaces around the main staircase include the meeting rooms to the right where wood doors from the previous interior were re-used, in some cases as doors to nowhere.

236

ABOVE In evolving the design, we built physical working models for the 500,000 SF campus in Mountain View. Page and Brin reviewed them and gave their input, especially with the fabric yurt structure. We also tested colored glass for its screening effects.

MIDDLE Model study.

BELOW The early design iteration included four-story meeting room towers made of shipping containers, floating within the very tall two-storey space. Unfortunately, the value engineering hammer deleted them.

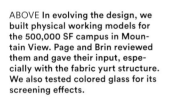

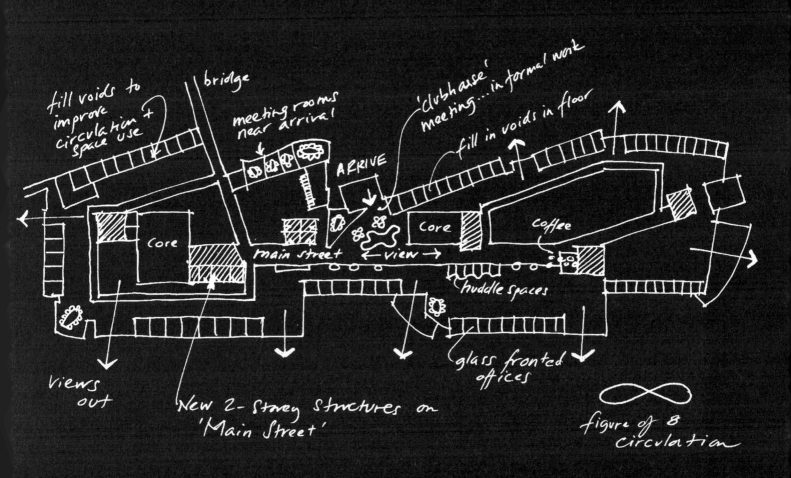

fill voids to improve circulation + space use

bridge

meeting rooms near arrival

'clubhouse' meeting...informal work

fill in voids in floor

ARRIVE

Core

Core

coffee

main street

← view →

huddle spaces

views out

New 2-storey Structures on 'Main Street'

glass fronted offices

figure of 8 circulation

Apertures were cut in the slab to improve connections between the floors, and a grand staircase that invites hanging out celebrates the main entry point.

ABOVE Typical tented work rooms along the building perimeter.

BELOW Sketch section through building 43.

OPPOSITE PAGE The entire perimeter of the two large buildings was furnished with glass workrooms to accommodate three to four senior Google engineers. Glass was necessary to permit excellent light and view connection for the interior work areas but also posed an acoustic challenge. We solved this by custom fabricating absorbent acoustic tent roofs and delivering services through a central collar element, which also functioned to support and provide tension to the roof form.

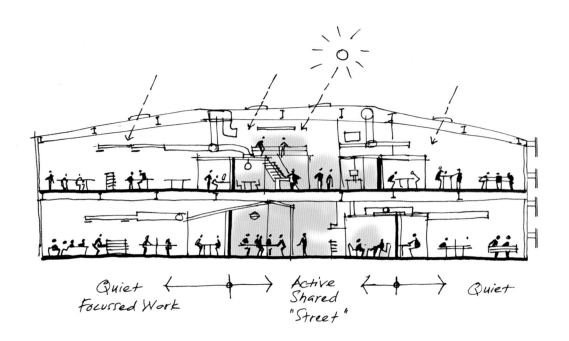

Quiet Focussed Work   Active Shared "Street"   Quiet

ABOVE Our masterplan followed a simple distribution of work 'neighborhoods' along a 'Main Street' circulation plan. All shared resources are located along this street, and range from meeting rooms, to tech talk spaces, to micro-kitchens and library lounges. Here is a library hang-out with custom tent meeting room.

BELOW One of the larger meeting rooms with acoustic paneling and dual projection for internal brainstorming.

OPPOSITE PAGE ABOVE Tented workrooms with inboard open working. The tent ceilings created and undulating landscape.

241

After their post occupancy survey, Andrew Laing noted: "It's designed almost as a living environment – it's much more like being at a university than being in a conventional work environment."

Human Scale and Community Scale

Determining an optimum group and neighborhood size is essential to cohesive communities.

"The optimum group and neighborhood size is a major factor in corporate communication and engagement. Where corporations do no actively manage scale, rogue tribal groupings may occur which may not have corporate or community interests at heart."

CLIVE WILKINSON

The challenge of working for a large organization is fundamentally one of scale. The larger an organization becomes, the harder it is for employees to understand their role and contribution to the company without the form of decentralization of neighborhoods and team scales. In the days when large companies were primarily employing people for routine and repetitive work, the question of social engagement in the workplace was of lesser importance. An employee was a productive entity that could be easily replaced. As computers assumed these repetitive routine tasks, the roles of humans transformed. Non-routine work was ascendant. Beyond the capabilities of mechanization, the knowledge worker became the most valuable type of employee, and the extent to which a worker was positively engaged in their work was directly proportional to his or her creative and productive results.

Companies began to ask more of the workers, and workers began to ask more of their companies. Everybody was asking more about everything, which is entirely commensurate with radically transformed work conditions. The workplace became a subject for massive transformation.

Several years ago we observed that the problems of many large organizations were not repeated in small organizations. With variants between different business typologies, we have discovered through experience, that team sizes are generally best when limited to four to 16 people. People have social capabilities that are not infinite. This fact is represented globally, in the size of typical office meeting rooms, regardless of what a company does. We know that larger groups peak at around 100 – 150 people because it becomes impossible to maintain meaningful and productive relationships with greater numbers of people. Extensive data supports this point.

It is significant that 100 was the unit for basic divisions of the Roman army. The Roman soldier was a 'Centurion' and this number has been used for the military company since Roman times. The word company of course extended into the modern business enterprise. Its etymology was originally from the Old French 'compagnie' – a military term which had origins in the Latin 'companio' meaning 'one who eats bread with you'. Hence its communal function is recognized in the word itself.

Robin Dunbar, the anthropologist and behavioral psychologist, proposed a theory known as Dunbar's Number. That number is 150 and he suggested that number was the limit to the number of people with whom one can maintain stable social relationships – relationships in which you can know who each person is and how each person relates to the next within that numerical community. The actual number will vary somewhat from person to person, but the concept is valuable, when considering large corporate space planning.

The small company, which is anything from a few people to perhaps 80 or 100, operates on familiarity and trust between all the members of the community. People quite simply get to know each other well and can operate instinctually and with deeper knowledge can readily predict their colleagues' behaviors and actions. They can therefore move quickly in knowledge sharing and decision-making processes. In essence, they operate as 'extended families.'

Larger organizations have always struggled with employee engagement. Alienation, the sense of detachment or estrangement from the group, the loss of identity that comes with an inability to see or comprehend one's place in or contribution to a large company are problems that were identified early in the Industrial Revolution, and which Marxists attributed to Capitalistic decadence, or the unsustainability of the Capitalist machine. With the advent of the knowledge worker, the challenge of scale has become a critical business issue. Corporations are finally listening and observing. Human Resources is conducting surveys, board directors are debating, and engagement initiatives are coming to the forefront. Structural ideas in the physical environment, like neighborhood formations, are becoming common in an authentic place-making effort. After all, employees do not engage in numbers or statistics – they want and need human environments which resonate, which support manageable and accessible communities, and which inspire them. None of this is provided by a magic formula.

The two case studies that follow provide a window into two very different scenarios. The Intuit building project begins with a single 'centreing action' in the form of a large sculpted atrium, which invites large company meetings, as well as a number of shared communal spaces including food service. The building furthermore supports and encourages work on the outside edges of the building, blending terraces and garden landscapes. From our first concepts about workplace, we promoted the idea that a building should reveal its purpose on entering, or as soon as possible after entering. With Intuit, we evolved that idea to the next level. The building is about community first and foremost, hence the first experience is of the atrium which acts as a vertical street.

In a very different vein, The Barbarian Group operates at the tipping point of a small company. We designed a workspace for 125 people with the ability to expand to 175. Ensuring connectivity between all 'Barbarians' was paramount. For that, we designed a single 4,400 square foot table to connect everyone, so the physical vibration of a community could literally be felt.

244

"The natural state of animal brain is one of distractedness. This is due to the need to react to changes in the environment instantly in order to find food or to avoid danger."

NICHOLAS CARR – THE SHALLOWS: WHAT THE INTERNET IS DOING TO OUR BRAINS

LOCATION Mountain View, California, United States
COMPLETED October 2016
FLOOR AREA 185,400 square feet
POPULATION 1,080

Intuit Marine Way Building

The new Marine Way Building (MWB) was the first to be owned and developed by the business and financial software company Intuit, and was therefore of symbolic importance in their multi-building Mountain View campus. Intuit recognized that the success of their new workplace would hinge on the extent to which the building created a strong sense of community, in addition to the extent to which it would help provide a centre and focus to their larger campus community. Community as an idea would need to work on these two opposed notions: the building's internal workplace community required its own definition and characterization, while at the same time, the building would need to act as a new hub of an existing campus community.

The new building was projected as an antidote to the insular campuses going up throughout Silicon Valley. Intuit's human-centreed, urban-minded, deep-green workplace design promoted a more sustainable, publicly-engaged community-based development pattern. In collaboratively conceiving a new workplace building from scratch, our project for Intuit was a first for us. We were appointed by Intuit for the interior architecture with WRNS Studio of San Francisco for the Site Planning and Core and Shell architecture. A driving factor was the need to respond to the unusual conditions of Silicon Valley: a formerly quiet semi-agricultural area that has been progressively transformed into the world's largest tech development centre. In the process, the developer-driven basic office park zone had become the modern commercial equivalent of an industrial precinct.

Compounding this homogenous trend, Silicon Valley lacks the infrastructure and amenities of an urban location, despite being at the heart of America's digital economy. Intuit's campus planning aims to redress the balance by providing an environmentally sustainable, walkable, networked precinct that offers choice and diversity in amenities with two new key buildings, of which MWB is the first. The strategy would support growth, attract and retain top talent, foster collaboration, and provide a place for the community to come together.

Following contextual analyses, staff surveys, visioning sessions and workshops with Intuit, the design team developed a site, building and interior design response for the Marine Way Building to create a centrally positioned hub for the increasingly global Intuit community and a workplace that feels like home. The planning and geometry of the building, spread over four floors, can be described as low, wide, connected and flexible – a strategy that addresses the specific programmatic and collaborative needs of Intuit's employees, reinforces campus patterns and cohesion, and creates interest along the street.

With a ground floor that emerges from the landscape as a solid, textured base, glazed loft-like upper levels, extensive terraces, and amenities located at the building perimeter, the building creates a dynamic new edge along the campus's main pedestrian and vehicular spine. The structure will join, via pathways, program, and a shared street edge, with the office building planned for phase two, creating a new campus gateway and centre of gravity. Reflecting the client's longstanding, employee-driven commitment to take care of the environment, sustainability is woven into every aspect of the site and building. Design strategies of the LEED Platinum building enhance resource efficiency, expand the natural habitat, ensure good indoor environmental quality, reduce water consumption and waste, and enable the expanded use of transit options.

The large floor plates, which accommodate a variety of places for people to collaborate, concentrate, socialize, and reflect, are organized into human-scaled neighborhoods and connected by clear circulation. Cores are pulled to the perimeter of the building, allowing for maximum connectivity and flexibility in team configuration and workflow between individual desks, breakout areas, lounge spaces, and conference rooms. A café, living rooms, bike facilities, showers, and terraces radiate off of a highly visible atrium that welcomes up to 500 people at a time and opens out onto the campus's main internal street. Reflecting Intuit's mission to empower small businesses and individuals, much of the furniture was purchased from small businesses, and local artists created the art and wind sculptures.

The four-story main atrium space draws activity from the east and west sides of the campus. Each landing and bleacher stair along the atrium connects directly to a large 'living room' with pantry functions and generous inter-team collaborative workspace. Full workspace neighborhoods are located at the edge of the atrium, while intimate breakout spaces such as balconies and casual soft-furniture settings, offer a range of work opportunities to encourage users to take advantage of the whole building. This variety of programmatic functions along the perimeter of the atrium helps generate consistent activity throughout the workday. With a large blue colored staircase that serves all levels, clerestory windows that span 60 feet to pull in daylight, and a built-in ventilation stack, the atrium plays a key role in supporting Intuit's wellness and energy efficiency goals.

Designed to embrace the mild climate of Mountain View's North Bayshore Area, the building connects to both nature and the public realm. Extensive terraces with views to the bay offer an indoor/outdoor workplace experience that fosters choice, authenticity, and wellbeing while helping to knit the campus together. The terraces and green roofs act as mediated spaces, or porches, between the natural environment and the workplace. Here, native and adapted plant species support biodiversity and help manage rainwater.

The MWB advances the trajectory of Intuit's Mountain View campus, helping it interact positively with its neighbors, connect to the public realm, conserve natural resources, accommodate flexibility and mobility, and support both collaborative and concentrated work. In a region that must become more efficient and sustainable to support the flexibility and work/life integration that knowledge workers seek, Intuit projects a model workplace design that addresses employees needs for a community centreed architecture, while anticipating a denser, more networked future for the Valley.

246

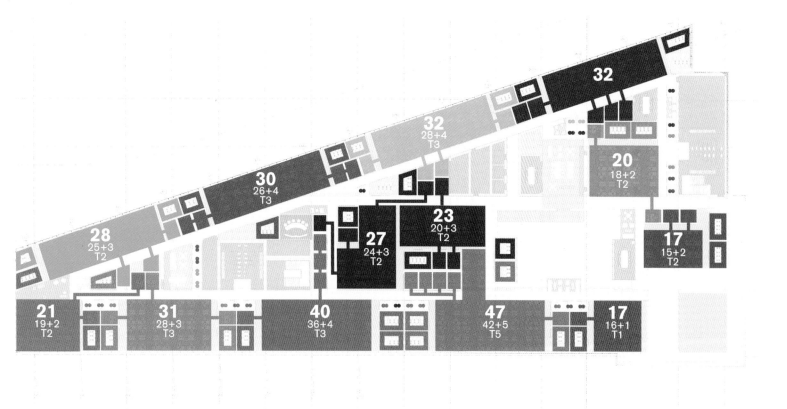

CAMPUS – CONNECTING AMENITIES   3 FL

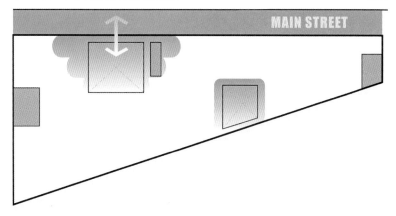

MAIN STREET

OCCUPANCY – NEIGHBORHOODS   3 FL

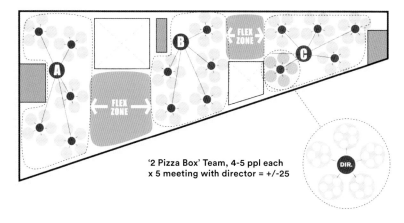

FLEX ZONE

FLEX ZONE

DIR.

'2 Pizza Box' Team, 4-5 ppl each
x 5 meeting with director = +/-25

OPPOSITE PAGE **A low, wide and connected building assists community bonding.**

ABOVE **Group planning.**

MIDDLE **Connecting to campus.**

BELOW **Neighborhood occupancy.**

HUMAN SCALE AND COMMUNITY SCALE

The central atrium forms the hub of the community and hosts events at different scales. Its architecture allows constant re-configuration for different functions including large scale campus community meetings.

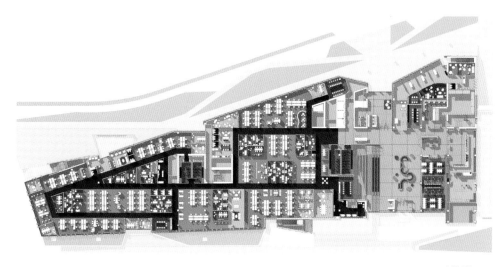

LEVEL 1

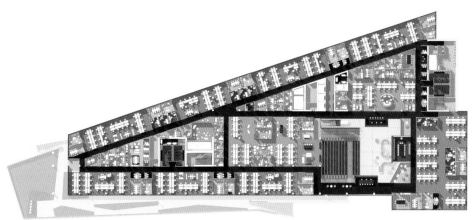

LEVEL 2

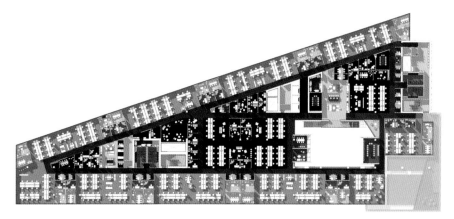

LEVEL 3

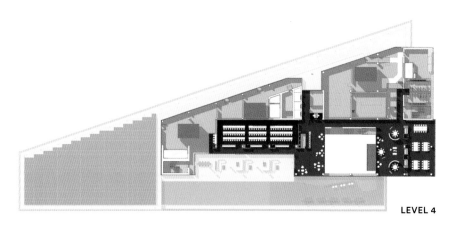

LEVEL 4

THE THEATRE OF WORK

ABOVE Movement paths are continuously in vision, offering a clear sense of orientation.

BELOW Terraces provide for outdoor working in the benign Silicon Valley climate.

HUMAN SCALE AND COMMUNITY SCALE

252

ABOVE **Living room zones encircle the atrium and provide undesignated spaces for both group and individual work.**

OPPOSITE PAGE **The architecture of the atrium perimeter includes balconies for working.**

254

ABOVE **The atrium café.**

OPPOSITE PAGE **The atrium is
carved from the concrete
building structure and achieves its visual
interest from the variety of
different functions that inhabit
its periphery.**

HUMAN SCALE AND COMMUNITY SCALE

OPPOSITE PAGE **People use the atrium seating for spontaneous meetings.**

ABOVE **Workplace areas are punctuated with social breakout spaces.**

HUMAN SCALE AND COMMUNITY SCALE

LOCATION New York, New York, United States
COMPLETED January 2014
FLOOR AREA 20,000 square feet
POPULATION 125-175

The Barbarian Group

258

The Barbarian Group emerged from successful early experiments in digital marketing and represented one of the most progressive forms of the new digital creative company. Part ad agency and part film production studio, it had the capabilities to generate and produce content, soup to nuts. These were knowledge workers who operated independently on the creative edge with a tendency to disappear down rabbit holes. There was the potential for community to pull them together, to ground individuals and increase synergies between groups. Since this was a relatively small organization of 125 people, and there was an opportunity to collocate everyone in one space, we searched for a unifying iconic concept to bring the community together.

The project for the Barbarian Group was unique in that the Barbarian community had a strong independent alternative culture that embraced new technology, but had been fractured into siloed dysfunctional groups in their last offices. Our task was to take their loose company structure and develop a truly flexible, non-hierarchical solution that addressed human scale by being intimate and personal, but also unifying and team oriented, making an effective community space for a midsized organization. When they grew out of their old fragmented Tribeca offices, we were commissioned to design their new workspace. They secured a lease of the seventh floor of a building on 20th Street, Manhattan. Working with a constrained budget, we retained the existing perimeter offices and services to work as acoustically controlled spaces, while surgically clearing the central zone for a flexible community space.

The early conversations with Barbarian leadership questioned all aspects of why an office should be conventional, or why one needed an office at all. In discussion, we reduced the brief to its most fundamental basics. People need to connect to other people: they need flat surfaces to work on with laptops or monitors or other equipment, and easily accessible places to meet and collaborate. We got excited about the idea of massively simplifying the concept to show how radically different an office could be when you alter the 'job description'. They were keen on conceiving of their office from a blank slate and drilling down into what a community meant for them. Connection was valuable, audial space was

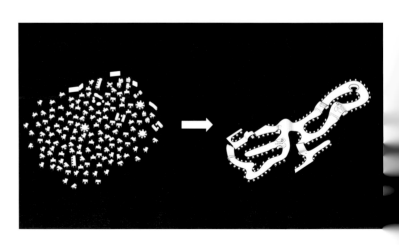

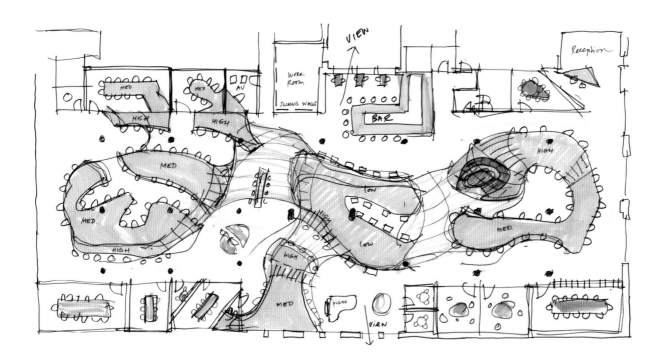

The first sketch plan, with labels including VIEW, Reception, MED, HIGH, LOW, BAR, WTR ROOM, SLIDING WALLS, AV, piano, VIEW.

valuable, tech infrastructure was valuable. Many conventional office furnishings and appurtenances were deemed irrelevant.

With these clear requirements in mind, we prioritized openness and transparency. Extending the idea we had developed ten years earlier with Mother in London, we imagined of a kind of endless uninterrupted table that connects everyone. The surface you work on should be the same as the surface your colleagues work on, and that surface could connect everyone in the company in a single mission. Like an electrical wire, the table surface itself becomes a medium for connecting and centreing a community. Surface vibration can be empathetically felt across a hundred feet. It was no surprise when long after the project was finished, the staff were referring to the table as having a life and character of its own.

The first sketch plan presented to the client showed an enormous table absorbing most of the room. We marked out the desire lines or cow paths that would directly connect all the peripheral functions, like a desire-line network. This map became the organizing principle for the table. Where paths crossed the table, we needed to lift the table up so people could move underneath it. Once we studied this we realized that the places where the table lifted up made for protected grotto-like spaces, shielded from the community, to meet or hang out.

A detailed computer model was constructed within our office and provided an initial cutting schedule for production. We worked with the computational design guru, Andreas Froech, and his company Machineous to plan production of the table. Machineous laser-cut plywood panels in sections in Los Angeles by customized automotive robots and shipped components to New York where the table was assembled on site. Layers of Masonite and MDF formed the surface which was finished with surfboard resin, applied in a continuous pour over 30 hours. It had to be continuous in order to avoid joint lines.

Feedback that we received from both employees and leadership proved the validity of the concept. Working groups were better connected and production processes more efficient. People knew what was going on as it happened. In fact, the only drawback expressed was that for a short time they became widely known more for their table than for their work.

259

OPPOSITE PAGE **175 individual desks can morph into one 'superdesk'.**

ABOVE **The first sketch plan presented to the client: an enormous table absorbing most of the room. This map became the organizing principle for the table and the space.**

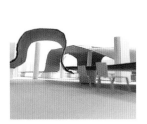

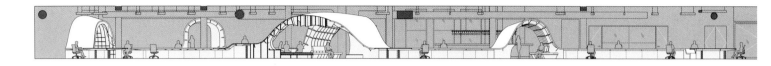

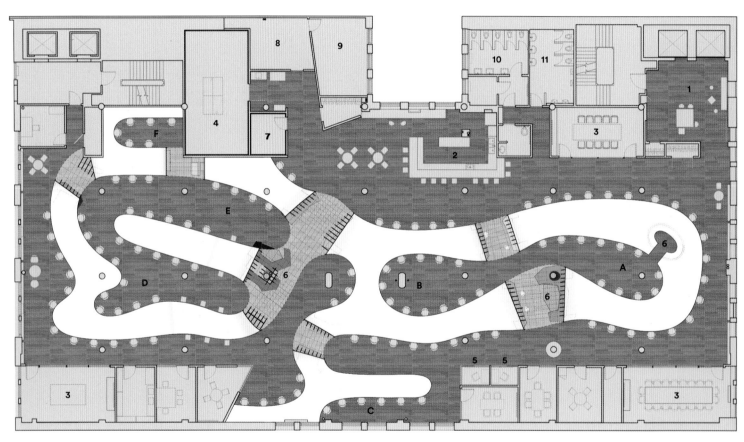

ABOVE Model tests, early computer model and long section through the seventh floor space. Following the initial hand sketches, we produced measured drawings and built physical models to analyze the spatial effects. Photographing the physical model also enabled us to better understand how the underside of the table could be used.

BELOW Floor plan: the space is entered from the elevators in the upper right.

1. Entry
2. Kitchen/bar
3. Conference room
4. Studio
5. Phone booth
6. Breakout meeting area

7. AV room
8. IT
9. Mechanical
10. Women's bathroom
11. Men's bathroom

NEIGHBOORHOODS
A. Business development
B. Product/social/strategy
C. Executives
D. Creative
E. Production
F. Technology

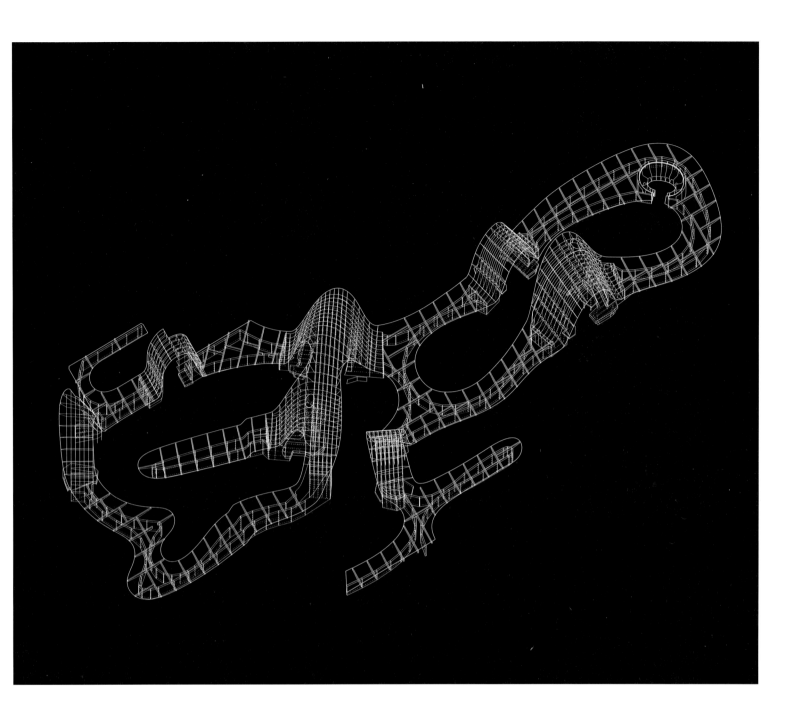

ABOVE After being initially drawn by hand and then molded in physical models, the plywood supporting structure was thereafter entirely shaped by the computer.

BELOW Initial physical model: The plywood structure rises from the existing oak floor as pony walls supporting the table. Because the movement routes bisect the space, we lifted the table to fly over pathways and maintain surface continuity. The resulting grotto-like spaces underneath these 'arches' are characterized by a vigorous plywood coffer structure and offer a variety of amenities. They can accommodate meetings up to eight people, provide private focused workspace, or high counter work-space, and house bookshelves and other storage.

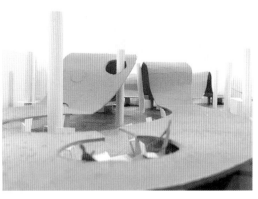

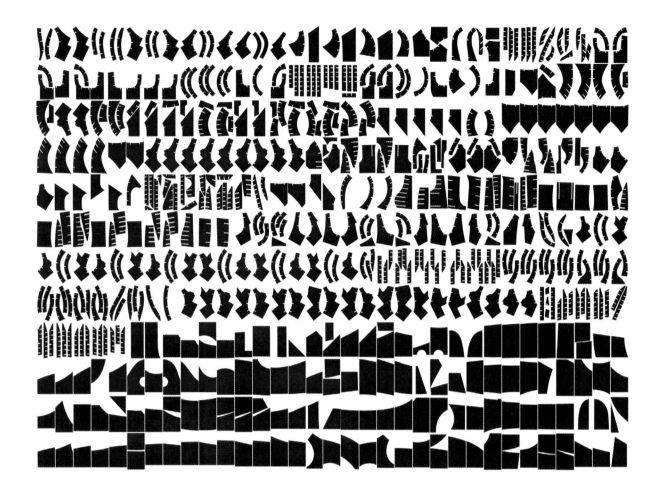

ABOVE Diagram of the 870 unique plywood sections that make up the table.

BELOW Application of the top finish was achieved 'in a single pour' over 24 hours. It needed to be a continuous application to avoid creating seams in the surface.

OPPOSITE PAGE The plywood egg crate structure formed grottos under the table for meeting and private work.

264

ABOVE Inevitably, the question of what happens if the table acquires a crack was raised. We agreed that the best method was to accept and celebrate the material fragility. We proposed the Japanese concept of Kintsugi Repair: if the table is broken, the repair should amplify the fissure by adding gold dust or similar to the glue product used. This highlights the material failure as part of the effects of nature on life forms.

CENTRE AND OPPOSITE PAGE The plywood frame was assembled and then skinned with a combination of MDF board and Masonite, depending on curve conditions. The top surface of the table is an ethereal pearlescent white, with a clear epoxy coating, so the fluid nature is emphasized.

HUMAN SCALE AND COMMUNITY SCALE

266

267

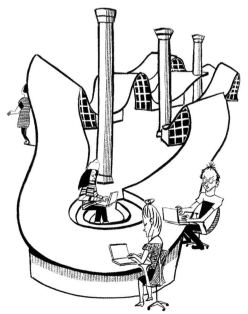

OPPOSITE PAGE LEFT The executive team in the hot tub meeting space.

OPPOSITE PAGE RIGHT The kitchen functioned as a coffee bar, lunch spot, and beverage service bar during parties.

ABOVE The superdesk in action.

BELOW Superdesk Illustration, Tom Bachtell, *The New Yorker*, April 14, 2014.

HUMAN SCALE AND COMMUNITY SCALE

ABOVE **Spatial effects from lifting the superdesk.**

CENTRE AND OPPOSITE PAGE **Meeting areas under the table.**

NEXT PAGE **Spaces below the desk resulted from planning circulation paths – and offered great spaces for meeting or private work.**

269

Postscript – The Endless Workplace Concept

September 2015

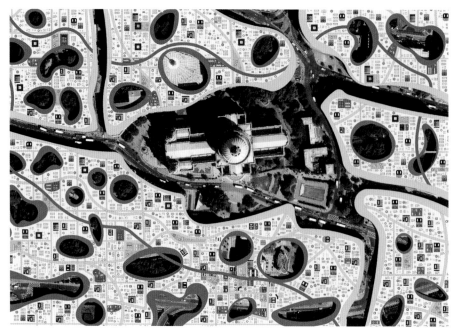

ABOVE AND BELOW **The Endless Workplace at St Paul's Cathedral – aerial view. Drawings by Humberto Arreola.**

In the Summer of 2015, the studio was approached by *Flaunt Magazine* with a request to imagine an architectural cross-pollination of the two very separate and unique cultural milieus of California, USA, and London, UK. Their special Fall 2015 issue, called *Califuk*, looked at a variety of provocative crossovers in fashion, art and culture in general.

From our unashamedly sun-bleached Californian point of view (with a great tendency to oversimplify), we chose to investigate the systemic transportation problems of London, which has become almost paralyzed by the clogged arteries of the city, with consequently debilitating commute times for its workers. The underground rail system is overloaded and prone to frequent system failures, the roads are almost grid-locked and escalating land prices have compelled the work force to live further and further away from their workplaces so that from two to four hours of commuting periods a day is normal and progressively increasing.

Given that technology now supports new ways of working, our starting point challenges the need to collocate workers in individual business locations. Our theoretical proposal was to 'carpet bomb' the city with a new type of workplace in a single, horizontally-connected level. The proposition imagines a mobile work mode where anyone can work anywhere, since technology now supports that, and so workers living in the existing infrastructure below can simply 'go upstairs to the office'. The argument for a single level derives from workplace studies that show multi-level working creates undesirable disconnections and silos.

This of course solves massive commute times and avoids the numbing isolation of working at home by ensuring that you are part of a real live community, who also happen to be your neighbors downstairs. With this concept, one recovers something of the medieval model of collaborating with multiple disciplines in your local village and leveraging the healthy cross-pollination aspects of that.

A further suggestion implicit in this idea is that our current urban model may be ill suited to the technologically liberated future. And it may be a more invasive form of surgery that ultimately delivers new opportunities to spend time on things that we value: namely local, tribal communities, multi-disciplinary working, and unfettered connectivity to social and business communities without the enormous friction, stress and tedium resulting from poor 'flow' in a city.

"The zoning of areas will break down, as it becomes increasingly anachronistic to think of places as somewhere you work or somewhere you live. Cities will become dotted with local communities where housing, office space, retail and leisure uses are mixed up and people move around different environments as the need, or urge takes them."

ANTHONY SLUMBERS – THE IMPACT OF TECHNOLOGY ONCORPORATE REAL ESTATE: A PANGLOSSIAN FUTURE

"Since work is now independent of time and location, we proposed a design concept that asks why home should be separated from work, or how we might physically contract the distance between home and work, entirely ignoring questions of land ownership or the existing urban fabric."

CLIVE WILKINSON

274

Original text for *Flaunt Magazine*:

"It's no secret that Californians love London, but they also would love to correct its horrendous problems with one quick solution before surfs up. Almost every Londoner wastes about two to three hours a day on commuting past each other to offices in all sorts of odd corners of the metropolis. The Endless Workplace proposition solves this instantly, and breaks down all business silos, by making getting to work no more taxing than climbing the stairs or shuffling into the odd elevator. This new workplace is a single layer of open office space that sits light as a feather over all the buildings in the city, and by its shear horizontal extremity, absorbs the City's entire workplace space requirement. Access to light and views is achieved with deferential circular court-yards that look down at the sights of London and open to the sun above. With a pervasive mobile working paradigm, you are no longer stealing someone's desk, but parking wher-ever feels good. Hence working anywhere means working just above your kettle and teabag collection, a short hop from the couch into the future. And everyone you would want to know is a short walk away."

Rethinking the urban roofscape. Modern workplace efficiency with the museum of the city of London below you.

List of References

Managing Creativity and Innovation. Harvard Business Essentials. Compiled by *Harvard Business Review*. Boston: Harvard Business Press, 2003.

Abu-Lugbod, Janet L. *Before European Hegemony: The World System A.D. 1250-1350*. Reprint, Oxford: Oxford University Press, 1991.

Artaud, Antonin. *The Theatre and Its Double*. Translated by Victor Corti. London: Calder, 1970.

Bachelard, Gaston. *The Poetics of Space*. Translated by Maria Jolas. Rev. ed. New York: Penguin, 2014.

Bacon, Edmund N. *Design of Cities: A Superbly Illustrated Account of the Development of Urban Form from Ancient Athens to Modern Brasilia*. New York: Penguin, 1978.

Barthes, Roland. *Mythologies*. Translated by Annette Lavers. New York: Farrar, Straus and Giroux, 1972.

Becker, Franklin. *Offices at Work: Uncommon Workspace Strategies That Add Value and Improve Performance*. Hoboken: John Wiley & Sons, 2005.

Benjamin, Walter. *The Arcades Project*. Edited by Rolf Tiedemann. Translated by Eland, Howard, and Kevin McLaughlin. Rev. ed. Reprint, Cambridge: Harvard University Press, 2002.

Benjamin, Walter, and Marcus Paul Bullock. *Selected Writings, Volume 4, 1938-1840*. Edited by Eiland, Howard, and Michael William Jennings. Translated by Rodney Livingstone. Cambridge: Harvard University Press, 2003.

Bishop, Morris. *The Middle Ages*. Reprint, Boston: Houghton Mifflin Harcourt, 2001.

Block, Peter. *Community: The Structure of Belonging*. Reprint, Oakland: Berrett-Koehler, 2009.

Brook, Peter. *The Empty Space: A Book About the Theatre: Deadly, Holy, Rough, Immediate*. Reprint, New York: Simon and Schuster, 1996.

Brunner, Robert, Stewart Emery, and Russ Hall. *Do You Matter? How Great Design Will Make People Love Your Company*. Upper Saddle River: FT Press, 2008.

Brynjolfsson, Erik, and Andrew Mcafée. *The Second Machine Age: Work, Progress, and Prosperity in a Time of Brilliant Technologies*. New York: W. W. Norton & Company, 2014.

Collins, Jim. *Good to Great: Why Some Companies Make the Leap... And Others Don't*. New York: HarperCollins, 2011.

Davenport, Thomas H., and Laurence Prusak. *Working Knowledge: How Organizations Manage What They Know*. Boston: Harvard Business Press, 2000.

De Botton, Alain. *The Pleasures and Sorrows of Work*. Reprint, London: Penguin, 2009.

Debord, Guy. *The Society of the Spectacle*. Translated by Ken Knabb. Rev. ed. Berkeley: Bureau of Public Secrets, 2014.

Drucker, Peter F. *The Essential Drucker: The Best of Sixty Years of Peter Drucker's Essential Writings on Management*. Reprint, New York: HarperCollins, 2003.

Duffy, Francis. *Work and the City*. The Edge Futures. London: Black Dog Press, 2007.

Ehrenhalt, Alan. *The Great Inversion and the Future of the American City*. Reprint, New York: Vintage Books, 2013.

Florida, Richard. *The Rise of the Creative Class*. Christchurch: Hazard Press, 2003.

Friedman, Ron. *The Best Place to Work: The Art and Science of Creating an Extraordinary Workplace*. Reprint, New York: Penguin, 2015.

Friedman, Thomas L. *The World Is Flat: A Brief History of the Twenty-first Century*. 3rd ed. London: Picador, 2007.

Gates, Bill. *Business @ the Speed of Thought: Succeeding in the Digital Economy*. New York: Grand Central Publishing, 1999.

Gehl, Jan. *Life Between Buildings: Using Public Space*. Washington, D.C.: Island Press, 2011.

Glaeser, Edward. *Triumph of the City: How Our Greatest Invention Makes Us Richer, Smarter, Greener, Healthier, and Happier*. Reprint, New York: Penguin, 2011.

Goffman, Erving. *The Presentation of Self in Everyday Life*. Harmondsworth: Penguin, 1971.

Handy, Charles B. *Understanding Organizations*. Reprint, Oxford: Oxford University Press, 1976.

Hawken, Paul. *The Ecology of Commerce (Revised Edition): A Declaration of Sustainability*. Rev. ed. New York: Harper-Collins, 2010.

Hillman, James. *A Blue Fire*. Reprint, New York: Harper-Collins, 1991.

Hillman, James. *The Soul's Code: In Search of Character and Calling*. New York: Random House, 2013.

Huizinga, Johan. *Homo Ludens: A Study of the Play-Element in Culture*. Reprint, Eastford: Martino Publishing, 2014.

Huizinga, Johan. *The Waning of the Middle Ages*. Reprint, Eastford: Martino Publishing, 2016.

276

Illich, Ivan D. *Celebration of Awareness: A Call for Institutional Revolution*. New York: Doubleday, 1970.

Jacobs, Jane. *The Death and Life of Great American Cities*. Harmondsworth: Penguin, 1972.

Jaworski, Joseph. *Synchronicity: The Inner Path of Leadership*. Oakland: Berrett-Koehler, 1996.

Kelley, Tom, and Jonathan Littman. *The Ten Faces of Innovation: IDEAO's Strategies for Beating the Devil's Advocate and Driving Creativity Throughout Your Organization*. New York: Doubleday, 2006.

Laugier, Marc-Antoine. *An Essay on Architecture*. Translated by Wolfgang Herrmann. Reprint, Los Angeles: Hennessey & Ingalls, 1977.

Lewis, Michael. *The Future Just Happened*. London: Hodder & Stoughton, 2001.

Lewis, Richard D. *When Cultures Collide: Leading Across Cultures*. 3rd ed. London: Nicholas Brealey Publishing, 2010.

Linklater, Andro. *Owning the Earth: The Transformation History of Land Ownership*. London: Bloomsbury Publishing, 2013.

Lynch, Kevin. *Good City Form*. Rev. ed. Reprint, Cambridge: MIT Press, 1984.

Lynch, Kevin. *The Image of the City*. Reprint, Cambridge: MIT Press, 1960.

McLuhan, Marshall. *The Mechanical Bride: The Folklore of Industrial Man*. 50th ed. Berkeley: Gingko Press, 2002.

McLuhan, Marshall, and Bruce R. Powers. *The Global Village: Transformations in World Life and Media in the 21st Century (Communication and Society)*. Reprint, Oxford: Oxford University Press, 1992.

McLuhan, Marshall, and Quentin Fiore. *The Medium is the Massage*. Produced by Jerome Agel. Berkeley: Gingko Press, 2001.

Mihaly Csikszentmihalyi. *Creativity: Flow and the Psychology of Discovery and Invention*. Reprint, New York: HarperCollins, 1996.

Mihaly Csikszentmihalyi. *Flow: The Psychology of Optimal Experience*. New York: HarperCollins, 2009.

Mills, C. Wright. *White Collar: The American Middle Classes*. Reprint, Morrisville: Lulu Press, 2018.

Moore, Alan. *No Straight Lines: Making Sense of Our Non-linear World*. Cambridge: Bloodstone Books, 2011.

Neumeier, Marty. *The Brand Gap: Revised Edition*. 2nd ed. San Francisco: Peachpit Press, 2006.

Papanek, Victor J. *Design for the Real World: Human Ecology and Social Change*. 2nd ed. Reprint, Chicago: Academy Chicago, 1984.

Perec, Georges. *Species of Spaces and Other Pieces*. Edited by John Sturrock. Rev. ed. New York: Penguin, 1997.

Perez, Carlota. *Technological Revolutions and Financial Capital: The Dynamics of Bubbles and Golden Ages*. Reprint, Cheltenham: Edward Elgar Publishing, 2002.

Peters, Thomas J. *Thriving on Chaos: Handbook for a Management Revolution*. Reprint, New York: Knopf, 1987.

Pinker, Steven. *The Blank Slate: The Modern Denial of Human Nature*. Reprint, New York: Penguin, 2003.

Rosen, Evan. *The Culture of Collaboration: Maximizing Time, Talent and Tools to Create Value in the Global Economy*. San Francisco: Red Ape Publishing, 2007.

Ross, Alec. *The Industries of the Future*. New York: Simon and Schuster, 2016.

Rowe, Colin, and Fred Koetter. *Collage City*. Reprint, Cambridge: MIT Press, 1983.

Rybczynski, Witold. *Makeshift Metropolis: Ideas About Cities*. New York: Simon & Schuster, 2010.

Rybczynski, Witold. *Waiting for the Weekend*. Reprint, New York: Penguin, 1992.

Senge, Peter M. *The Fifth Discipline: The Art & Practice of the Learning Organization*. Rev. ed. New York: Doubleday, 2006.

Schein, Edgar H. *Organizational Culture and Leadership*. 3rd ed. Hoboken: John Wiley & Sons, 2006.

Shiqiao, Li. *Power and Virtue: Architectural and Intellectual Change in England 1660-1730*. Abingdon: Routledge, 2007.

Shirky, Clay. *Here Comes Everybody: The Power of Organizing Without Organization*. Reprint, New York: Penguin, 2008.

Spary, E. C. *Utopia's Garden: French Natural History from Old Regime to Revolution*. Chicago: University of Chicago Press, 2010.

Surowiecki, James. *The Wisdom of Crowds: Why the Many Are Smarter Than the Few and How Collective Wisdom Shapes Business, Economies, Societies and Nations*. Reprint, New York: Doubleday, 2004.

Thompson, Clive. *The Best of Technology Writing 2008*. Ann Arbor: University of Michigan Press, 2008.

Van Doren, Charles L. *A History of Knowledge: Past, Present, and Future*. Reprint, New York: Ballantine Books, 1992.

Veldhoen, Erik. *The Art of Working*. Den Haag: Academic Service, 2004.

Vidler, Anthony. *The Scenes of the Street and Other Essays.* New York: Monacelli Press, 2011.

Waber, Ben. *People Analytics: How Social Sensing Technology Will Transform Business and What It Tells Us about the Future of Work*. Upper Saddle River: FT Press, 2013.

Waldron, Arthur. *The Great Wall of China: From History to Myth*. Cambridge: Cambridge University Press, 1990.

Whyte, William H. *The Social Life of Small Urban Spaces*. Reprint, New York: Project for Public Spaces, 2001.

Zittrain, Jonathan. *The Future of the Internet—And How to Stop It*. New Haven: Yale University Press, 2008.

Photo Credits

All images copyright to Clive Wilkinson and Clive Wilkinson Architects unless otherwise noted.

PHOTOGRAPHY

PART 1

24	Musée Carnavalet/Roger-Viollet/ The Image Works
34	Courtesy of the U.S. National Archives and Records Administration
35	Courtesy of the United Press International/ Cornell University Library
36	Courtesy of the Buffalo History Museum
37	Courtesy of the National Museum of American History
39_2	Courtesy of the U.S. Air Force
40_1	Marshall Gerometta/CTBUH
40_2	Ezra Stoller/Esto
42	Courtesy of the Herman Miller Archives
43_1	Les Films de Mon Oncle – Spectacle Films C.E.P.E.C.
44	Jan Ainali

INTERMEZZO

59_2	Peter de Ru
61_1	Benny Chan/Fotoworks

PART 2

76-79	Benny Chan/Fotoworks
82-86_1	Benny Chan/Fotoworks
86_2	Francesco Radino
86_4	Benny Chan/Fotoworks
92-103_1	Michael Moran Photography
106_2	MGM/Alamy Stock Photo
107_1	Karl Kost/Alamy Stock Photo
107_2	Benny Chan/Fotoworks
109_1	Benny Chan/Fotoworks
110-117	Benny Chan/Fotoworks
123-125	Benny Chan/Fotoworks
127-129	Benny Chan/Fotoworks
136-138_2	Benny Chan/Fotoworks
140-143_1	Benny Chan/Fotoworks
144-145	Benny Chan/Fotoworks
148_2	Centro Storico Fiat
150_1	Francesco Radino
150_2-151	Adrian Wilson/Interior Photography
152	Francesco Radino
153-154	Adrian Wilson/Interior Photography
155_1	Francesco Radino
155_2	Adrian Wilson/Interior Photography
157_2	Courtesy of Woods Bagot Eric Sierins Photography
165-169	Shannon McGrath
172-177	Shannon McGrath
179_1-2	Daniela Duncan/Getty Images
182-189	Michael Moran Photography
196-203	Riddle-Stagg
206	Ema Peter Photography
207_2-213	Ema Peter Photography
219-225	Paul Warchol Photography
234-235	Benny Chan/Fotoworks
238_1-2	Benny Chan/Fotoworks
239-341	Benny Chan/Fotoworks
246	Jeremy Bittermann Photography
248-249	Jeremy Bittermann Photography
251-257	Jeremy Bittermann Photography
263	Michael Moran Photography
264_2-267_1	Michael Moran Photography
268-271	Michael Moran Photography
280	Josh Franklin

ILLUSTRATIONS/DRAWINGS

PART 1

15	The National Gallery, London
38	Courtesy of the Smithsonian Libraries
41_1	Courtesy of HENN

PART 2

71	Museum of London
106_1	L'Établissement public du château, du musée et du domaine national de Versailles
267_2	Courtesy of Tom Bachtell, *The New Yorker* Condé Nast

The CWa Design Community

All of our design and production work is highly collaborative, and the community that produced it includes the following people, since the firm's inception, who deserve appropriate credit.

Adams, Crystal
Altchech, David
Arreola, Humberto
Avshman, Melanie
Bainter, Jane
Bandi, Christian
Bard, Alison
Baron, Maria
Beauter, Bill
Beissel von Gymnich, Bertram
Berry, John
Binfet, Nancy
Bliss, Evan
Bornstein, David
Bozer, James
Breeden, Josh
Bu, Yinan
Burns, David
Cannon, Nicole
Carpenter, Brad
Cerilla, Xavier
Cerrilla, Alex
Chang, Gerome
Chang, Jonathan
Cheung, Henry
Chow, Nelson
Christensen, Anne
Chumakova, Ksenia
Colcleugh, Keely
Cole, Sandy
Conn, Susan
Corbett, Chris
Corbin, Marico
Craig, Ashley
Currington, Jasmine
Daly, Kevin
Dang, Tiffany
Dowling, Nancy T
Duncan, Caroline
Elander, Tom
Eun, Grace
Farhang, Sam
Febres-Cordero, Juan
Feuer, Miwako
Fletcher, Jeremy
Fong, Ho-Yu
Fontiveros, Jose
Garrison, Catherine
Gehle, Shawn
Ghaemi, Ailin
Gilio-Tenan, Matthew
Giordano, Andrea
Girone, Christine
Goldklang, Jacklyn
Gordon, Nora
Gould, Stefan
Green, Lindsay

Griffith, Roy
Guardado, Juan
Gulin, Iain M
Hahn, Kristina
Hammond, Richard
Herzl, Reuben
Hiller, Laurie H.
Hocek, Ali
Hoefter, Claudia
Hongo, Miya
Hovsepyan, Ara
Howell, Ben
Hsin, Bob
Huang, Jenny
Hudson, Mark
Hughhet Hiller, Laurie
Hwang, Maggie
Isoda, Airi
Jakus, Nathaniel
Jee, Eunsung
Jeevanjee, Ali
Johnson, Mark
Jordan, Richard
Kalenik, Ben
Keller, Andrea
Kelly, James
Kerr, Robert
Kes, Meghan
Ketcham, William
Khudyakova, Yana
Koizumi, Wayne
Komatsu, Mitsuhiro
Kropac, Martin
Kubota, Yuna
Lai, Nancy
Landsberg, Garrick
Larson, Carter
Law, Jacqueline
Lee, Monica
Lee, Rachel
Lesko, Steve
Leung, Michael
Lo, Yu-Ngok
Loescher, Ben
MacDonald, Katie
MacDonald, Michael
Macduff, Ian
Madrid, Jesse
Mandell, Shiva
Manio, Kayla
Marasso, Lorenzo
McDaniel, Meredith
McKee, Carmen
Meachem, John
Mecava, Andrej
Merit, Byron
Milton, Matthew
Moerland, Peter

Mokgubu, Mokgadi
Momtahen, Sheila
Moran, Matthew
Morimoto, Chris
Morris, Caroline
Mullen-Carey, Jess
Muntzel, Neil
Murphey, John
Myers, Jenny
Myers, Melisa
Myers, Tom
Nagel, Thomas
Name, Valerie
Nelco, Marni
Nesser, Anna
Nielsen, Chester
Norr, Tom
Oberherr, Daniela
Ogosta, Ed
Pan, Jonathan
Pare, Phillippe
Pastrana, Jeanette
Pauly, Michelle
Plomb, Jacqueline
Poirier, Michael
Quirmbach, Nadine
Ramsey, Sarah B
Rappaport, Alexis
Regnier, Ben
Ringo, Christopher
Ritz, Annie
Rowe, Leslie
Ruppert, Vance
Rybicki, Andrew
Saxe, Vernon
Schoening, Andrea
Scott, Cheryl
Shaffner, Danielle
Shumyatsky, Sasha
Simmer, Colin
Smith, Renee
Smith, Sarah
Smith, Scott
Smudde, Ruben
Song, Ying
Soren, Hailey
Stein, Alex
Su, Tony H.
Suzuki, Akiko
Sylianteng, Nicole
Tan, Yong
Terayama, Thomas
Tryhane, Andrew
Tsin, Robert
Vivien, Michael
Volger, Nina
Vuong, Audrey
Walkszek, Meredith

Wang, Christie
Wei, Reiko
Wernick, Amber
Wise, Kate
Wong, Amelia
Wu, Jennifer
Wuu, Jane
Yang, Chia-Ching
Yang, Jiahui
Yoshida, Riko
Zeroth, Lawrence
Zunzunegui, Pablo

Publication Credits

**THE THEATRE OF WORK
CLIVE WILKINSON**

PUBLISHER
Frame Publishers

AUTHOR
Clive Wilkinson

EDITOR
Andrew Mackenzie /
URO Publications, Australia

PRE-PRODUCTION
Christie Wang

PRODUCTION
Sarah de Boer

GRAPHIC DESIGN
Zoe Bar-Pereg

PREPRESS
Edward de Nijs

PRINTING
IPP Printers

SPECIAL THANKS TO
The community of excellent architects and
designers at Clive Wilkinson Architects.

TRADE DISTRIBUTION USA AND CANADA
Consortium Book Sales & Distribution, LLC.
34 Thirteenth Avenue NE, Suite 101
Minneapolis, MN 55413-1007
T +1 612 746 2600
T +1 800 283 3572 (orders)
F +1 612 746 2606

TRADE DISTRIBUTION BENELUX
Frame Publishers
Luchtvaartstraat 4
1059 CA Amsterdam
the Netherlands
distribution@frameweb.com
frameweb.com

TRADE DISTRIBUTION REST OF WORLD
Thames & Hudson Ltd
181A High Holborn
London WC1V 7QX
United Kingdom
T +44 20 7845 5000
F +44 20 7845 5050
ISBN: 978-94-92311-36-8

© 2019 Frame Publishers, Amsterdam, 2019

The Koninklijke Bibliotheek lists this publication in the Nederlandse Bibliografie: detailed bibliographic information is available on the internet at http://picarta.pica.nl

Printed on acid-free paper produced from chlorine-free pulp. TCF ∞

Printed in Poland

987654321

Clive Wilkinson is an architect, interior designer and workplace strategist. In 1991, he established his eponymous firm in Los Angeles, which undertakes a variety of design projects across the globe. He was born in South Africa, and educated there and in England, before moving to California. His firm has won over 150 design awards, including Induction to the Interior Design Hall of Fame (2005) and the Smithsonian Cooper-Hewitt National Design Award for Interior Design (2012). He lives in Los Angeles with his two children, a stepdaughter and a glorious wife named Elisabeth.